Praise for *Reading the Margins*

Gilmour's book expertly traces the indelible and ubiquitous imprint of the Bible on classic literature and pop culture alike. Through his sensitive readings of literature, Gilmour argues that one's empathy for the marginalized can be enhanced by bringing literature and Scripture into conversation with each other. His winsome prose will spark your desire to read more widely in literature and more deeply in the biblical text that has so masterfully shaped culture.

—David Anonby, assistant professor of English, Trinity Western University, and author of *Shakespeare on Salvation: Crossing the Reformation Divide*

This isn't a book that parses this or that obvious biblical citation in well-known, highfalutin pieces of literature. Those books have their value, but Michael Gilmour is aiming for something different. In *Reading the Margins: Encounters with the Bible in Literature*, Gilmour examines often offbeat and uncommon examples to show that creative writing can encourage readers to reflect deeply and can challenge us to develop empathy. His work illuminates allusions to and echoes of the Bible in the service of directing the reader to ponder profoundly and dialogically Scripture's call to embrace a more selfless inclusivity of those on the margins. Gilmour's chapter on Woody Guthrie's *Bound for Glory* demonstrates his approach nicely, as he mines Guthrie's quasi-memoir and discovers how it stresses compassion for the downtrodden, how it foregrounds the importance of learning oppressed people's stories, and how its characters model charity and kindness to "the least of these." Gilmour's deeply researched and compellingly written message is one we'd do well to heed in our time of divisiveness, partisan politics, and religious nationalism.

—Dan W. Clanton Jr., associate professor of religious studies, Doane University, and author of *God and the Little Grey Cells: Religion in Agatha Christie's Poirot Stories*

In *Reading the Margins,* Michael Gilmour is an exemplary host who models gracious and knowledgeable engagement with texts and their contexts. His wide-ranging but biblically moored exploration of a delightful array of literary and cultural works offers insights not only into these particular works, but also into what it means more generally to read widely and read well.

—Karen Swallow Prior, author of *The Evangelical Imagination: How Stories, Images, and Metaphors Created a Culture in Crisis*

Michael J. Gilmour demonstrates with flair and imagination that, as he claims, stories do indeed "shape the way we view the world." Wide-ranging, personal, authentic, and discursive, his book challenges the way we encounter the Bible in literature and literature in the Bible.

—Alison Jack, professor of Bible and literature, and principal of New College, School of Divinity, University of Edinburgh

Michael J. Gilmour's *Reading the Margins: Encounters with the Bible in Literature* is an engaging and intriguing exploration of how reading literature can constitute a "spiritual discipline." Gilmour shares with us his delightfully wide and eclectic library—ranging from Charles Dickens, Hugh Lofting (creator of Doctor Dolittle), Woody Guthrie, and Bob Dylan, to Salman Rushdie—and demonstrates how literature dialogues with the Bible not just through allusions and parallels, but by compelling us to feel empathetically for those on the margins. As a result, *Reading the Margins* offers us a thoughtful and erudite study in compassion and ethical thinking.

—Mark Libin, professor of English, theatre, film and media, University of Manitoba

Reading the Margins

Reading
THE MARGINS

Encounters with the Bible in Literature

Michael J. Gilmour

FORTRESS PRESS
MINNEAPOLIS

READING THE MARGINS
Encounters with the Bible in Literature

Copyright © 2024 Fortress Press, an imprint of 1517 Media. All rights reserved. Except for brief quotations in critical articles or reviews, no part of this book may be reproduced in any manner without prior written permission from the publisher. Email copyright@1517.media or write to Permissions, Fortress Press, PO Box 1209, Minneapolis, MN 55440-1209.

Library of Congress Control Number: 2024933662 (print)

Cover image: Silhouette of library, vector stock illustration by kovalto1/Getty Images
Cover design: Kristin Miller

Print ISBN: 978-1-5064-6935-5
eBook ISBN: 978-1-5064-6936-2

Contents

	Preface	ix
	Introduction: Love Your Neighbor as Yourself	xv
1.	Poverty and Woody Guthrie's Train Bound for Glory	1
2.	Anne Brontë Confronts Domestic Unrest: Reading Wisdom's Diary	23
3.	Daniel Defoe's Shipwrecked Bible and Jean Rhys's Cardboard World	41
4.	Joy Kogawa and Salman Rushdie "Verses" Racism	59
5.	The Lion, the Witch, and the Rock Star: Bob Dylan in Narnia	81
6.	An Old Curiosity Shop and an Old Copy of Bunyan's *Progress*	109
7.	The Meek Shall Inherit the Earth: Richard Adams's Rabbit Theologians	127
8.	The Gospel of the Imagination, or the Imaginary Gospel	155
	Afterword: Censorship and The Far Side *of Religion*	169
	Works Cited	185
	Index of Names	193
	Index of Subjects	195

When the Son of man shall come in his glory, and all the holy angels with him, then shall he sit upon the throne of his glory: And before him shall be gathered all nations: and he shall separate them one from another, as a shepherd divideth his sheep from the goats: And he shall set the sheep on his right hand, but the goats on the left. Then shall the King say unto them on his right hand, Come, ye blessed of my Father, inherit the kingdom prepared for you from the foundation of the world: For I was an hungred, and ye gave me meat: I was thirsty, and ye gave me drink: I was a stranger, and ye took me in: Naked, and ye clothed me: I was sick, and ye visited me: I was in prison, and ye came unto me. Then shall the righteous answer him, saying, Lord, when saw we thee an hungred, and fed thee? or thirsty, and gave thee drink? When saw we thee a stranger, and took thee in? or naked, and clothed thee? Or when saw we thee sick, or in prison, and came unto thee? And the King shall answer and say unto them, Verily I say unto you, Inasmuch as ye have done it unto one of the least of these my brethren, ye have done it unto me. Then shall he say also unto them on the left hand, Depart from me, ye cursed, into everlasting fire, prepared for the devil and his angels: For I was an hungred, and ye gave me no meat: I was thirsty, and ye gave me no drink: I was a stranger, and ye took me not in: naked, and ye clothed me not: sick, and in prison, and ye visited me not. Then shall they also answer him, saying, Lord, when saw we thee an hungred, or athirst, or a stranger, or naked, or sick, or in prison, and did not minister unto thee? Then shall he answer them, saying, Verily I say unto you, Inasmuch as ye did it not to one of the least of these, ye did it not to me. And these shall go away into everlasting punishment: but the righteous into life eternal.

—Jesus (Matt 25:31–46, AV)[1]

---

1 I cite the Authorized (King James) Version of the Bible at times because it is the version used by some authors discussed. When using this translation, I include the abbreviation AV after the reference. Where no abbreviation appears, I use the New Revised Standard Version.

Blessed are the poor in spirit: for theirs is the kingdom of heaven.
Blessed are they that mourn: for they shall be comforted.
Blessed are the meek: for they shall inherit the earth.
Blessed are they which do hunger and thirst after righteousness: for they shall be filled.
Blessed are the merciful: for they shall obtain mercy.
Blessed are the pure in heart: for they shall see God.
Blessed are the peacemakers: for they shall be called the children of God.
Blessed are they which are persecuted for righteousness' sake: for theirs is the kingdom of heaven.
Blessed are ye, when men shall revile you, and persecute you, and shall say all manner of evil against you falsely, for my sake.
Rejoice, and be exceeding glad: for great is your reward in heaven: for so persecuted they the prophets which were before you.
Ye are the salt of the earth: but if the salt have lost his savour, wherewith shall it be salted? it is thenceforth good for nothing, but to be cast out, and to be trodden under foot of men.
Ye are the light of the world. A city that is set on an hill cannot be hid.

—Jesus (Matt 5:3–14, AV)

Preface

The only thing better than reading good books is sharing the experience with others. In the summer of 2022, my colleague Nicholas Greco and I each purchased and read a lovely set of Charles Williams's seven novels, published by the Society that bears his name. This wasn't an academic exercise. The rigor of our two-person book club consisted entirely of text messages traded back and forth with random observations about the latest pages read. I was working on the present volume at the time and had no expectation these strange books would connect with its theme. We only bought them on a lark as an end-of-semester diversion. But here is Williams, making an appearance on the first page.

His is a wild imagination. Strange stuff. Entertaining stuff. Williams, I mean, though I suppose it's true of said colleague as well. And yet one curious insight stayed with me long after putting those novels back on the shelves. I'd never read anything by him before but had come across others mentioning the Williamsian concept of substitution. C. S. Lewis, for one, does so in a letter addressed to Sheldon Vanauken, dated November 27, 1957: "I forget if I had begun my own bone disease (osteoporosis) when you were with us. Anyway, it is much better now and I am no longer in pain.... The intriguing thing is that while I (for no discoverable reason) was losing the chalcium [*sic*] from my bones, [my wife] Joy [Davidman Lewis], who needed it much more [owing to bone cancer], was gaining it in hers. One dreams of a Charles Williams substitution! Well, never was a gift more gladly given: but one must not be fanciful."[1]

He's not fully persuaded, but Lewis still seems to appreciate his late friend's inclination to allow theology to break free of the merely theoretical and

---

1 C. S. Lewis, *The Collected Letters of C. S. Lewis*, vol. 3, *Narnia, Cambridge, and Joy 1950–1963*, ed. Walter Hooper (New York: HarperCollins, 2007), 901.

abstract and enter the realm of the literal. Calcium lost, calcium gained. It's measurable. It's tangible.

Owing to his association with Lewis, J. R. R. Tolkien, Owen Barfield, and others in the Oxford literary fellowship called the Inklings, many recognize the name Charles Williams (1886–1945), though fewer, I suspect, are familiar with his writings. He was a longtime editor with the Oxford University Press, and during World War II, when the Press moved its offices from London to Oxford, Williams moved, too, and began his association with that famous circle of friends gathering in Lewis's rooms at Magdalen College or The Eagle and Child or Lamb and Flag pubs to read their scribblings over pipes and drinks.

Williams was not a formally trained or full-time academic by profession, but he was very much a scholar, often lecturing in London and Oxford in addition to his editorial duties. He was a poet, playwright, and novelist; an expert on the Arthurian legends, Dante, and Milton; and an amateur—but nonetheless for that a complex and insightful—theologian. He was also "a swirling mass of contradictions," as one biography has it, and with respect to his religious views, "he was orthodox but heretical, a devout Anglican who practiced magic."[2] This may account for Williams's declining popularity after his death, at least among Christian readers. Perhaps a more significant reason is the strangeness of his books. His works defy simple genre classification; they jumble fantasy, science fiction, mystery, and horror and often involve a gothic mingling of "the Probable and the Marvellous," as Lewis observes.[3]

Though I found these books challenging and weird, this notion of substitution struck a chord. The biographer Grevel Lindop suggests Williams offered the first hints of his theory to a London student named Thelma Mills in 1929. She later wrote about the conversation they had and an experiment Williams proposed to her: "An inspector, he said, was to visit his class, and he was worried about it: 'The projected visit interferes; intrudes awkwardly; will not be dismissed; in fact, makes of the lecture a burden, which it is not, or certainly should not be.' Would Thelma, he asked, be willing to take on the worry for him? If she would set herself to worry a little about the inspection,

---

2 Philip Zaleski and Carol Zaleski, *The Fellowship: The Literary Lives of the Inklings* (New York: Farrar, Straus and Giroux, 2015), 221.

3 C. S. Lewis, "The Novels of Charles Williams," in *On Stories: And Other Essays on Literature*, ed. Walter Hooper (1949; New York: Harcourt, 1982), 21. Full essay, 21–28.

then he could get on with preparing the lecture, and giving it, without anxiety, knowing that she was taking care of it on his behalf."[4]

Williams builds this idea on Galatians 6:2 (AV): "Bear ye one another's burdens, and so fulfil the law of Christ."[5] As Lindop explains it, one person "could voluntarily take over the suffering—mental or physical—of another, and so relieve it. He had long felt that everything—everyone—was connected. And he had wondered about the implications of such biblical passages as St. Paul's 'Bear ye one another's burdens, and so fulfill the law of Christ' and 'we, being many, are . . . every one members one of another' [Rom 12:5]. The ultimate example of the process was the Atonement, in which Christ had redeemed mankind from the burden of sin by taking it upon Himself."[6] One imagines Williams wondering what such verses meant in practice. To bear another's burdens is a nice sentiment, but how does it happen? What are the practical implications of being one in Christ?

Williams grapples with these questions in his fiction. In his 1937 novel *Descent into Hell*, in the chapter titled "The Doctrine of Substituted Love," a character named Pauline is in conversation with the poet Peter Stanhope. She tells him of the fear and distress she experiences because of a recurring vision. He does not dismiss her anxieties but instead offers a very practical solution.

> "Haven't you heard it said that we ought to bear one another's burdens?" "But that means—" she began, and stopped. "I know," Stanhope said. "It means listening sympathetically, and thinking unselfishly, and being anxious about, and so on. Well, I don't say a word against all that; no doubt it helps. But I think when Christ or St. Paul, or whoever said *bear*, or whatever he Aramaically said instead of *bear*, he meant something much more like carrying a parcel instead of someone else. To bear a burden is precisely to carry it instead of. If you're still carrying yours, I'm not carrying it for you—however sympathetic I may be."[7]

---

4 Grevel Lindop, *Charles Williams: The Third Inkling* (Oxford: Oxford University Press, 2015), 155. Lindop cites here a 1984 letter by Thelma Shuttleworth (nee Mills) recalling the incident.

5 I grossly oversimplify Williams's concept here, aiming merely to illustrate how fiction urges readers to reflect on biblical ethics. For more on this intriguing idea, see e.g., Nancy C. Hanger, "The Excellent Absurdity: Substitution and Co-Inherence in C. S. Lewis and Charles Williams," *Mythlore* 34 (1983): 14–18; and Barbara Newman, "Charles Williams and the Companions of the Co-inherence," *Spiritus: A Journal of Christian Spirituality* 9.1 (2009): 1–26.

6 Lindop, *Charles Williams*, 156.

7 Charles Williams, *Descent into Hell* (1937; London: Charles Williams Society, 2018), 88. Italics original.

Pauline is skeptical at first, but like the episode recalled by Thelma Mills, she puts it to the test. Sure enough, her outlook transforms, and she recognizes, "She wouldn't worry; no . . . she couldn't worry. That was the mere truth—she couldn't worry. She was, then and there, whatever happened later, entirely free. She was, then and there, incapable of distress. . . . He had been quite right; he had simply picked up her parcel. God knew how he had done it, but he had."[8]

This is not his only fictional work touching on the subject: "Her hand closed round the [injured] ankle; her mind went inwards into the consciousness of the Power which contained them both; she loved it and adored it: with her own thought of Aaron in his immediate need, his fear, his pain, she adored. Her own ankle ached and throbbed in sympathy, not the sympathy of an easy proffer of mild regret, but that of a life habituated to such intercession." And it is more than physical pain Sybil carries for her brother Aaron in this 1932 Williams novel, *The Greater Trumps*: "She throbbed for an instant not with pain but with fear as his own fear passed through her being. It did but pass through; it was dispelled within her, dying away in the unnourishing atmosphere of her soul, and with the fear went the pain."[9]

Williams reads Galatians 6:2 literally, insisting sympathy alone falls short of carrying another's burden. Instead, it is beyond mere listening, thinking unselfishly, and being anxious about, as Stanhope puts it; it suggests rather something more akin to an actual encounter with another's distress. Stanhope suffers with and for Pauline as "the body of his flesh received her alien terror, [as] his mind carried the burden of her world."[10] Sybil does the same for her brother Aaron. *Empathy* seems a better term. Williams finds in Paul's remark a glimpse of Christ's incarnation, of Christ participating in creation and carrying the burden of a broken world. Christians in turn are to be Christlike, following his lead in sacrificial service to others. When Stanhope carries Pauline's burden, I think he approaches the heart of the gospel: "He endured her sensitiveness, but not her sin; the substitution there, if indeed there is a substitution, is hidden in the central mystery of Christendom which Christendom itself has never understood, nor can."[11]

---

8 Williams, *Descent into Hell*, 93, 94. Pauline later discovers this capacity to carry another's burden is not even limited by time (139–140).

9 Charles Williams, *The Greater Trumps* (1932; London: Charles Williams Society, 2019), 223, 224. Cf. 231 for a recollection of the scene as an act of healing.

10 Williams, *Descent into Hell*, 91.

11 Williams, *Descent into Hell*, 91.

The apostle's charge in Galatians 6:2 is weighty, especially given the second clause about fulfilling the law of Christ in this way. There may well be something of the "fanciful" in Williams's literalism, as Lewis suspects, but it's his process of exploring the meaning of biblical teachings through storytelling I highlight here. Right or wrong, Williams gets us thinking about sacrificial service. He shows us what enacting Galatians 6:2 might look like. For my part, these encounters with fictional studies of Paul's charge proved both moving and thought-provoking on first reading; a writer pushed me to think more deeply about what it means to love others as Christ loves me. Since reading these stories, I've even found myself praying on occasion—rather shyly, I confess, because unlike Sybil, mine is hardly a life habituated to such intercession—that God would allow me the privilege of carrying, literally carrying, the worries and pains of others. Fanciful? Maybe. But either way, we see here the capacity of works of fiction to inform and inspire Christian thought and praxis, which is the subject considered in the following pages.

Along with Professor Greco, there are others I must thank for reading with me. I regularly teach a course called Religious Themes in Literature at Providence University College in Manitoba, Canada. The list of novels, poems, plays, and short stories considered changes each time around, but most works of fiction considered in the following chapters appeared in one or another iteration of the syllabus during the last twenty or so years. My thanks to the generations of students in Religious Themes who've considered the intersections of art, theology, and ethics with me—who've looked to the margins with me. I'm sure their wisdom and idealism inform what follows in more ways than I realize. Among this thoughtful and talented bunch, I'm especially grateful to Christina Duerksen, who kindly read through earlier drafts of this book and offered numerous suggestions for improvement.

Introduction

Love Your Neighbor as Yourself

I take it for granted most picking up a book with the subtitle *Encounters with the Bible in Literature* are readers of both the Bible and literature. But maybe not. Some may be readers of the Bible but less interested in creative writing, while for others, the reverse may be true. My aim is to affirm what the first group already knows and to persuade those in the second and third of the same, namely, that reading widely, reading both secular and sacred, the creative and the canonical, is an enriching experience that enhances appreciation of both. There are plenty of good scholarly resources exploring the influence of religion generally and the Bible specifically on the creative writings of the Western world.[1] There are also many insightful works considering literature as a resource for those seeking to deepen their faith. I hope this book contributes to both conversations, but it is also narrower in scope. The specific issue I consider is how storytellers help us define discipleship and understand better the moral imperatives of Scripture, which explains the lead title, *Reading the Margins*.

---

1 See, e.g., Northrop Frye, *The Great Code: The Bible and Literature* (1981; San Diego, CA: Harvest, 2002); David Lyle Jeffrey, *Houses of the Interpreter: Reading Scripture, Reading Culture* (Waco, TX: Baylor University Press, 2003); David Lyle Jeffrey, ed., *A Dictionary of Biblical Tradition in English Literature* (Grand Rapids, MI: Eerdmans, 1992); Robert Detweiler and David Jasper, eds., with S. Brent Plate and Heidi L. Nordberg, *Religion and Literature: A Reader* (Louisville, KY: Westminster John Knox, 2000); and the "Further Reading" sections they include throughout; Andrew W. Hass, David Jasper, and Elisabeth Jay, eds., *The Oxford Handbook of English Literature and Theology* (Oxford: Oxford University Press, 2007); Paul Cavill and Heather Ward, with Matthew Baynham, Andrew Swinford, John Flood, and Roger Pooley, *Christian Tradition in English Literature: Poetry, Plays, and Shorter Prose* (Grand Rapids, MI: Zondervan, 2007); and Rebecca Lemon, Emma Mason, Jonathan Roberts, and Christopher Rowland, eds., *The Blackwell Companion to the Bible in English Literature* (Chichester, UK: Wiley-Blackwell, 2012).

INTRODUCTION

For Christians, the Bible is the inspired word of God, a unique revelation, but it is no less for that a human document. The cultures, languages, experiences, and personalities of the prophets and apostles are very much present in the writings of the Christian Old and New Testaments. God speaks, God reveals, through individuals and communities, through the processes of history as seen in the stories of ancient Israel and the early church. For Darren J. N. Middleton, the inspiration of Scripture "denotes each biblical writer's *graced* desire and attempt to comprehend the world in light of God's revelation," and though God is indeed "at the center of this interpretive process," this does not mean the works they produced "lose their human, fallible flavor during their composition."[2] He goes further, suggesting inspiration occurs outside biblical literature as well. It appears also among authors who, "whether inside or outside the traditional circle of Christian faith . . . have used and continue to use their creative imagination to gesture toward Mystery." They, like many others, Christian or otherwise, "sometimes find themselves engaged in a graced search for theological meaning."[3] I am similarly curious about such gestures toward Mystery.

Stories shape the way we view the world. We learn and teach, we interpret and evaluate, we urge caution and seek to persuade through narration. "How was your day?" "What's new?" "You won't believe what I just saw!" Our speech is constantly offering and requesting stories. But there is more. The artists producing the poems and novels and plays and songs and paintings and television shows and films we consume create other worlds for us to enter—and ones often contributing meaning to and resources helping us make sense of our lives. Some religious readers may question this or at least add a caveat. Yes, I read novels for entertainment and a bit of escapism, but the Bible alone gives shape to my worldview. Fair enough. But is this maybe a both/and situation? Is it possible the religious reader's biblically informed worldview has much to gain by reading or watching those entertaining and escapist fantasies? Is it possible fiction provides resources needed for navigating complicated

---

2 Darren J. N. Middleton, *Theology after Reading: Christian Imagination and the Power of Fiction* (Waco, TX: Baylor University Press, 2008), 2. Italics original. Among other books considering ways fiction enhances the religious life and theological contemplation, see, e.g., Karen Swallow Prior, *On Reading Well: Finding the Good Life through Great Books* (Grand Rapids, MI: Brazos, 2018); Ralph C. Wood, *Literature and Theology* (Nashville, TN: Abingdon, 2008); and Frederick Buechner, *Speak What We Feel (Not What We Ought to Say): Reflections on Literature and Faith* (New York: HarperSanFrancisco, 2001).

3 Middleton, *Theology after Reading*, 3.

lives, whether those producing them hold to a religious worldview or not?[4] To explore these possibilities further, I turn in the next few pages to excerpts from the works of two literary preceptors leading me to think so. I borrow the term from Canadian theorist Northrop Frye, who directed the following word of wisdom to students: "I think it advisable for every critic proposing to devote his life to literary scholarship to pick a major writer of literature as a kind of spiritual preceptor for himself, whatever the subject of his thesis. I am not speaking, of course, of any sort of moral model, but it seems to me that growing up inside a mind so large that one has no sense of claustrophobia within it is an irreplaceable experience in humane studies. Some kind of transmission by seed goes on here."[5]

Frye is not prescriptive regarding which author or authors qualify. Presumably William Blake functioned this way for him. Several writers fill this role for me, and I try to reinforce Frye's idea of "growing up" inside such minds by intentionally returning to some of them throughout this book, which explains recurring discussions of the Brontë sisters, Woody Guthrie, Charles Dickens, Bob Dylan, and Salman Rushdie. But at this point, I turn to two others whose works *gesture toward Mystery*. When I engage them, the resulting "transmission[s] by seed" occasionally take root and awaken new perspectives. In the first we see how works of the imagination mingle with real-world experiences and provide a means by which we interpret them. The second illustrates how fiction with an ethical impulse turns our gaze outward, beyond the self. Such reading experiences serve as prompts, redirecting the mind toward spiritual matters.

C. S. LEWIS'S BOOKS AND BATTLES

Real Life and the Life of the Imagination. It's 1917. The Great War rages on the Continent, and an eighteen-year-old C. S. Lewis settles into his new environs as a student at the University of Oxford. This is more than a decade before his conversion to Christianity. Studies are on hold, the school nearly empty. Most of his peers are on the battlefield, many already dead. He himself will reach the trenches of France within a few months, arriving there on his nineteenth

---

4 On the matter of religious scruples leading to censorship, see further the afterword.
5 Northrop Frye, "The Search for Acceptable Words," in *Spiritus Mundi: Essays on Literature, Myth, and Society* (1973; Bloomington: Indiana University Press, 1976), 15.

INTRODUCTION

birthday. He will sustain injuries and return to England to convalesce, after which he will resume his academic pursuits and launch his career as a scholar and writer. But not yet, not now as he writes a letter to longtime friend Arthur Greeves back in Ireland.[6] It is July 8. In this latest of many missives to Arthur, he tells of a moving experience occurring the night before.

These days he spends most of his time at nearby Keble College training for military service, living there in temporary barracks but returning to his rooms at University College on weekends. Though Irish and exempt from conscription, Lewis chose to serve anyway, entering the army through the University Officers' Training Corp. Military service seems an odd fit for him. The teenage Lewis was bookish, by his own admission fat, not particularly patriotic, and seems to have little respect for the army and soldiering. "Write me a nice long letter and help keep up other interests amid all this damned military show," he instructed Arthur a few weeks earlier.[7]

He is understandably afraid of what's to come but also resigned. His father is anxious his son should be in the artillery, assuming this to be safer. Jack, as he was known, is more realistic, seeing the more dangerous infantry to be his fate. He lacks the "advanced mathematics" required for an artillery appointment for one thing, and he is uncomfortable with the idea of gaining protections others do not enjoy: "It is true that you might get me in by influence. But would it not be very wrong for mere reasons of safety, to push me into a responsible position for which I know I am absolutely unfit?"[8] He later reports his respect for the commanding officer of the Third Somerset Light Infantry and comradeship with other soldiers as further reasons to stay where he is.

With an uncertain future ahead, just months before reaching France, Lewis settles into his letter. Last night, he tells Arthur, "I wandered out into the deserted quad. [of University College] & after 'strolling' for some time went up a staircase where nobody ever goes in these days into the oldest part of the College." There is an artistic flair to his account, as he establishes an eerie, lonely, gothic atmosphere, complete with tiny, ivy-covered windows, gloomy halls and rooms, and a descending darkness. "I walked up & down long passages," he continues, "with locked rooms on each side, reveling in 'desolation.'" Most of the student rooms are inaccessible but—readers see this

---

6   C. S. Lewis, *Collected Letters*, vol. 1, *Family Letters, 1905–1931*, ed. Walter Hooper (London: HarperCollins, 2000), 323–325.

7   Letter of June 10, 1917, in *Collected Letters*, 1:321.

8   Letter of July 22, 1917, in *Collected Letters*, 1:328.

coming after the dramatic setup—"by good luck I found one open & went in." He observes the name Carter inscribed on the door.

There is a deep sense of melancholy at this moment. It seems "almost sacrilege to turn on the lights in such a forsaken place, but I simply had to inspect it." The furniture is just as its former resident left it; "his photos were there on the wall," his books in place. A copy of Laurence Sterne's *Tristram Shandy*, one of Henry Fielding's *Tom Jones*. A snapshot of a young student's life, one now in the trenches instead of Oxford's lecture halls. Lewis finds the experience moving and tells Arthur, "I suppose this sounds trivial to you: but perhaps you can picture the strange poetry of the thing in such a time & place. I wonder who Carter is, and if he has been killed yet, & why he left his pile of music so untidily on the dressing table?" After continuing his evening rambles with a visit to the clock tower with its "cobwebs," he returns to his rooms for some relief from wartime worry, finding the empty school "a bit creepy." And once there, he turns to fiction, finding comfort in Edmund Spenser's *Faerie Queene* (1590, 1596), an epic poem of knights in armor, heroism, and service to queen and country. An interesting choice, given his circumstances.

Lewis closes this letter, as he often does in correspondence with Arthur, discussing his literary ambitions, the hope of getting "my stuff" published.[9] There's a connection here, I think, between the brief glimpses of Lewis-the-soldier and Lewis-the-would-be-author in letters around this time. To his mind, both careers seem doomed to failure. With respect to his longing to write books, he admits to Arthur, "What castles in the air—but still better have a cloud castle than no castle at all."

Quite an admission. He recognizes his extravagant, ambitious desire to publish is likely nothing more than a pipe dream, especially since the odds of returning from the war are not good. Yet the dreaming itself is what really matters. At the same time, the fat, bookish, unlikely soldier destined for a dangerous infantry position retreats into Edmund Spenser's *Faerie Queene*, of all things. Though unfit for the artillery and in many other ways a less than ideal candidate for service, this frightened soldier on the eve of battle finds comfort in a chivalrous romance about knights slaying dragons and other enemies of the realm. A bit of escapism, yes, but also an embrace of the heroic at a time when most needed. Real life and fiction meet. My career as a

---

9 He would eventually release his first book, a collection of poems titled *Spirits in Bondage: A Cycle of Lyrics*, in 1919.

soldier is not likely to end any better than my efforts to publish, but duty calls, and I must try my best. Imagination, those castles in the sky, as inspiration. Imagination, sparked by Spenser's tales of the Redcrosse Knight and others, as solace to one about to face his own dragon.

Jump ahead a few years and we find him still processing major life events through stories read and stories told. On one of the branches of the River Cherwell, near Magdalen College of the University of Oxford, there is an area once reserved for male students to bathe. In a 1922 diary entry, Lewis reports swimming there, adding a sobering observation: "Amid so much nudity I was interested to note the passing of my own generation: two years ago every second man had a wound mark, but I did not see one today."[10] Such a disturbing indicator of the extent of damage to the bodies of his peers that the *absence* of war wounds among younger students who did not fight warrants a passing remark in a diary entry.

We know something of the physical injuries he himself sustained while in France from a message sent to his father in 1918, with perhaps some understatement to minimize a parent's anxiety: "I was . . . hit in the back of the left hand, on the left leg from behind and just above the knee, and in the left side just under the arm pit. All three were only flesh wounds."[11] While recovering in London, he again downplays the situation in a letter to Arthur Greeves: "There are still two pieces of shrapnel in my chest, but they give me no discomfort."[12] Others in Lewis's circle had similar experiences. Fellow Inkling Hugo Dyson, for one, fought in the Battle of the Somme (1916), the Battle of Arras (1917), and the Battle of Passchendaele at Ypres (1918) and was badly wounded in the last.[13]

As mentioned, Lewis was not a Christian when he wrote those letters or that 1922 diary entry, but even after his conversion sometime around 1930, that close connection between his "real" life and the life of the imagination, both as a reader and a writer, continued.[14] It's now 1946, and those war wounds

---

10 C. S. Lewis, *All My Road before Me: The Diary of C. S. Lewis 1922–1927*, ed. Walter Hooper (San Diego, CA: Harvest, 1991), 39.

11 Lewis, *Collected Letters*, 1:367.

12 Lewis, *Collected Letters*, 1:374.

13 See Hooper's entry on Dyson in the Biographical Appendix of Lewis, *Collected Letters*, 1:988–990.

14 For some fascinating biographical sleuthing and a reappraisal of the date usually assigned to Lewis's conversion, see Alister McGrath's *C. S. Lewis—A Life: Eccentric Genius, Reluctant Prophet* (Carol Stream, IL: Tyndale House, 2013), 141–159.

sustained decades earlier are still an issue. When writing to a friend, he lists these physical scars alongside emotional ones that torment him: "The early loss of my mother, great unhappiness at school, and the shadow of the last war [World War I] and presently the experience of it [World War II], had given me a very pessimistic view of existence."[15] Lewis's letters of the 1930s and '40s reflect continual reminders of aging, mortality, and vulnerability, among them the failing health of his "mother" Janie Moore (a friend's mother he lived with and cared for), his brother's return to active military service during wartime and struggles with alcoholism, food shortages and rationing, his own worsening rheumatism, and the sudden death of friend and fellow Inkling Charles Williams in 1945. All the while, interestingly, Lewis was writing fiction with conspicuous attention to the damage of bodies and minds and their recovery.

Lewis turned forty-one on November 29, 1939, thus avoiding conscription, but his writing at the time suggests deep concern about war and human fragility. In *Perelandra* (1943), which draws loosely on the biblical creation narratives, the protagonist, Elwin Ransom, uses his "middle-aged, sedentary body" to fight a demonic enemy on another planet (Perelandra, or Venus). Ransom, like Lewis and like J. R. R. Tolkien, on whom he bases this character, has memories of "very dangerous job[s] in the last war" and is aware another one rages back on Earth. The Germans "'may be bombing London to bits at this moment!'"[16] Wars past and present—World Wars I and II—intrude on the fantasy. The story culminates in a great battle between Ransom and the devilish Professor Edward Rolles Weston, a fight of good against evil. Ransom is victorious but badly hurt. His injuries include a vicious bite to the foot, recalling humanity's struggle with the serpent in Genesis 3:15. This wound does not heal, but the rest of his body does and "surprisingly quickly" when he enters an Edenic garden.[17] Ransom rejuvenates in this sinless, new world. Hints of real life and longing, of fear and faith, subtly woven into a fantastic tale.

After returning home, an astonished friend finds Ransom "glowing with health and rounded with muscle and seemingly ten years younger," despite the bleeding foot. Spending time on Perelandra reverses the usual decrepitude

---

15 C. S. Lewis, *The Collected Letters of C. S. Lewis*, vol. 2, *Books, Broadcasts, and the War, 1931–1949*, ed. Walter Hooper (New York: HarperCollins, 2004), 747.

16 C. S. Lewis, *Perelandra* (1943; London: HarperCollins, 2005), 180, 184, 208.

17 Lewis, *Perelandra*, 236.

and decay known back on Earth. In *That Hideous Strength* (1945), the sequel to *Perelandra*, Ransom appears a young man even though "nearer fifty than forty."[18] It is a both/and situation, a paradox. Younger yet aging, healed yet bleeding and broken. Our frail bodies are prone to all manner of illnesses and injuries, and ultimately death, but in the most important sense, which is to say *spiritually*, the Christian sings, it is well with my soul. We have this treasure in earthen vessels (2 Cor 4:7). Real life, fantasy, and reflection on religious themes intermingle in Lewis's wartime storytelling.

Lewis struggled with his own "bleeding heel" at this stage of his life. He, too, was sound in spirit yet broken in body: "I've finished another book [*The Hideous Strength*] wh. concludes the Ransom trilogy," he writes to a friend. He then adds in the very next sentence, *suggesting a connection with the book just mentioned, whether consciously or otherwise*, "I've had an operation for the removal of a piece of shell I got into me in the last war, which, after lying snug and silent like an unrepented sin for 20 years or so, began giving me trouble."[19] An interesting simile, one hinting that battle with a physical enemy (during World War I) is somehow analogous with battling spiritual ones. Sometimes the enemy scores a blow (shrapnel, sin), and we suffer as a result. Paul thinks in similar terms, urging readers to put on a soldier's armor when combating spiritual foes (Eph 6:10–20).

Tolkien also writes about bodily restoration for those broken by war. Thus spake Ioreth, wise woman of Gondor, "*The hands of the king are the hands of a healer, and so shall the rightful king be known.*"[20] After the king's ministrations, Faramir opens his eyes and says,

> "My lord, you called me. I come. What does the king command?"
> "Walk no more in the shadows, but awake!" said Aragorn.[21]

King Aslan in Lewis's later Narnia tales heals the victims of war, too, as does Lucy Pevensie. When Father Christmas distributes gifts in *The Lion, the*

---

18 Lewis, *Perelandra*, 30; C. S. Lewis, *That Hideous Strength: A Modern Fairy-Tale for Grown-Ups* (1945; London: HarperCollins, 2005), 186. Lewis turned forty-seven the year he published this book, Tolkien fifty-three.

19 Lewis, *Collected Letters*, 2:624.

20 J. R. R. Tolkien, *Return of the King* (1955; London: HarperCollins, 1999), 157. Italics original.

21 Tolkien, *Return of the King*, 161.

Witch and the Wardrobe (1950), he gives her a cordial: "'If you or any of your friends is hurt [fighting the enemy], a few drops of this will restore them.'"²²

Without appealing to allegory to interpret these books, it is enough to suggest they resemble elements of the Christian story. Faith-inclined readers recognize in Tolkien's returning king, who brings healing to a broken world, something of the Christian hope of Christ returning as king to wipe away every tear (Rev 21:4). Father Christmas is one of the few overt references to Christianity in the Chronicles of Narnia. Like Tolkien's Middle Earth, Narnia also has its share of war, injury, illness, and death. The devout Roman Catholic Tolkien and the devout Anglican Lewis allow Christian longing for *ultimate* healing and restoration, even resurrection, to permeate their fantasies. These soldiers' stories about lingering scars and restored bodies hint at deep faith. As they well know, Christ's own resurrected body still bore the scars of battle (John 20:27).

Lewis and Tolkien are hardly alone weaving personal experience into the fiction they read and write, though the degree to which authors do it naturally varies.²³ But more important than mining occasional clues about writers' lives, fiction reveals much about the broader world and presents us with questions about the way we live and our interactions with others. This often has ethical import, as our next literary preceptor shows.

HUGH LOFTING'S PARADISE AND A PIFFILOSAURUS

Imagining a Kinder, Gentler World. While the teenage C. S. Lewis contemplated literary castles in the air amid bullets and bombs, Hugh Lofting (1886–1947) was not that far away doing much the same thing. As origin stories for fictional characters go, Doctor Dolittle's is rather unexpected. Hugh Lofting first put pen to paper, bringing his most famous creation to life, while on the battlefields of World War I. It is unexpected because Dolittle is the very embodiment of peaceful coexistence. As a soldier in Flanders and France, Dolittle's creator engaged in a form of literary resistance. The resulting books (published 1920–1952) present an alternate reality in which aggression gives

---

22 C. S. Lewis, *The Lion, the Witch and the Wardrobe* (1950; New York: HarperCollins, 1994), 160.

23 For a very different blending of the imaginative and the autobiographical, see chap. 5.

INTRODUCTION

way to affability, hostility to hospitality. He turns from the ugliness of battle toward a utopian dreamworld where animals and people alike are treated kindly. According to Gary D. Schmidt, "None of the novels can ever be read outside the context of . . . the trenches of the First World War, where horses, unprotected against the green billows of gas that belched across the fields and cascaded into the trenches, died screaming out of burning lungs." This is where Lofting's longing for a gentler connection with nature begins: "While he could somehow avoid despair and place the war in the context of a reasonable explanation—these were apparently rational creatures who had consciously decided to commit atrocity—he could not accept the destruction of horses. While the troops could protect themselves against the green gas that poured into the trenches and coated the landscape, the horses could not. It sprang into their lungs, blistered their tissues, and led to agonizing death."[24]

The books, Lofting later explained, began as letters home to his children during the war, and the idea of a medical person caring for animals has direct connection to what he saw: "One thing . . . that kept forcing itself more and more on my attention was the very considerable part the animals were playing in the World War and that as time went on they, too, seemed to become Fatalists. They took their chances with the rest of us. But their fate was far different from the men's. However seriously a soldier was wounded, his life was not despaired of; all the resources of a surgery highly developed by the war were brought to his aid. A seriously wounded horse was put out by a timely bullet."[25] Lofting's contributions to the modern animal welfare movement are not easily overstated.[26]

Consider a brief illustration of the imaginative force of these (on the surface) lighthearted tales. The good doctor visits the people of Fantippo, who believe fire-breathing dragons inhabit an island just off the coast. They call it No Man's Land. According to legend, a magic spell turned the mother-in-law

---

24 Gary D. Schmidt, *Hugh Lofting*, Twayne's English Authors Series 496 (New York: Twayne, 1992), 13.

25 As cited in Schmidt, *Hugh Lofting*, 6. See, too, M. Daphne Kutzer, *Empire's Children: Empire and Imperialism in Classic British Children's Books* (New York: Garland, 2000), 81. For her full discussion of Lofting and his Dolittle stories, see 80–94. In addition to the Great War, she demonstrates ways Lofting's experiences at colonial outposts in Cuba and Lagos, working as a civil engineer, influenced his writing.

26 I celebrate this aspect of Lofting's writing throughout *Creative Compassion, Literature and Animal Welfare* (Basingstoke, UK: Palgrave Macmillan, 2020). See esp. 3–8; 247–248. See, too, chap. 7 below regarding Lofting's influence on the English novelist Richard Adams.

of an ancient king into one, and after banishment to the island, she had offspring. Hundreds of years later, the residents of Fantippo still believe the island to be full of dragons, and no one dares visit the place. Predictably, Doctor Dolittle is curious. He and his dog, Jip, swim toward No Man's Land, but the currents are too strong. They are close to drowning, but suddenly a large creature rises from the water beneath them and carries them the rest of the way. It is a piffilosaurus. Once safely ashore, Jip and Dolittle's remarkable host shows them around the island and explains its residents' unique situation. The doctor, of course, can speak to animals.

Doctor Dolittle is the first human visitor to the island in a thousand years and so the first in an age to see a piffilosaurus. They were thought to be extinct. The secret to their preservation lies in their refuge away from human encroachment: "'We didn't want the locals to see us,' said the strange beast. 'They think we are dragons—and we let them go on thinking it. Because then they don't come near the island and we have our country to ourselves.... They think we live on men and breathe fire! But all we ever really eat is bananas.'"[27]

The truth is, the creature explains further, this is the only part of the world where we now live, "'where we are left—where we can live in peace.'" Human interference is more than a nuisance: "'Whatever happens, we mustn't be seen from the shore and have the [locals] coming here. It would be the end of us if that should ever happen, because, between ourselves, although they think us so terrible, we are really more harmless than sheep.'"[28]

What specifically the piffilosaurus has in mind—whether his species fears human hunters, destruction of their habitat, enslavement for labor, or some combination of these—is left to the reader's imagination, but their extinction would be the inevitable outcome of intrusion. All these options involve cruelty and forms of oppressive dominion. It is pure fantasy, but Lofting's disdain for human aggression is subtly present, beneath the story's surface just as the friendly piffilosaurus was hidden beneath the waves. The story reflects unease with humanity's proclivity to destroy habitats and harass wildlife (cf. chap. 7). This human-free island is an animal heaven on earth. It is a place where violence simply doesn't exist.

This chapter of *Doctor Dolittle's Post Office* (1923), titled "The Animals' Paradise," offers a reenactment of Edenic peacefulness. Like the Genesis story,

---

27 Hugh Lofting, *Doctor Dolittle's Post Office*, in *Doctor Dolittle: The Complete Collection*, vol. 1 (1923; New York: Aladdin, 2019), 478–479.

28 Lofting, *Doctor Dolittle's Post Office*, 479, 480.

this island paradise is no longer accessible to people. As the biblical story goes, after God drives Adam and Eve from Eden, he places an angel waving a flaming sword to guard against their return to the tree of life (Gen 3:24). Here, instead of a fiery sword, it is the lore about fiery dragons that keeps visitors away. In addition, the high cliffs along the shore of the island hide the beautiful bowl-shaped valley from the view of those on shore. To Jip, the island is like a plum pudding in appearance.[29]

The Edenic character of the island continues to emerge as the piffilosaurus shows Dolittle around. This island is entirely populated by harmless, vegetable-feeding creatures. "'If we had the others,'" he continues, "'of course, we wouldn't last long.'"[30] The scene recalls the first biblical creation story: "God said, 'See, I have given you every plant yielding seed that is upon the face of all the earth, and every tree with seed in its fruit; you shall have them for food. And to every beast of the earth, and to every bird of the air, and to everything that creeps on the earth, everything that has the breath of life, I have given every green plant for food.' And it was so" (Gen 1:29–30). Lofting emphasizes the plant-eating character of this strange world Jip and Dolittle visit:

> Down by the banks of the streams the Doctor was shown great herds of hippopotami, feeding on the luscious reeds that grew at the water's edge. In the wide fields of high grass there were elephants and rhinoceri browsing. On the slopes where the forests were sparse he spied long-necked giraffes, nibbling from the trees. Monkeys and deer of all kinds were plentiful. And birds swarmed everywhere. In fact, every kind of creature that does not eat meat was there, living peaceably and happily with the others in this land where vegetable food abounded and the disturbing tread of man was never heard.[31]

The absence of predation also echoes the prophet Isaiah, who writes of a kingdom of peace involving people and animals (Isa 11:1–9).

As the lone human on the island, Doctor Dolittle is, in effect, Adam in the garden of Eden: "Out of the ground the Lord God formed every animal of the field and every bird of the air, and brought them to the man" (Gen 2:19; cf. Mark 1:13). And indeed, the animals do approach the Adam-Doctor: "He

---

29 Lofting, *Doctor Dolittle's Post Office*, 480–481. For further description of the geography and cultures of Fantippo and No Man's Land, see the entries in Alberto Manguel and Gianni Guadalupi, *The Dictionary of Imaginary Places* (Toronto: Vintage, 2001), 213–214 and 473–474, respectively.
30 Lofting, *Doctor Dolittle's Post Office*, 480.
31 Lofting, *Doctor Dolittle's Post Office*, 481.

was kept busy from morning to night with all the animals who wanted to consult him about different things."[32]

The capacity of stories to sketch out worlds that do not exist, or exist yet, is part of the magic of fiction. There is an ethical impulse in this Lofting flight of fancy. We may not be able to hide animals, to create spaces for them beyond all human intrusions. Human-caused climate change, for instance, touches all living things on earth. But the ability to imagine safe places where animals flourish is evidence humans can do *some things* to ameliorate conditions for *some animals*. While standing on a hill with Jip and the piffilosaurus, the doctor gazes down over the wide bowl of the island, filled with its contented animals, and sighs. He then pronounces what amounts to a benediction: "'This beautiful land could also have been called the "Animals' Paradise,"' he murmured. 'Long may they enjoy it to themselves! May this, indeed, be *No Man's Land* forever!'"[33]

Some things are in our power, Lofting seems to suggest. Some things we can do to alleviate animals' suffering, and the Adamic Doctor Dolittle, who constantly protects other species from human cruelties, offers a model of kindness.

Lofting is a children's author so of course needed to mask his pacifist rejection of war in the whimsy of the Dolittle tales.[34] But there is one work in the Lofting catalog, the only one he wrote for adults, in which the mask comes off. He published the book-length poem *Victory for the Slain* in 1942, during the dark days of another conflict, and though the writer during his lifetime never emerged from the shadow cast by his portly doctor, and likely never will, this rarely read poem is a remarkable example of artistry as advocacy, of creative writing striving to awaken our better angels.

This passionate and troubling antiwar jeremiad is more despairing than optimistic. The shift in form and tone in this late-in-life work is jarring

---

32 Lofting, *Doctor Dolittle's Post Office*, 481, 482.
33 Lofting, *Doctor Dolittle's Post Office*, 481.
34 There are hints of Lofting's antiwar sentiments in the children's books. For instance, when Tommy Stubbins meets Colonel Bellowes, this military figure has a red, angry face; yells at the boy in keeping with his name; makes him go to the backdoor servants' entrance; and calls him "boy." When he first meets the nonviolent Dolittle in the near context, however, we're told he has a kind face, speaks civilly to his new young friend, welcomes him through the front door of his home, and calls him by his surname as though an adult acquaintance, much to the boy's delight (see Hugh Lofting, *The Voyages of Doctor Dolittle*, in *Doctor Dolittle: The Complete Collection*, vol. 1 [1922; New York: Aladdin, 2019], 21–34).

compared with his more familiar animal stories as the author shifts from child-friendly prose to adult poetry and from the playful to the poignant. As the title phrase suggests, one repeated across these pages, the narrator contemplates humanity's fragility and considers death as less an evil to be dreaded than a solace for the world-weary:

> Wholesome, friendly Death,
>   You are no grim or morbid Reaper here.
>   Give me your hand again, as once you did
>   In Flanders, such a little time ago,
>   Some score of years and five.[35]

Lofting published this poem in 1942 during World War II. Looking back twenty-five years takes us to 1917 during the First. Lofting was a soldier in Flanders in what was supposed to be the war to end all wars and badly wounded. The narrator's anguish in *Victory for the Slain* stems from the never-ending return to conflict: "Wars to end wars?—War again!"[36] But as he discovered a quarter century earlier, and continues to reflect now as Europe's new conflict rages, the dead know peace.[37] It is the only form of escape from violence.

The poem opens with the narrator walking along a town's high street and coming upon a soldier dressed in hospital blues. The patient struggles to light a cigarette because he is missing a hand. The narrator helps him do so, then continues his walk, "a weary peasant" seeking refuge from "the Now and Present" in "this edifice."[38] The edifice is a grand old church where for centuries the music of *"Come unto me!"* supported generations of the faithful.[39] That refrain is Jesus's invitation to approach and find rest in him (see Matt 11:28), but therein lies a disturbing reality for the author-narrator.

Across the sixty or so pages of the poem, Lofting describes the architecture of that medieval church and the tombs of the honored dead who fell during conflicts in the remote past. The narrator thinks of the prayers uttered in that

---

35 Hugh Lofting, *Victory for the Slain* (1942; Sandness, UK: Walmer, 2020), 21–22. Cf. 32.
36 Lofting, *Victory for the Slain*, 39.
37 Lofting, *Victory for the Slain*, 27, etc.
38 Lofting, *Victory for the Slain*, 3.
39 Lofting, *Victory for the Slain*, 5.

place throughout the centuries by those responding to Jesus's invitation and their recollections of venerated saints. But as the pilgrim-narrator immerses himself in this holy space, a persistent anxiety intrudes: "What if their *planes* come over this"; "Planes? . . . . The walls are strong. / The roof is frail . . . . They must not come!"; "[Birds,] I've seen your instinct do the same / When silver of an aeroplane / Has flashed against the sunlit blue."[40] The narrator's fear is warranted because as the poem draws to a close, the worst happens:

> Listen! . . . . A drone!
> That's it . . . . But is it in my ears alone?
> A drone! That's it: a droning in the sky! . . . .
> A drone of aeroplanes!
>
> At last, with whistling screams, it strikes.
> Cutting through the chancel-roof like paper,
> The bomb
> Explodes before the tabernacle of our dreams![41]

Lofting is unsparing when confronting the horrors of war—"I saw the incendiaries flash, / The bombs like rain!"; "children's bodies broken, rent"—and the memories of conflict never leave him.[42] Twenty-five years after his own battlefield experiences, the left-right-left-right marching orders still come to mind constantly, and the bombs continue to fall.[43] The poem closes with the narrator's plea to the victorious slain, now more enlightened for having passed beyond the "madness" of the perennial return to war. "Direct" the living "to the Peace that must endure."[44]

In both forms of writing—the whimsical Dolittle tales and the despairing antiwar verse—we find Lofting's art confronting humanity's darkest inclinations. A gentler world, a peaceful world, is elusive but still within the reach of our imaginations, and this is a necessary first step if we are to realize those dreams. In both forms of writing, Lofting also draws on religion, its imagery and worldview, to articulate his values. The writings considered throughout

---

40 Lofting, *Victory for the Slain*, 5 (italics original), 16, 23.
41 Lofting, *Victory for the Slain*, 54.
42 Lofting, *Victory for the Slain*, 55.
43 Lofting, *Victory for the Slain*, 1, 2, 7, 31, 33.
44 Lofting, *Victory for the Slain*, 60.

INTRODUCTION

the present book are as different from one another as *Doctor Dolittle's Post Office* is from *Victory for the Slain*, but also like both, the underlying ethical concerns are pressing and deadly serious. They also interact with sacred themes and texts.

READING AND THE EMPATHETIC GAP

Reading fiction and poetry is a slow process. The time it takes to interact with creative writing is a kind of meditation. To read thoroughly and carefully requires patience, across many hours and days depending on the length and complexity of the work in question. We live with stories and the characters in them for that duration, momentarily giving them our full attention and shutting out all else. Of course, not all books offer the kinds of spiritual nourishment I have in view, but many do, turning our thoughts to what is true, noble, right, pure, lovely, admirable, excellent, and praiseworthy, to borrow St. Paul's terms (Phil 4:8).

Furthermore, literature is directive. Authors make decisions for readers, forcing them to submit to plots and outcomes. They take us places we might not otherwise go, given the choice, and put us in company with people we might otherwise avoid or never have occasion to meet. In addition, writers impose certain interpretations of events, which we may or may not share. We see things from points of view not our own. Sometimes this includes perspectives on religious matters with which we disagree. Authors are not necessarily beholden to the creeds or convictions of the religious reading communities with which we associate. Most books considered in the following chapters interact with the Bible in one way or another and often in a highly original fashion. If we differ in opinion with their interpretations, this forces us to think through our reasons why. This is never a bad thing. Confronting difference is an opportunity. Maybe there is something to learn from that alternative viewpoint, but even if not, the process of reviewing why we hold certain positions is an important one. Inevitably, our theology is incomplete, at times even erroneous. Now we know only in part (1 Cor 13:9). There is always more to learn, a need for deeper comprehension, and this is certainly true with reference to ethics. Literature is a potential resource. Through fiction we learn about the struggles of others and often in the process discover prejudices and gaps in our moral reasoning and commitment to care. When it functions this way, it is prophetic.

Empathy and sympathy are related but not identical. Empathy connects to the German term *Einfühlung*, a feeling *into*, which "signifies an identification of oneself with an observed person or object which is so close that one seems to participate in the posture, motion, and sensations that one observes." It is a kind of inner mimicry, to the extent that in our absorbed contemplation "we seem empathically to pirouette with a ballet dancer, soar with a hawk, bend with the movements of a tree in the wind, and even share the strength, ease, and grace with which a well-proportioned arch appears to support a bridge."[45] Sympathy involves not a feeling *into* a physical state and sensations but rather a "feeling-along-with the mental state and emotions" of others, whether human or nonhuman beings "to whom we attribute human emotions."[46] Instances of sympathy are common enough in biblical texts. When Lazarus dies, many neighbors comfort his sisters, Mary and Martha (John 11:19). They know what it is to grieve so can feel along with others who lose a loved one, even though their own connection to the deceased is at some remove. It is possible some of those mourners did not even know Lazarus but were yet able to comfort Mary and Martha because grief is an experience shared by all. They've lost siblings too. But it seems the Bible often urges a fellow feeling going beyond that, something better described as empathy:

- Love your neighbor as yourself (Lev 19:18; cf. Mark 12:31; Rom 13:9).
- Weep with those who weep (Rom 12:15).
- Bear one another's burdens (Gal 6:2).
- If one member of the body of Christ suffers, all suffer together with him or her (1 Cor 12:26).

When Jesus weeps with the sisters (John 11:33–35), we know it is a grief different in kind from the larger crowd.[47] He, too, loved Lazarus (11:36) so can empathize with the sisters in ways others cannot. His is a shared experience,

---

45 M. H. Abrams with Geoffrey Galt Harpham, *A Glossary of Literary Terms*, 11th ed. (Stamford, CT: Cengage, 2015), 105–106.

46 Abrams and Harpham, *A Glossary of Literary Terms*, 106–107.

47 For contexts regarding death and burial customs in the Roman and Jewish worlds, see, e.g., Everett Ferguson, *Backgrounds of Early Christianity*, 3rd ed. (Grand Rapids, MI: Eerdmans, 2003), 244–250; and Craig A. Evans, *Jesus and the Ossuaries: What Jewish Burial Practices Reveal about the Beginning of Christianity* (Waco, TX: Baylor University Press, 2003), esp. chap. 1. Those bereaved sometimes hired professional wailers. Of course, employed mourners would not experience the loss of Lazarus in the same way as Mary, Martha, Jesus, and others close to the man.

a feeling-into the sisters' sorrow. Biblical texts regularly call for and model forms of empathy, but empathy requires a degree of understanding, an ability to connect with other people and share in their situation. But how is this possible with respect to those we do not know or those in situations we know nothing of firsthand?

At the risk of overstatement, I argue we do well to approach reading fiction as a kind of spiritual discipline or spiritual exercise because it provides a way of moving toward such empathetic connection. In the Christian tradition, the term *spiritual discipline* usually refers to acts of devotion such as prayer, meditation on Scripture, fasting, corporate and private worship, and singing and chanting. I argue there is value in approaching stories with a similar attitude to that associated with contemplation of religious mysteries and approach to the altar rail. In the context of worship, the devotee is attentive to the divine presence, prepared and willing to hear God's voice and to be led by the Spirit into greater understanding and a more robust commitment to fulfill their calling. This ought to be true of all aspects of our lives: "Whatever you do, in word or deed, do everything in the name of the Lord Jesus" (Col 3:17). I do not mean all books on our shelves are likely to facilitate some profound insight or that we should only read with such an agenda. I turn to Douglas Adams for laughs, to Stephen King for chills, and to Jane Austen for romance. Still, whatever pages I flip through ("whatever you do"), I try to be open to anything that feeds the soul. As a spiritual discipline so defined, it is one especially suited for spurring reflection on ways we treat others, even to the point of awakening something approaching empathy.

I marvel at the capacity of creative writers to nurture bonds between readers and fictional characters. "A work of literary fiction . . . can show its readers how an experience feels—what that experience is like," writes Mitchell S. Green. To the degree the information provided by the author is reliable and the one receiving it comprehends, there is reason to think "a reader can learn what that experience is like from reading a work of fiction. That learning process will in turn result in their knowing what that experience is like. As a result, the reader will be in a position to empathize with an individual—be they fictional or real—who is undergoing the experiences so described."[48] Identification with the plight of others, while a powerful motivator for positive

---

48 Mitchell S. Green, "Learning to Be Good (or Bad) in (or through) Literature," in *Fictional Characters, Real Problems: The Search for Ethical Content*, ed. Garry L. Hagberg (Oxford: Oxford University Press, 2016), 298.

action on their behalf, is not always an easy thing to achieve, and yet the prophets insist we do. *Weep with those who weep*. For this reason, there is much for those committed to biblical ethics to gain from storytellers able to relate effectively the distresses leading to those tears.

Here's an example of the challenge I have in view. The author of Hebrews instructs readers, "Remember those who are in prison, as though you were in prison with them; those who are being tortured, as though you yourselves were being tortured" (13:3). These mandates presuppose the audience's ability to identify with certain experiences, and indeed, those originally addressed understood the plight of the incarcerated and tortured owing to past harassments they survived: "Recall those earlier days when . . . you endured a hard struggle with sufferings, sometimes being publicly exposed to abuse and persecution, and sometimes being partners with those so treated" (10:32–33). Having gone through a similar trial positions the readers to do what is asked. Previous experience permits empathy, something for which this community has a reputation, as is evident in the next verse: "You had compassion for those who were in prison" (10:34). The author issues the imperative of 13:3 to readers who lived through the traumas described in 10:32–34. Support those going through horrors you experienced years before.

How are later readers to approach Hebrews 13:3? Those who engage biblical texts within faith communities usually make a hermeneutical leap from first contexts to contemporary relevance. The author of Hebrews knew the original readers' background of oppression and instructed them to recall those earlier events and respond to those now facing similar trials. But how am I to empathize with those imprisoned and tortured "as though" I were going through the same things when I have no idea—not *really*—what such persecution is like experientially? Literally translated, Hebrews 13:3 tells us to remember the tortured as though "being in the body" with them. General assent to the notion that prisoners and victims of religious persecution deserve compassion seems insufficient.[49] The writer urges something more profound. Empathy is not easy and requires knowledge and deep connection with others. I confess to struggling with several of the Bible's ethical

---

49 Those addressed "are not to avoid a share in such suffering but are to act as though they themselves were in the bodies of those undergoing such hardship. The phrase . . . is a bit odd but . . . is clearly intended to express intense identification with those who are suffering" (Luke Timothy Johnson, *Hebrews: A Commentary*, NTL [Louisville, KY: Westminster John Knox, 2006], 341).

demands for the same reason. How do we fulfill the call to empathize with others whose situations are ones we know nothing of? How do we close that empathetic gap? Fiction can provide *a kind of commentary* on canonical literature that provides at least some resolution to this conundrum. To the extent the prophets and apostles ask us to empathize with others, not just sympathize, they ask us to do something we are not always able to do owing to the circumstances of our lives. I don't know what it is to be a prisoner or tortured, so asking me to remember them to the extent I imagine what it is to be *in their bodies* is asking the impossible.

Consider another example. According to Deuteronomy 24:21–22, the Israelites are not to take all the grapes from the vines, instead leaving some for the stranger in the land, the orphan, and the widow, and they are to do so because they remember what it was like being slaves in Egypt. There is more to it than merely providing food for the vulnerable. There is need for a deeper connection. Not just helping but helping because I understand something of the specific challenges they face. There is a conspicuous emphasis on this idea in Torah, with the Israelites' memory of their maltreatment serving to inspire empathy for others similarly abused and displaced:

> You shall not oppress a resident alien; you know the heart of an alien, for you were aliens in the land of Egypt (Exod 23:9).
> The alien who resides with you shall be to you as the citizen among you; you shall love the alien as yourself, for you were aliens in the land of Egypt (Lev 19:34).
> . . . when you send a male slave out from you a free person, you shall not send him out from you empty-handed. Provide liberally out of your flock, your threshing floor, and your wine press, thus giving to him some of the bounty with which the LORD your God has blessed you. Remember that you were a slave in the land of Egypt, and the LORD your God redeemed you; for this reason I lay this command upon you today (Deut 15:13–15).

I am not likely to experience imprisonment or starvation, but others do. I differ from the first readers of Hebrews and those addressed in Torah in ways that limit my ability to connect deeply with others, even to love them, the way such passages seem to require. At the same time, with Green, I believe it is possible to enter forms of empathetic connection with others by hearing or reading their stories. Literature nurtures empathy, and that in turn helps us better understand certain biblical injunctions.

Instruction in the church takes many forms: creeds, catechisms, stained-glass windows, icons, hymns, and more. For some, however, the idea of finding moral guidance and theological insight in the arts and not exclusively in the canon and the official teaching of the church is troubling. John Bunyan (1628–1688) anticipated some would find his *"mode"* of teaching in *The Pilgrim's Progress*, which is a highly imaginative, extended allegory of the Christian journey toward salvation, offensive, so he began with a poetic apology:

> *For those that were not for its coming forth* [i.e., his book];
> *I said to them, Offend you I am loth;*
> *Yet since your Brethren pleased with it be,*
> *Forbear to judge, till you do further see.*
> . . . .
> *May I not write in such a stile as this?*
> *In such a method too, and yet not miss*
> *Mine end, thy good? why may it not be done?*[50]

Bunyan's intent is unambiguous, with *"thy good"* indicating religious instruction leading to a right relationship with God. What is needed is an openness to spiritual light in whatever form it reaches us.

Ethical awakening is one potential benefit of creativity, *"such a stile,"* in service of religious instruction. We find examples of this in the Bible itself. The prophet Nathan tells Israel's king a fictional story in 2 Samuel 12, and one clearly with a serious purpose: "The thing that David had done displeased the LORD, and the LORD sent Nathan to David" (11:27–12:1). The "thing" in question is a series of moral lapses. It begins with his lustful attraction to Bathsheba and the adulterous affair that followed. On learning of the resulting pregnancy, he brings her soldier husband, Uriah, home from the battlefield on the assumption he would sleep with his wife, thus concealing the fact David is the true father. When this plan fails, David makes matters worse, effectively murdering Uriah by arranging the battle in a way that puts the man in danger. Uriah dies, but even that is not enough to shield the king from the consequences of his actions. God knows what happened and sends his prophet to confront him. When the commissioned storyteller is before the

---

50 John Bunyan, *The Pilgrim's Progress*, Oxford World's Classics, ed. W. R. Owens (1678, 1684; Oxford: Oxford University Press, 2003), 4. Italics original. For more about this book, see chap. 6.

monarch, it is straight to business: "He came to him, and said to him, 'There were two men in a certain city'" (12:1). Prophetic proclamation presented as once-upon-a-time.

Nathan's parable tells of a poor man and his pet ewe lamb. He loves her dearly; "'it was like a daughter to him'" (12:3). But things go horribly wrong when a rich man takes and kills the animal to feed a guest, even though he has flocks of his own. At first, David does not realize the story is fictional, and he is outraged. With his sense of justice kindled, he is prepared to act: "'the man who has done this deserves to die; he shall restore the lamb fourfold'" (12:5–6). The lesson, of course, concerns David's adultery described in the preceding verses. The king's behavior is the real moral outrage, the real injustice. Nathan makes this plain when he answers David's angry response with, "'You are the man!'" (12:7). The episode suggests different ways of knowing. On the one hand, David's reaction to the parable indicates a sense of what constitutes right and wrong, justice and injustice, and even knowledge of the Law (see Exod 22:1 regarding the fourfold restitution), but on the other, he obviously fails to connect that sense of moral outrage to his own actions. A fiction, a tale about an imagined poor man and ewe lamb, confronts him with the guilty verdict, which he eventually accepts: "'I have sinned against the LORD'" (12:13). The story helps David see his behavior in a new light.

Engaging stories and reflecting on their meaning is a valuable exercise because stories often present us with ambiguities (see further chap. 2). We need to pause and consider interpretive options. One such ambiguity in this case concerns the alignment of our sympathies. All likely agree the rich man is in the wrong, but what about David and Bathsheba? We need to decide whether we view the king as one brought down by a temptress, an interpretation evident in many paintings of the scene, or as the aggressor, meaning Bathsheba is the victim.[51] The latter is certainly the case. After all, what other option is available to her when faced with the most powerful man in the realm? But we need to choose, and such decision-making, forced on readers by storytellers, is often instructive. At times, the process urges readers to look beyond the text, to consider analogous situations. Despite the tendency of many to

---

51 In addition to many paintings, the 1951 film *David and Bathsheba*, starring Gregory Peck and Susan Hayward, is a striking example of an adaptation of the story highlighting Bathsheba's sensuality. For analysis of this and other artistic representations, see J. Cheryl Exum's *Plotted, Shot, and Painted: Cultural Representations of Biblical Women*, 2nd rev. ed. (1996; Sheffield, UK: Sheffield Phoenix, 2012), chap. 1.

blame Bathsheba, there is no evidence in the text she is a seductress. The issue is David's behavior, not hers.[52] As we work that out, perhaps we question whether *we* ever behave in like manner. Do we abuse power? Take advantage of those who are vulnerable? Do our actions have negative consequences for others? Approached this way, we see storytelling's prophetic function (see further chap. 7). In that role, literature is a chaotic force, upsetting the *status quo* and critiquing the establishment.

THERE ARE SHEEP, AND THERE ARE GOATS

The response given by the goat spokesperson in Matthew 25:31–46 (see the front matter) is damning. *When were you hungry, Lord? When thirsty?* Being unaware or claiming to be is no defense. They are goats whether this assertion is indeed the case or a last desperate attempt to dodge the looming verdict. To admit not seeing the needy is, in effect, an admission of indifference. And that is the terrifying heart of this passage. Sometimes we really are deaf and blind to the plight of others. There are forms of deprivation and abuse, of injustice and need, of which we are only vaguely aware, if aware at all. Empathetic connection is entirely absent. Literature can put before us categories of the overlooked, the hidden, the erased, and in that sense, it serves as a form of commentary on values espoused in this Matthean passage; it reminds us there are some in need we fail to recognize.

In Jesus's lesson about the sheep and goats (Matt 25:31–46),[53] righteousness expresses itself through care of those who are vulnerable, and those who provide for the hungry, thirsty, and naked, who attend to the needs of those who are sick, imprisoned, and strangers in their midst, are favored by

---

52 "In the story of the adultery of David with Bathsheba, he is the one the narrative regards as the sole guilty party. The death of their child and the subsequent sexual and political chaos of his household are his punishment (2 Samuel 11–12), while Bathsheba bears David's ultimate heir, Solomon, and helps engineer his ascent to the throne (1 Kings 1–2)" (Gail Corrington Streete, *The Strange Woman: Power and Sex in the Bible* [Louisville, KY: Westminster John Knox, 1997], 14).

53 Though some refer to Matthew 25:31–46 as a parable, it is not the best descriptor for this passage. As Donald A. Hagner observes, "Unlike the preceding parables . . . this narrative is based not on a fictitious story but on the description of a very real, though future event. Despite some clear parabolic elements, the passage with its future tense forms is more properly categorized as an apocalyptic revelation discourse" (*Matthew 14–28*, WBC 33B [Dallas, TX: Word, 1995], 740).

God. Those who turn away from such as these are condemned. The message appears straightforward enough. It is another version of the call to love our neighbors as ourselves.

My interest in these pages is primarily the reception of the Bible in works of the imagination, as opposed to historical-critical readings of those ancient writings. The focus is how later authors understood and/or adapted biblical texts as opposed to their original contexts. However, a few additional remarks on the sheep and goats lesson may be useful because it provides a loose guide for the chapters that follow, and it is possible for a few errors to creep into our reflections on it.

First, thinking of the ethical mandates in terms of individual response—*I need to feed the hungry*, or *I will be condemned*—is understandable, especially in contexts where solitary reading is the norm. However, the sheep and goats are nations or gentiles (Matt 25:32), and the image of God judging them is a familiar one in the Bible (e.g., Isa 66:18; Joel 3:11–12; Zeph 3:8). Israel is also among the nations (e.g., Deut 32:8; Isa 40:15–17; Acts 10:22), though Matthew does at times distinguish Israel from other peoples (e.g., 4:15 [citing Isa 9:1–2]; 5:47; 6:32). Also interesting in this context is Matthew 21:43, which suggests Jesus's followers, the church, are a nation (same term as 25:32, translated as *people* in NRSV): "'the kingdom of God will be taken away from you and given to a people that produces the fruits of the kingdom.'" The simple point I take from this, regardless of the exact meaning of "nations," is that *sheep* and *goats* are collective terms. The ethical message of the passage operates on a systemic, community level. *We* must feed the hungry, or *we* will be condemned. This need not rule out individual response. Jesus and Matthew celebrate individual actions in service of the kingdom of God as well (e.g., 19:27–29), and it is the kindness and faithfulness of individuals within the collective who embody and often enact the ideal behaviors called for in these verses.[54]

A second potential error is an inclination among religious readers of the Bible—I think this is a fair assessment, however much a broad generalization—to assume they are among the sheep. But Matthew places this lesson in a longer unit of teaching specifically addressed to his closest

---

54 On this, see further Craig L. Blomberg, *Interpreting the Parables*, 2nd ed. (Downers Grove, IL: IVP Academic, 2012). He argues on grammatical grounds that "them" in Matthew 25:32, translated in the NRSV as "people"—"All the nations will be gathered before him, and he will separate people one from another"—refers to "all *individuals* of all nations or ethnic groups" (398; italics original).

followers: "His disciples came.... Then he asked them.... The disciples came to him privately.... Jesus answered them" (24:1–4). This dialogue prefaces a longer unit of instruction that runs through 25:46 and marked, as is Matthew's habit, with a clear transition at its close ("When Jesus had finished saying all these things" [26:1; cf. 7:28; 11:1; 13:53; 19:1]). If there is no risk of those identified as disciples being numbered among the goats, there would be no need for Jesus to tell the story or for Matthew to include it for his Christian readers' consideration. Merely identifying as Jesus's follower does not ensure inheritance of the kingdom (25:34). It is a challenging but useful exercise to approach the biblical prophets without assuming we are among the heroes in the stories they tell.

A facet of the sheep and goats teaching pertinent for the argument of this book is the attention it gives to knowing and not knowing. The sheep respond to those in need, though they do not recognize it is Jesus himself they serve: "'when was it that we saw you sick or in prison and visited you?'" (25:38, etc.). The goats also lack understanding, but unlike the sheep, this is presumably the basis for their inaction and the reason for their eventual condemnation: "'Lord, when was it that we saw you hungry or thirsty or a stranger or naked or sick or in prison, and did not take care of you?'" (25:44). The sheep are embodiments of the kingdom ideals Matthew describes throughout. They are selfless and loving, faithful and generous. But to read the passage with humility, as suggested above, is to recognize that goat-like oversights are a possibility even for the best-intentioned.

One final note about the passage is in order. When Jesus refers to the beneficiaries of the sheep's acts of compassion, and in the negative the goats neglect, it is likely he has a specific group in view. He refers to *"toutōn tōn adelphōn mou tōn elachistōn"* (25:40), which becomes "the least of these brothers [and sisters] of mine" in the New Revised Standard Version (brackets added) and "the least [*elachistōn*] of these" in 25:45. Elsewhere in Matthew, similar language applies specifically to Jesus's followers: "'Whoever welcomes you welcomes me, and whoever welcomes me welcomes the one who sent me. Whoever welcomes a prophet in the name of a prophet will receive a prophet's reward, and whoever welcomes a righteous person in the name of a righteous person will receive the reward of the righteous, and whoever gives even a cup of cold water to one of these little ones [*tōn mikrōn toutōn*] in the name of a disciple—truly I tell you, none of these will lose their reward'" (10:40–42; cf. 11:11; 18:6, 10, 14).

INTRODUCTION

It is possible, then, Jesus's remarks do not refer to care of a broad, undefined category of those poor and imprisoned but rather to ways others treat his followers. At the same time, the response of the sheep and goats deserves notice. They do not recognize Jesus in the people they help or ignore, respectively. *When were you hungry, Lord?* The "least of these brothers and sisters" are to the sheep and goats simply people in need they either stop to help or pass by.[55] So despite this caveat about the specific referent of the "least," it is still appropriate, I suggest, to read the sheep and goats lesson as distinguishing meritorious behavior from its counterpart. We are to treat all with kindness, whether we recognize Jesus in them or not. There's something in it of the "treating angels unaware'" motif we find elsewhere in the Bible (see, e.g., Gen 18–19; Tobit; Heb 13:2).

What has all this to do with literature? Jesus's remarks about knowing and not knowing warrant further consideration. To speak only for myself as one privileged in many ways, they raise uncomfortable questions. I don't know what it is to be hungry (on which, see chap. 1). I don't know what it is to be an immigrant, the modern-day equivalent to a stranger in the land, or to be a racial minority (on which, see chap. 4). I am sometimes blind to ways Christianity is weaponized and coercive, generating fear where there ought to be love. I trace my ancestral roots back to empire-builders rather than those colonized so know nothing by experience of traumas endured by the stifling of my culture or an imposed language or religion (on which, see chap. 3). I don't know what it is to be the victim of child or spousal abuse (on which, see chaps. 2 and 6), and my anthropocentrism makes it difficult to respect the land and its nonhuman animals (about which, see chap. 7). I have some understanding of struggling faith, but there is always more to learn about the nature of Christian discipleship and the need to respond to the call of God (on which, see chap. 5). Within the setting of church life, I don't know what it is to be excluded from positions of authority based on gender or to be marginalized, even demonized, based on sexual orientation or gender self-identity and self-expression. Such a list of *I don't knows* is both humbling and

---

55 For a brief overview of the passage with attention to these and other interpretive questions, see Stanley E. Porter, "Sheep and the goats, Parable of the," in *Dictionary of the Bible and Western Culture*, ed. Mary Ann Beavis and Michael J. Gilmour (Sheffield, UK: Sheffield Phoenix Press, 2012), 485–486. For a more detailed analysis, see Klyne R. Snodgrass, *Stories with Intent: A Comprehensive Guide to the Parables of Jesus*, 2nd ed. (Grand Rapids, MI: Eerdmans, 2018), 543–563.

frightening. Are the goats in Jesus's lesson necessarily lying when they say they didn't recognize the needs, when they failed "'to take care of'" (25:44) others the way the sheep did?

The world's storytellers offer much to readers of faith who want to work toward fulfilling Jesus's call to love their neighbors as themselves. As said, fiction takes us to places we've never been and introduces us to people we've never meet. The authors examined here are not necessarily Christian, but their stories involve dialogue with the Bible and engagement with religious themes, and they offer in their various ways insights about Jesus's teaching. Old wine in new wineskins.

ETHICAL CRITICISM AND THE MARGINS

Stories disarm. As we suspend disbelief, we open ourselves to new ways of seeing the world. Stories permit vicarious encounters with what is otherwise unknown. The prosperous meets the poor, the colonizer meets the colonized, and so on. Such encounters disrupt assumptions—it's harder to hate someone you know—and often invite reassessment of our values. Am I among the sheep or the goats? Stories force us to listen rather than speak. Occasionally, they illuminate the moral visions of Scripture in ways other authorities fail to do. Reading is a solitary exercise, one leaving us alone with our thoughts, and without the din of competing voices that would challenge or stifle moral reasoning. Reading involves sustained engagement with characters and situations. It takes time to follow narratives to their close. *In literature, as Lewis reminds us, we find real life and the life of the imagination meeting. In literature, as Lofting reminds us, we find visions of a kinder, gentler world.*

The kind of ethically focused examination of creative writing attempted here is not acknowledged by all as a valid interpretive exercise. The interaction of literature and religion inevitably takes us into the realm of ethics, but for some, this is problematic. The formalism that dominated literary criticism in the mid-twentieth century still has influence. New Criticism, associated with such scholars as I. A. Richards and Cleanth Brooks, urged close reading of poetry and prose without attention to external matters, including consideration of the author, the reader's experience of a text, or the circumstances shaping either. One of the cautions put forward by the New Critics is the need to avoid the affective fallacy, which William K. Wimsatt Jr. and Monroe C.

Beardsley define as "a confusion between the poem and its *results* (what it is and what it *does*)." The interpreter guilty of this "begins by trying to derive the standard of criticism from the psychological effects of the poem and ends in impressionism and relativism."[56] The formal features of the poem, not its potential influence on those reading it, are all the critic ought to be concerned with, and if this is the case, ethical interests are of little matter. But the ethical impulse for authors and critics never entirely disappeared, and certainly by the 1980s this aversion to an emotional engagement with texts and the willingness to connect imaginative works to lived experience began to wane. "Whenever any human practice refuses to die, in spite of centuries of assault from theory," Wayne C. Booth observes, "there must be something wrong with the theory." Indeed, ethical criticism may be "clumsy" and strike some as old-time moralism or censorship, but "no one seems to resist ethical criticism for long."[57] His objective in *The Company We Keep* is to show "there are many legitimate paths open to anyone who decides to abandon, at least for a time, the notion that an interest in form precludes an interest in the ethical powers of form."[58]

Margins. Reading the margins. The term appeals to me for a few reasons. It is a *non sequitur*, of course, because margins are the usually blank spaces on the pages of books. There is nothing there to read. But the term's metaphoric potential and the constant visual cue provided by the book or tablet or monitor you're looking at helps pinpoint key themes in what follows. The first concerns connections between many of the fictions we read and the *marginalized* people they put before us. Margins surround the pages of novels that incline our thoughts toward contemplation of the Gospels, and we see those margins constantly during the hours spent with a book in hand. Those blank spaces on the edge of the page often go unnoticed. There's nothing there to

---

56 William K. Wimsatt Jr. and Monroe C. Beardsley, "The Affective Fallacy" (1949), reprinted in *The Norton Anthology of Theory and Criticism*, ed. Vincent B. Leitch et al. (New York: Norton, 2001), 1388. Italics original. Terry Eagleton highlights one of New Criticism's limitations: "To call for close reading ... is to do more than insist on due attentiveness to the text. It inescapably suggests an attention to *this* rather than to something else: to the 'words on the page' rather than to the contexts which produced and surround them .... it encouraged the illusion that any piece of language, 'literary' or not, can be adequately studied or even understood in isolation" (*Literary Theory: An Introduction*, Anniversary Edition [Minneapolis: University of Minnesota Press, 2008], 38).

57 Wayne C. Booth, *The Company We Keep: An Ethics of Fiction* (Berkeley: University of California Press, 1988), 5, 6.

58 Booth, *Company We Keep*, 6–7.

see, after all. Marginalized people are often unnoticed, too, on the fringes of our societies. Those in hospitals, the homeless, the hungry, the abused hidden away behind closed doors, those harassed because of their sexuality or preferred gender identification. Others, like the margins between columns in a newspaper, are between worlds, displaced by war or famine, seeking a better life. Migrant workers, refugees, the victims of discrimination. Good storytellers encourage us to see them too.

A margin is also a *blank space*, meaning there is room to write alongside the story told on the page (on which, see further afterword). Reading is not a passive activity. We visualize, interpret, emotionally respond, criticize, cheer, compare, and more as we follow an author's lead, and so it is we add something to their story. With reference to ethical concerns, stories (like Nathan's) spark outrage or reinforce our values. To the extent writers incorporate religious or political themes, here, too, we experience stories as conversations with an ideology. A margin is also a blank space where others provide explanatory information as in Bibles with cross-references or suggested interpretations. Creative writing as margin notes on biblical themes, providing a form of commentary on the teachings of the prophets and apostles.

Finally, another key term found throughout the present book is *novel*. Obviously, it indicates a literary category, referring to a long work of prose in contrast to poetry or shorter narratives. Most of the works considered here are novels in that sense. But *novel* also indicates something new, something unexpected. Creative writers often introduce novel ideas, novel perspectives that challenge existing ways of seeing the world. Many invite a shift in our sympathies. The kinds of stories considered here do that by introducing us to marginalized people we may rarely or never meet and presenting new ways of thinking about biblical religion. This newness, this novel encounter, is potentially one that nurtures compassion and furthers our understanding of Christian discipleship.

CHAPTER ONE

Poverty and Woody Guthrie's Train Bound for Glory

Blessed be ye poor: for yours is the kingdom of God.

—Luke 6:20, AV

Jesus tells a story about the deaths of a rich man, often referred to as Dives, and a poor man (Luke 16:19–31). Luke places the tale in the immediate context of remarks about wealth and the abuse of it (e.g., 16:13–15), which is fitting because the rich man's guilt is obvious. He feasts while the poor man, Lazarus, goes hungry. He receives a proper burial, but there is no one willing to provide this last dignity for the poor man on his death, which presumably explains why angels carry him away (16:22). More damning yet is something revealed in the postmortem cry for help Dives directs to Abraham, when he asks him to "send Lazarus" (16:24). The rich man knows the poor man's name. It's just a subtle detail but one troubling in its implications. Dives knew Lazarus was starving and sick. Dives knew Lazarus was friendless, something stressed by mention of dogs licking his sores and angels taking his corpse. There was no human to care for him. Some poverty we know about, and this is certainly the case in this instance. Lazarus sat at the rich man's gate (16:20). To know and do nothing is vile. But need within our midst is not always so obvious. In this chapter, we consider Woody Guthrie's *Bound for Glory* (1943) as our primary example of imaginative writing inviting us to *see* the poor whom Jesus calls blessed and cautioning us to be *wary* of the Dives-like behavior of those who pass them by: "Blessed are you who are poor. . . . But woe to you who are rich" (Luke 6:20, 24). But before turning to that classic of American literature, a few remarks about an earlier English one.

A LITTLE TWIST ON JESUS'S PARABLES BY CHARLES DICKENS

The first seven chapters of Charles Dickens's *Oliver Twist* (1838) move quickly from the account of the titular child's birth through to his escape from a coffin maker.[1] This section closes with the first truly compassionate words Oliver hears, the "blessing" from a boy named Dick. An interesting feature of this part of the novel is its ironic use of biblical teachings. On two occasions, this is explicit. The first is the description of Oliver as "'a porochial 'prentis, who is at present a dead-weight—a millstone, as I may say—round the porochial throat,'" a clear allusion to Jesus's words in the Gospels (Matt 18:6; Mark 9:42; Luke 17:1–2).[2] Significantly, in the verse immediately preceding the millstone comment, Jesus holds children up for special honor. He says that the greatest in heaven are like them and "whoso shall receive one such little child in my name receiveth me" (Matt 18:5, AV). For the beadle Mr. Bumble to describe a child as a burden, using the very words Jesus spoke when honoring children, is to make that Gospel passage say the opposite of its original intent. The second such use of Scripture is found in the description of Bumble's coat buttons, which are cast with the parochial seal of the Good Samaritan (Luke 10:30–37).[3] Since his indifference to Oliver resembles the heartless priest and Levite of that story (and the title *beadle* is also a religious descriptor), and not the compassionate Samaritan, his claim to model the parable's ideals by parading the story on his clothing is rather hollow.

In addition to these obvious uses of the New Testament, a third passage, not explicitly mentioned, provides a possible backdrop for the novel's introductory chapters. Matthew alone records Jesus's teachings about the sheep and goats (25:31–46) discussed in the introduction. In this passage, Jesus distinguishes the righteous and the wicked based on their willingness to feed

---

1 Charles Dickens, *Oliver Twist* (1838; London: Penguin, 2002), 3–57.
2 Dickens, *Oliver Twist*, 29.
3 Dickens, *Oliver Twist*, 29. The proud Bumble, glancing at the large brass buttons embellishing his coat, explains to Mr. Sowerberry that it is a depiction of "'the Good Samaritan healing the sick and bruised man.'"

those who are hungry, provide drink for those thirsty, welcome strangers, clothe those who are naked, care for sick people, and visit those in prison. In each case, Jesus uses the first person—"I was hungry, and you gave me food" (v. 35, etc.)—and so this passage resembles the blessing on children noted above in that he claims to be the beneficiary of charitable acts: "Whoever welcomes one such child in my name welcomes me" (Matt 18:5). Oliver Twist is, of course, a needy child who was not welcomed early in the novel, one whose plight resembles the vulnerable ones described in Matthew 25:31–46 as the following excerpts illustrate:

- Oliver is hungry: "without the inconvenience of too much food" (cf. Matt 25:35, AV: "I was an hungred, and ye gave me meat").[4]
- Oliver is alone in the world: "you've got no father or mother" (cf. Matt 25:35, AV: "I was a stranger, and ye took me in").[5]
- Oliver is "naked": "without the inconvenience of ... too much clothing" (cf. Matt 25:36, AV: "I was ... Naked, and ye clothed me").[6]
- Oliver is in "prison": "Oliver remained a close prisoner in the dark" (cf. Matt 25:36, AV: "I was in prison, and ye came unto me").[7]

There is clear mockery of the parish's so-called charitable activities here. They show greater concern for outward appearance than they do provision of substantive care for the boy. There are recurring references to Oliver's loneliness,[8] but the parish gives him no companionship or meaningful sense of community (cf. "ye visited me not" [Matt 25:43, AV]). The subtle allusions to the sheep and goats lesson represent a clever critique of these hypocritical parish practices. The parable's warning is directed to those feigning to be Jesus's followers—just look at Bumble's shiny buttons—but not recognizing him among those who were poor and needy: "Lord, when saw we thee an hungred, or athirst, or a stranger, or naked, or sick, or in prison, and did not minister unto thee?" (Matt 25:44, AV).

Dickens's critique culminates in the brief blessing mentioned above, offered by Dick (*hear Dickens?*). His speech recalls key terms from the

---

4 Dickens, *Oliver Twist*, 6.
5 Dickens, *Oliver Twist*, 12.
6 Dickens, *Oliver Twist*, 6.
7 Dickens, *Oliver Twist*, 17; see also 54, 79.
8 Dickens, *Oliver Twist*, 11, 32, 34, 59, 162.

Matthew passage ("heaven," "angels," "blessing"), and indeed his kind words to Oliver model true charity. Dick's blessing, "the first that Oliver had ever heard," left an impression on the orphan, who "never once forgot it."[9] Dick is a model of virtue, a child to be emulated according to the context of the millstone passage Bumble ironically cites: "Whosoever therefore shall humble himself *as this little child* [a little child like Oliver's friend Dick], the same is greatest in the kingdom of heaven" (Matt 18:4, AV, italics added).

This brief episode illustrates fiction's capacity to illuminate biblical values, sometimes in subtle ways. We come to know Oliver across the hours spent reading his story, and to the extent he becomes the embodiment of one of Jesus's "least of these" (Matt 25:40), we gain at least one writer's understanding of what such vulnerability looks like. Dickens's Oliver is put into "conversation" with Matthew's Jesus, and it is possible readers of both stories move beyond mere abstract concepts like poverty, neglect, and need and come to appreciate ways such labels attach to actual people deserving love and care.[10] A similar prodding toward compassion occurs in the next work we consider, where again we meet people who, like Oliver, encounter individuals and institutions failing to care.

THIS TRAIN IS BOUND FOR GLORY

The tale Woody Guthrie tells in his autobiographical novel *Bound for Glory* (1943) similarly turns our attention to society's margins. The story begins sometime after the 1941 attack on Pearl Harbor as the singer-songwriter rides in a boxcar with sixty-some "hoboes," as he calls them. It is a dusty, noisy, crowded setting as the train in question travels through Minnesota. Some in that crowd are good-natured folk, swapping stories, sharing cigarettes,

---

9   Dickens, *Oliver Twist*, 57; cf. 429: "'Oh Dick, Dick, my dear old friend, if I could only see you now!'"

10   For discussion of Charles Dickens's religious views and engagement with biblical texts, see, e.g., Gary L. Colledge, *God and Charles Dickens: Recovering the Christian Voice of a Classic Author* (Grand Rapids, MI: Brazos, 2012); and Jennifer Gribble, *Dickens and the Bible: "What Providence Meant"* (New York: Routledge, 2021). See, too, chap. 6 below. Dickens's interest in the ethical teachings of Jesus is perhaps most evident in his book *The Life of Our Lord*, which he wrote for his children. It was not published in his lifetime.

supporting those who are ill, and protecting others unable to defend themselves. Others are violent and cruel, throwing empty bottles, lighting a sleeping man's foot on fire. All are desperate. All impoverished. There is talk of lost jobs, and those aboard are clearly in search of work and opportunities for a better life. We don't know yet the circumstances that brought Guthrie, guitar in hand, to that boxcar but soon will.

Guthrie befriends a Black man during that ride, and the two sit at one of the boxcar's open doors when a fight breaks out. Someone pushes them out, but they grab the ladder of the slowing train, climb it to the top, and continue their journey on the boxcar's roof. While there, two runaway children join them. It is an odd foursome. Strangers to one another. A mix of age and race but all traveling together with the rabble below, inside the boxcar. And then a wild storm hits. All four strip off their sweaters and shirts and wrap them around Guthrie's guitar to protect it from the rain, suggesting they recognize that instrument's significance. Guthrie refers to it as his "meal ticket,"[11] but it is more than that to the others. To Guthrie's new friends, the music that comes from that guitar matters because it tells *their story*. A quick web search for Woody Guthrie brings up images of the singer's guitars, which he marked with the phrase "This Machine Kills Fascists." His music aims to protect those who are vulnerable from bullies, from those who exploit people who are weak and downtrodden. No wonder the runaways and the Black man on the top of the boxcar with Woody do what little they can to protect his "machine."[12]

The opening chapter of *Bound for Glory* begins and ends with fragments from one of Guthrie's songs:

This train don't carry no gamblers,
Liars, thieves and big-shot ramblers;
This train is bound for glory,
This train!

---

[11] Woody Guthrie, *Bound for Glory* (1943; New York: Penguin, 1983), 33.

[12] For further discussion about Guthrie's guitar slogan and its influence on a later activist musician, see Michael J. Gilmour, "Raging against the Machine: Tom Morello's Nightwatchman Persona and the Sound of Apocalypse-Inspired *Schadenfreude*," in *Anthems of Apocalypse: Popular Music and Apocalyptic Thought*, ed. Christopher Partridge (Sheffield, UK: Sheffield Phoenix Press, 2012), esp. 43–45.

> This train don't carry no rustlers,
> Whores, pimps, or side-street hustlers;
> This train is bound for glory,
> This train.[13]

Structurally, these song fragments are parenthetical, in effect wrapping the stowaways riding that boxcar whose story Guthrie tells in the chapter. The fragments begin and end this section of the novel. The song, therefore, tells us something about the singer's traveling companions. But there's an interesting detail about the song that deserves notice. In the opening stanza, we're told it is "the righteous and the holy" who are the only ones bound for glory, who are the only ones bound for heaven on that gospel train. And the rest of the lyrics, including those in the novel cited above, list a broad cross section of those not welcome on that train: gamblers, thieves, liars, smokers, conmen, rustlers, hustlers, and more—in other words, the down-and-outers Guthrie travels with throughout the novel *Bound for Glory*. But therein lies the key insight of this book. Are the demarcations distinguishing the righteous and holy from the unrighteous and the wicked always so obvious? Those usually considered righteous and holy are not always righteous and holy, and the reverse is equally true. Guthrie challenges conventional thinking. He himself and the diverse cast of characters populating this travelogue are anything but the kind of respectable people we assume to be welcome on a train bound for heaven. And yet there they are. They are the ones with whom we sympathize as we read this book. Guthrie's song "This Train Is Bound for Glory" and its namesake novel are deeply ironic, inviting us to meet and even care about outsiders, those marginalized, the underdogs. They also encourage us to be wary of those considered respectable, powerful, and well-off and to be suspicious of institutional power.

Biblical authors often refer to poor people, and it is a prominent theme in Jesus's teaching. Consider "many who are first will be last, and the last will be first," "the last will be first, and the first will be last" (Matt 19:30; 20:16). These two phrases frame Jesus's parable about laborers in a vineyard. A landowner hires some early in the day. Those workers agree to a wage. Others the landowner hires a few hours later, and still more he hires near the end of the workday, but when it comes time to pay them, all receive the same amount.

---

13 Guthrie, *Bound for Glory*, 19, 36. For the full lyrics to "This Train Is Bound for Glory," see woodyguthrie.org.

Those who worked the longest grumble about this: "'These last worked only one hour, and you have made them equal to us who have borne the burden of the day and the scorching heat.' But he replied to one of them, 'Friend, I am doing you no wrong; did you not agree with me for the usual daily wage? Take what belongs to you and go; I choose to give to this last the same as I give to you. Am I not allowed to do what I choose with what belongs to me? Or are you envious because I am generous?'" (Matt 20:12–15). Those who seem least deserving are unexpectedly blessed, and it is often an occasion for grumbling among those who see themselves as more deserving.

Or consider Jesus's story of the prodigal son. With whom do we identify? Is it the prodigal or the brother who stays with the father all along? Jesus's audience when telling that story includes "sinners" as well as Pharisees and scribes (Luke 15:1). We may naturally align ourselves with the penitent prodigal, suggesting we are like those sinners who "were coming near to listen to him," but when we return to the story after being part of the community of Jesus's followers, are there still lessons to take from his brother as well? He is unwilling to accept the wastrel sibling. The prodigal son squanders his inheritance, and yet his father celebrates his return with a feast. This does not sit well with the one who stayed behind: "He became angry and refused to go in [for the feast]. His father came out and began to plead with him. But he answered his father, 'Listen! For all these years I have been working like a slave for you, and I have never disobeyed your command; yet you have never given me even a young goat that I might celebrate with my friends. But when this son of yours came back, who has devoured your property with prostitutes, you killed the fatted calf for him!'" (Luke 15:29–30). The gospel train bound for glory may have those obviously "righteous and . . . holy" on board, but they are not the only ones.

Again, with whom do we identify when reading the parables of the laborers and the prodigal son? I suspect most religious readers of these stories see themselves aligning with those receiving unmerited grace. We are the worker who deserves little but is given much; we are the prodigal whose return the father celebrates. But what about the complaining laborer who puts in a full day's work? What about the long-suffering brother who never left home? Do we ever see ourselves in them? The gospel musician Keith Green offers what I suspect is a common reading of the latter story. In his twelve-plus-minute retelling of the parable ("The Prodigal Son Suite," *The Prodigal Son*, 1983), there is no mention of the prodigal's brother at all. The song inevitably leads listeners to identify with the prodigal. It is a valid reading. All in the community of faith identify as sinners saved by grace. But we are often the prodigal's brother too.¹⁴ Maybe lifelong churchgoers, maybe those who work hard to build a comfortable life, maybe upright citizens and productive members of our communities. Do we ever look askance at those unemployed? Those outside the church? Those whose lifestyles do not align with what we consider respectable or moral? How dare the generous landowner pay them what he pays us! How dare our father prepare a feast for that wayward sibling!

When Guthrie is on top of that boxcar, riding in the cold, windy storm, he is reflective. The narrative aligns the angry storm with the circumstances faced by the unruly, desperate, brawling crowd inside: "The cloudbursts got madder and splashed through all of the lakes, laughing and singing, and then a wail in the wind would get a low start and cry in the timber like the cry for freedom of a conquered people."¹⁵

The simile clearly indicates the impoverished stowaways beneath and others in their situation are the conquered. They are in many cases victims of the Great Depression of the 1930s, an economy in ruins through no fault of their own. Guthrie listens to the voices below: "Through the roof, down inside the car, I heard the voices of the sixty-six hoboes. . . . Men fighting against men. Color against color. Kin against kin. Race pushing against race. And all of us battling against the wind and the rain. . . . Who's all of these crazy men down there howling out at each other like hyenas? Are these men? Who am I? How come them here? How the hell come me here? What am I supposed to do here?"¹⁶

And as these questions run through his mind, with his ear to the boxcar roof, he hears singing in the midst of the turmoil below: "This train is bound for glory." With this, Guthrie sets up the rest of his story. He asks a further series of questions—"Where was I? Where in the hell was I? Where was I when I was a kid? Just as far, far, far back, on back, as I can remember?"¹⁷—and then he begins at the beginning telling his story and explaining how it is he got

---

14 For analysis of the parable of the prodigal son with detailed attention to cultural and literary contexts, see Kenneth E. Bailey, *Jacob and the Prodigal: How Jesus Retold Israel's Story* (Downers Grove, IL: InterVarsity, 2003). On the older brother, whose "anger lies buried like a ticking bomb ready to explode" (154), as it does in the Jacob saga alongside which he reads Jesus's parable, see 177–194, etc. As opposed to the tendency to overlook the elder brother, Bailey gives due attention to this character as a central part of Jesus's lesson.

15 Guthrie, *Bound for Glory*, 35.

16 Guthrie, *Bound for Glory*, 35.

17 Guthrie, *Bound for Glory*, 36.

from his childhood home in Oklahoma to the roof of a boxcar in the early 1940s, somewhere in Minnesota.

The landowner in the parable finds some men "standing around" late in the day, and he asks them why they have been idle. Their answer: "'Because no one has hired us'" (Matt 20:7). That response is striking when read with attention to contemporary social justice as it puts the issue of opportunity before us. They are not lazy; there is simply no work offered to them. Guthrie's boxcar includes moments analogous to this. Most on that train are anxious to work, and some lost jobs for reasons beyond their control: "'I'm woikin' stiff, too, see? . . . I woiked thirteen years in th' same weave room! Breakout fixer on th' looms! Poil Harbor comes along. Big comp'ny gits alla de war orders. My place is a little place, so what happens? Just like dat! She closes down. An' I'm out on de freights. But I ain't nuttin' when I hit th' freights. Takes it all outta me. Nuttin'. But a lousy, dirty tramp!'"[18]

No one hired us, say those in Jesus's parable. No one hired them, writes Guthrie of the wandering "hoboes." Some equate prosperity with divine favor, a reward for faithfulness. They assume poverty is symptomatic of some character flaw or poor life choices, but there is nothing indicating this in Jesus's parables. Poverty and wealth are not moral categories, not indicators of righteousness or unrighteousness. Jesus announces the unexpected: blessed are the poor; woe to you who are rich (Luke 6:20, 24). There may well be holy "hoboes" aboard that train. After all, when he has his ear to the roof of the boxcar, Guthrie hears the misfits and social rejects inside singing "this train is bound for glory."[19]

A City on a Hill

Woody Guthrie was born in Okemah, Oklahoma, in 1912, a place that means, he explains, "Town on a Hill."[20] This is the first line of the second chapter of *Bound for Glory* as he begins answering the series of questions that close the first chapter regarding where he came from and how he got on that train. Providing that detail about the meaning of Okemah is conspicuous, given it recalls Jesus's words in the Sermon on the Mount (cf. front matter): "You are the light of the world. A city built on a hill cannot be hid" (Matt 5:14). Just

---

18 Guthrie, *Bound for Glory*, 26.
19 Guthrie, *Bound for Glory*, 36.
20 Guthrie, *Bound for Glory*, 37.

as Guthrie's train in the opening chapter operates on more than one level as both a literal journey through Minnesota and a metaphorical journey to glory, so, too, does Guthrie's life story. Though *Bound for Glory* includes autobiographical elements, the book includes much beside. He is an "everyman," his story representative of many others who struggle in similar ways. He introduces his family, remarking how they "seemed to be getting along all right" but then goes on to relate a series of setbacks.[21] It is a riches-to-rags trajectory that many facing the Great Depression experienced. To begin the story in that Town on a Hill, an image associated with Jesus's remark in the Sermon on the Mount, offers an interpretive key. Like Jesus's city on a hill, the stories of all those living in towns on a hill, which is to say those who fall on hard times like the Guthrie family, cannot be hidden. Their stories must be told. And repeatedly he reminds readers that hardships are not evidence of divine disfavor. There is grace in the boxcar too. There is grace on Skid Row and in all the other troubled places the singer visits.

Perhaps the most striking storyline illustrating this point is one beginning halfway through the book, in a chapter titled "Off to California." Guthrie receives a letter from his aunt Laura inviting him to escape the dust and poverty of Texas and join her in the West: "'You must be twenty-five by now, Woody. I know I can get you a job here in Sonora. Why don't you come?'"[22] He does, and the coming-of-age first half of the book now becomes a travelogue, a quest initiated by the desire to leave behind a troubled life in search of something better: "Yes, I'll go, I was thinking. This is a right nice day for hittin' th' road ... Good old Pampa [Texas]. I hit here in 1926. Worked my tail off 'round this here town. But it didn't give me anything. Town had growed up, strung itself all out across these plains. Just a little old low-built cattle town to start with; jumped up big when the oil boom hit. Now eleven years later it had up and died."[23]

He hitches a ride, answering the driver, who asks where he's heading, "'Cal'fornia,' I said. 'Hustlin' outta this dam dust! ... Enda this dam highway! *Ain't a-lookin' back!*'"[24]

Quest stories involving a protagonist struggling to overcome obstacles on the way to a desired destination are widely represented in English literature.

---

21 Guthrie, *Bound for Glory*, 38.
22 Guthrie, *Bound for Glory*, 191.
23 Guthrie, *Bound for Glory*, 191.
24 Guthrie, *Bound for Glory*, 191. Italics added.

The titles of Guthrie's book and the chapter introducing Laura's invitation (*Bound for*, "Off to"), place the stories he tells in a tradition involving such diverse travelers as Dante, Bunyan's Christian, and Tolkien's hobbits. But for quest narratives in the Western literary tradition, some crucial influences are ancient, not least among them the biblical story of the Israelites who journey out of slavery in Egypt, through the Red Sea and wilderness, and into the promised land:

> Then the LORD said to Moses . . . "I am the LORD, and I will free you from the burdens of the Egyptians and deliver you from slavery to them. . . . You shall know that I am the LORD your God, who has freed you from the burdens of the Egyptians. I will bring you into the land I swore to give . . . I will give it to you for a possession." (Exod 6:1, 6–8)
>
> Then the LORD said, "I have observed the misery of my people . . . I have heard their cry . . . I know their sufferings, and I have come down to deliver them from the Egyptians, and to bring them up out of that land to a good and broad land, a land flowing with milk and honey." (Exod 3:7–8)

In this archetypical narrative, there is escape from despair and progress toward an ideal, and that broad story arc is easily and often adapted. There are narratives of spiritual awakening (from darkness to illumination) and others depicting more mundane transformations (from poverty to prosperity, sickness to health, alienation to integration).

The account of the Israelites' wanderings toward the promised land informs some of the New Testament authors. A distinctive characteristic of Luke's Gospel, for instance, is the long section concerning Jesus's travels to Jerusalem (9:51–19:44), which begins with an unambiguous statement of intent: "When the days drew near for him to be taken up, he set his face to go to Jerusalem" (9:51; cf. Acts 19:21, which begins a second Lukan journey narrative, this time involving the apostle Paul). It is almost certain Luke understood Jesus to be "the prophet like me" Moses promised would come (Deut 18:15) and intended the extended travel narrative at the heart of his Gospel to reflect the stories about Israel's progress toward the promised land related in Exodus through Joshua and perhaps also the exodus themes in Isaiah 40–55.[25]

---

25 For a helpful discussion of the journey motif, see, e.g., James L. Resseguie, *Spiritual Landscape: Images of the Spiritual Life in the Gospel of Luke* (Peabody, MA: Hendrickson, 2004), 29–44. Resseguie discusses Luke 9:51–19:44 alongside the story of disciples traveling to Emmaus (24:13–35).

As noted above, gospel imagery informs some of the language in Guthrie's *Bound for Glory*, so mention of these biblical journey narratives seems fitting.[26] To be bound for glory is to be bound for heaven, and by using such language, Guthrie evokes a deep tradition of spirituals, sermons, and hymns that depict progress toward salvation in similar terms. It should come as no surprise Guthrie's most famous musical descendant, Bob Dylan, turns to the Guthriesque train-travel metaphor for his first gospel album, *Slow Train Coming* (1979; cf. discussion in chap. 5).[27] When Guthrie acts on the invitation from his wealthy aunt Laura, his phrasing takes us back into biblical texts. *Ain't a-lookin' back!* he tells the driver, a determination echoing several passages:

Flee for your life [said angels to Lot and his family]; do not look back . . . (Gen 19:17).

But Lot's wife, behind him, looked back, and she became a pillar of salt (Gen 19:26).

On that day . . . anyone in the field must not turn back. Remember Lot's wife (Luke 17:31–32).

. . . forgetting what lies behind and straining forward to what lies ahead, I press on toward the goal for the prize of the heavenly call (Phil 3:13–14).

The salvation he seeks is not a spiritual one, but the language of the gospel and the Gospels serves his purpose well. During his travels, others say the same thing to Guthrie. Police officers in one town tell him and others, "'Git on outta town there!' 'Keep travelin'!' 'Don't you even look back!,'" and again later, they cruelly force him to walk alone, out of town and into the dark, cold, and rain, while they follow in the squad car: "'We will have to ask you to get

---

26 Though he doesn't discuss *Bound for Glory* specifically, James Knight highlights various connections between Guthrie's musical oeuvre and the Gospels and concludes the singer "incarnated Jesus' itinerant ethics by standing in solidarity with the poor and dreaming of a better world, where the poor would be blessed and the hungry fed" ("'I Ain't Got No Home in This World Anymore': Protest and Promise in Woody Guthrie and the Jesus Tradition," in *Call Me the Seeker: Listening to Religion in Popular Music*, ed. Michael J. Gilmour [New York: Continuum, 2005], 31; full article, 17–33).

27 In addition, the title of D. A. Pennebaker's 1967 film *Don't Look Back*, which documents Dylan's 1965 tour of the United Kingdom, hints at these singers' shared interest in this biblical image. Pennebaker takes his title from the lyrics of Dylan's song "She Belongs to Me" (*Bringing It All Home*), which came out the same year as the tour documented in the film. Regarding gospel content in contemporary songs more generally, see, e.g., Michael J. Gilmour, "The Bible and Popular Music," in *The Bloomsbury Handbook of Religion and Popular Music*, ed. Christopher Partridge and Marcus Moberg, 2nd ed. (London: Bloomsbury, 2023), 67–76.

out in front of this car and start walking down this highway. And don't look back—.'"[28] When Guthrie says it, it signals his determination to follow the path wherever it leads. When in the mouth of those who try to stop him, it is an obstacle to overcome.

Like the journey taken by the Israelites, there are challenges along the way, but after setting his face toward California, just as Jesus "set his face" toward Jerusalem, Guthrie perseveres. But there is an unexpected twist in this journey narrative after he reaches his destination, and it reflects the author's concern for social justice. He hitchhikes; travels in and on boxcars; endures hunger, heat, and cold; and makes friends with the poor and unemployed ramblers he meets along the way. But on reaching his destination, the gated home of his aunt Laura, he has an epiphany of sorts. As he stands at the impressive double doors of the gated mansion, he does not see luxury and beauty but rather something disturbing: "Windows so high and wide that the sun got lost trying to find a way to shine through all of them big thick drapes and curtains. Iron braces in the windows built to keep the nice, good, healthy sunshine out for a long, long time. Big double doors with iron cross braces, handles like the entrance to a funeral parlor, locks bigger and stouter than any jail I'd ever slept in."[29]

After reading about Guthrie's hunger and thirst, exposure to the elements and other dangers, this is completely unexpected. We naturally assume the security and creature comforts that await him in Aunt Laura's home to be the prize. But of course, the Gospel themes woven into the stories he tells foreshadow this moment. Jesus himself has no place to lay his head (Matt 8:20; Luke 9:58). It is Lazarus, not the rich man, who is blessed (Luke 16:19–31). The first shall be last and the last first (Matt 20:16; Luke 13:30). That the mansion brings funeral parlors and jails to mind makes it clear money is not salvation. A butler answers his knock on the door, and the moment is revelatory for Guthrie:

> He was wearing a nice suit of clothes. An old man, thin-faced, and straight shoulders, gray hair, white cuffs, black tie. The air from the house sifted past him on its way out the door, and there was a smell that made me know that the air had been hemmed up inside that house for a long time. Hemmed up. Walled in. Covered away from the moon and out of the reach of the sun. Cut away from the drift of the leaves and the wash of the waters. Hid out

---

28 Guthrie, *Bound for Glory*, 234, 238.
29 Guthrie, *Bound for Glory*, 242.

from the going and the coming of the people, cut loose from the thoughts of the crowds on the streets. Lazy in there, sleepy in there, cool and pale and shady in there, dark and dreary in the book case there, and the wind under the beds hadn't been disturbed in twenty-three years. I know, I know, I'm on the right hill, but I'm at the wrong house. This wasn't what I hung that boxcar for, nor hugged that iron ladder for, nor bellied down on top of that high rolling freight train for. The train was laughing and cussing and alive with human people.[30]

Even though the butler assures Guthrie he is standing at the right address, the grubby visitor keeps repeating he is at the wrong house, certain he made a mistake in coming. Interestingly, after he leaves the gated, isolated compound and the home he described as a jail and funeral parlor only moments earlier—after listening "to that iron gate snap locked behind [him]"—he says, "I was alive again."[31] Being in community with the downtrodden, Guthrie seems to say, sharing in their burdens and serving them with what little we have, is preferable to the pursuit of creature comforts.

Guthrie finds life among those downtrodden, serving them by singing their stories. He is a secular Franciscan of sorts, and the parallels with Jesus's ministry are clear. When asked by some Pharisees—the "the righteous and the holy" of his day—why he chose to be in the company of tax collectors and sinners, Jesus explained, "'Those who are well have no need of a physician, but those who are sick; I have come to call not the righteous but sinners to repentance'" (Luke 5:30–32). The exercise of reading *Bound for Glory* alongside Gospel narratives accomplishes at least two things. For one, it reminds us of structural realities that impose hardships on vulnerable members of society. Not all who want to work are able to work. Governments, banks, businesses, militaries (the specter of war lurks in the background of the story), and other institutions wield a lot of power and are often indifferent to or unaware of ways they introduce harms. Second, *Bound for Glory* illustrates a life modeling compassion. The tough, grubby, wandering, cussing singer-songwriter is a secular dust bowl saint. That last descriptor is warranted as the values he espouses in the novel contrast sharply with at least some representatives of institutional religion he meets during his travels.

---

30 Guthrie, *Bound for Glory*, 243.
31 Guthrie, *Bound for Glory*, 244.

A Family in Crisis

I mentioned how the Guthrie family experienced several setbacks when Woody was a boy, the most tragic of which was the failing health of his mother, which Guthrie slowly weaves into the early chapters of the book. At the beginning of his recital of the family history, they "seemed to be getting along all right," but that *seemed* alludes to a shadow falling over them.[32] In these early moments of the tale, recounting the family history when he was a boy around three, the description of the broader setting is positive, even idyllic: "Peace, pretty weather."[33] But we soon learn this is not real and lasting peace. His mother is anxious about her husband's rough and precarious business dealings in the world of real estate. The setting is the early twentieth century, "fighting days" in Oklahoma, and the struggle to "outwit" others to make a living was "dangerous." "It kept Mama scared and nervous," Guthrie writes. She wants her husband to leave the land-trading business so they could "settle down to some kind of a better life of growing things and helping other people to grow."[34]

And then comes a fire that destroys the proud family's beautiful home.[35] No one knew how it started, but rumors circulate suggesting Mrs. Guthrie lit the match causing the blaze.[36] We begin to suspect either a nervous breakdown or some other form of mental illness. There are other signs of her declining health. On one occasion, Woody's sister finds her mother spilling boiling water while doing dishes without any reaction: "Clara looked over the hot-water reservoir on the wood stove and nobody in the house saw what she saw. Her eyes flared open when she seen that her mama wasn't listening [to their warnings], just washing the dishes clean in the scalding water. . . . Clara kept her quiet, and Papa took a deep breath, and bit his lip."[37] Woody's grandmother also suspects something is wrong, and when Nora Guthrie confirms she has "'little dizzy spells,'" she urges her daughter to call a doctor for help.[38] Woody's grandmother confirms what the boy suspects: "'Your mama is awful bad sick. And . . . it's going to get a whole lot worse.'"[39]

---

32 Guthrie, *Bound for Glory*, 38.
33 Guthrie, *Bound for Glory*, 39.
34 Guthrie, *Bound for Glory*, 39.
35 Guthrie, *Bound for Glory*, 40–41.
36 Guthrie, *Bound for Glory*, 49, 56.
37 Guthrie, *Bound for Glory*, 46.
38 Guthrie, *Bound for Glory*, 61.
39 Guthrie, *Bound for Glory*, 65.

For the child Woody, compassion is lacking in the very places where he might reasonably expect to find it. Two of his young uncles, the children of his grandmother's second marriage, despise Woody and his parents and siblings: "'Yore whole dam family ain't nuthin' but bad luck!'"[40] The boy is angered by their attitude, thinking to himself, "My family can't help what happened to them. My mama can't help what happened. You used to be friendly and nice to my mama [their stepsister] when she was pretty and healthy.... But then, when she had some bad things happen to her, and lost her pretty home, and got sick, and needed you to treat her nice, you stand off and howl and bark like a crazy bunch of coyotes, and laugh and poke fun at us."[41]

In the near context, we further learn that when Nora Guthrie was young, near the same age as her cruel stepbrothers, she was a good student and well loved by everyone.[42] The boys' disdain and callousness are unwarranted. What *Bound for Glory* illustrates in this and many other anecdotes is the importance of appreciating an individual's backstory. Nora Guthrie is a victim of unfortunate circumstances. She is not a bad person or undeserving of the kindness of others. In Woody's stories about her, we see she is loving and concerned for the well-being of her family. Too easily, those who fall on hard times are simply dismissed, even by those who ought to know better: "'Yore whole dam family ain't nuthin' but bad luck!'"

When Woody's sister dies from burns in a household accident, this latest in a series of family tragedies proves to be "the breaking point" for his mother.[43] He describes her erratic behavior, including shrieking at the top of her lungs, lost muscle control during bad spells, and inattention to the needs of home and family as well as her own appearance. The actual cause of the symptoms was never diagnosed; "The doctor called it insanity and let it go with that."[44] After she starts a fire in what appears to be a suicide attempt, authorities send her to an asylum, where she later dies.[45] There is a brief shift in the narrator's voice at this point that catches the reader a little off guard as it is unusual for the author of *Bound for Glory*

---

40 Guthrie, *Bound for Glory*, 71; cf. 81.
41 Guthrie, *Bound for Glory*, 70–71.
42 Guthrie, *Bound for Glory*, 72–73. Though not mentioned specifically, occasional references to her illness in connection with Woody's birth suggest his mother's health issues began with, or perhaps were exacerbated by, postpartum depression (76–77, 81).
43 Guthrie, *Bound for Glory*, 135. Full episode, 133–135.
44 Guthrie, *Bound for Glory*, 136.
45 Guthrie, *Bound for Glory*, 157, 171.

to address readers directly: "I hate a hundred times more to describe my own mother in any such words as these. You hate to read about a mother described in any such words as these. I know. I understand you. I hope you understand me, for it must be broke down and said."[46] It must be said. The town on a hill cannot be hidden. The stories of those who are downtrodden must be told.

There are occasions when biblical texts provide information about characters' histories, which encourages readers to take an interest in their plight. We learn, for instance, that Ruth is a foreigner whose husband died, which makes caring for her Israelite mother-in-law, Naomi, and her determination to stay with her all the more remarkable (Ruth 1:4–18). But on many other occasions, the ethical mandates of biblical texts do not include such a "backstory." The kindnesses called for by the prophets often involve broad but vague categories of those who are vulnerable: "You shall not deprive a resident alien or an orphan of justice; you shall not take a widow's garment in pledge. . . . When you reap your harvest in your field and forget a sheaf in the field, you shall not go back to get it; it shall be left for the alien, the orphan, and the widow" (Deut 24:17–19; cf. Lev 19:9; 23:22). Who are these widows and orphans and those whose very survival depends on the fruit of the land left behind after harvest? We don't know reading only Deuteronomy and Leviticus. And while the imperatives of Scripture *ought* to be sufficient motivation for right action in themselves, encountering individuals within those categories of vulnerability, even fictional representations of those marginalized, potentially deepens our sense of connection to the people God calls us to serve. In this instance, to read the Leviticus and Deuteronomy laws regarding harvest alongside the story about Ruth gleaning in Boaz's fields (Ruth 2:1–3) presents us with images of what poverty and vulnerability in the ancient world looked like. It's difficult to read those Torah mandates in quite the same way after meeting the widows Ruth and Naomi. Their story gives a face to those dependent on sheaves left in the field. As suggested throughout, creative writing is potentially instructive, at times awakening concern for others and modeling both the kinds of compassion biblical texts demand as well as illustrating the harms resulting from the absence of such care. Guthrie's stories are a case in point.

---

46 Guthrie, *Bound for Glory*, 137–138.

Woody Goes to Church

Our author-narrator Woody Guthrie knows firsthand what such failure to share the fruit of the land involves. This secular saint is not always welcomed by institutional religion. When hitching rides on trains, there was a stop in Tucson, Arizona. He soon discovers much of it, particularly the well-to-do part of town, is inhospitable. The situation is dire because he's gone a few days without food and is unable to move or think as usual. During this uncomfortable stayover, he approaches three churches with the plan of doing some work in exchange for a meal. The first has a sign saying "something about Brethren"; this looks promising to him, "and so, feeling like a Brethren," he approaches.[47] That sentiment about being among the brethren is noteworthy. He is not a religious person, but he seems to appreciate he's the kind of person that ought to be embraced by such communities of faith who hold to Jesus's teaching. Blessed are the poor, after all, and he is clearly one of them. Jesus also spoke about being hungry and being fed by the faithful. As it turns out, Woody understands such gospel messages better than the church representative who answers the door on which he knocks. There are lots of others just like you, the woman who answers responds, and "'if the minister starts out to feed one of you, you'll go off and tell a dozen others about it, and they'll all be down here wanting something to eat.'"[48] Well, yeah. She sends him on his way without a meal.

At the second church, no one answers his knock.[49] There are three things about this scene that deserve notice. For one, this moment reverses what Jesus promises: "'Ask, and it will be given to you; *search*, and you will find; *knock*, and the door will be opened for you. For everyone who asks receives, and everyone who *searches* finds, and for everyone who *knocks*, the door will be opened'" (Matt 7:7–8; italics added). Guthrie stresses the nonresponse by saying he knocked and waited two times. Next, Guthrie's reaction when no one answers the door is troubling: "So feeling ashamed of myself for even being there, I tiptoed out on to the swaying sidewalks and sneaked off across town."[50] The sidewalks sway because of his desperate hunger. The gospel message includes lifting the lowly, so the idea of someone leaving a church empty-handed and in desperate straits, and feeling worse for *seeking* help, is

---

47 Guthrie, *Bound for Glory*, 203.
48 Guthrie, *Bound for Glory*, 204.
49 Guthrie, *Bound for Glory*, 204.
50 Guthrie, *Bound for Glory*, 204.

a clear sign of that church's failure. Finally, Guthrie's remark about tiptoeing away is a sign of deference and respect to those inside, but we wonder how deserving of it they are. Two times there is mention of them being asleep. This building he knocks on "was sleepier" than the other, and after knocking the second time, "still nobody woke up."[51] But sleeping is a negative thing in several biblical passages (e.g., Isa 56:10; Mark 13:35–37). It indicates a failure to serve others or being ill-prepared for Christ's coming. The whole episode, with its door-knocking and emphasis on food, brings Revelation 3:20 to mind, in which Jesus is the speaker: "Listen! I am standing at the door, knocking; if you hear my voice and open the door, I will come in and eat with you, and you with me." This second church in *Bound for Glory* models a failed Christianity. *I was hungry, and you gave me nothing to eat.* The episode is a strong indictment.

The third church is no better. After Woody tells a priest he hasn't eaten for two days, that representative of the church refuses to give him food based on a heartless rationale:

> "Charity here is like charity everywhere; it helps for a moment, and then it helps no more. It is part of our policy to be charitable, for to give is better than to receive. You seem still to retain a good measure of your pride and dignity. You do not beg outright for food, but you offer to do hard labor in order to earn your meal. That is the best spirit in this world. To work for yourself is to help others, and to help others is to help yourself. But you have asked a certain question; and I must answer that question in your own words to satisfy your own thinking. You asked if there is work that you can do to earn a meal. My answer is this: There is no work around here that you can do, and therefore, you cannot earn a meal. And, as for charity, God knows, we live on charity ourselves." The big, heavy door closed without making even a slight sound.[52]

By means of a technicality, a theological loophole—*you didn't ask for a handout*—the priest excuses himself from a basic act of human kindness and yet has the nerve to mention this church's policy of being charitable. The scene is reminiscent of the parable of the Good Samaritan that describes religious leaders passing by a man in need.

There is one positive interaction with religious people in the novel. When traveling out of Los Angeles, Guthrie stops in a few restaurants asking if there is any work he could do in exchange for a meal. After being turned down a

---

51 Guthrie, *Bound for Glory*, 204.
52 Guthrie, *Bound for Glory*, 210.

few times, he at last finds "an old gray-headed couple" listening to the radio in their empty restaurant. They were listening to "some hollering being done by a lady name Amy Semple Temple, or something like that."[53] Presumably he means Pentecostal evangelist Aimee Semple McPherson (1890–1944). The couple have Guthrie do some cleaning in return for a generous meal, but this is not the end of the kindness they show. Just before he leaves, the old lady gives him a bag lunch, so he has a little additional food for his journey. Don't tell my husband, she adds. Then when he walks out of the establishment, the old man follows and hands him a quarter "'ta he'p ya on down th' road.'" Don't tell my wife.[54] This encounter with generous and humble religious folk contrasts sharply with the three churches Guthrie describes in the near context. Individuals succeed where institutions fail.

In the sheep and goats passage, some who fall short of Jesus's moral standards complain they had no knowledge of the needs around them. *When were you hungry?* The exercise of reading Woody Guthrie's *Bound for Glory* is an instructive one for readers, reminding them the hungry ones are often nearer than we think. It not only illustrates what Christianity looks like when solicitude is wanting (churches one, two, and three) but also its capacity for kindness when heeding the call of God (the elderly Pentecostals).

Just Me and You

The priest in Tucson justified withholding a meal, even while acknowledging it is better to give than to receive, on the grounds of Woody's dignity. There's no work, and clearly accepting a mere handout is beneath a man such as yourself. Others justify indifference to those who are desperate on ideological grounds. Announcement of a dam-building project near Redding, California, requiring twenty-five hundred workers brought more than eight thousand to the area, with more arriving each day.[55] A makeshift camp, with people building temporary shelters from whatever scraps they could find, sprang up nearby. Woody interacts with many of these unemployed and impoverished individuals, now waiting months for the project to commence and for the call to work.

---

53 Guthrie, *Bound for Glory*, 225.
54 Guthrie, *Bound for Glory*, 225–226.
55 Guthrie, *Bound for Glory*, 245.

One of these conversations is with a young man who reflects on the plight of these desperate souls, and when doing so, he invokes the teachings of Christ, wondering aloud what *he* would say about the terrible conditions of millions around this country if he were here: "'You just ask Jesus how the hell come a couple of thousand of us living out here in this jungle camp like a bunch of wild animals. You just ask Jesus how many million of other folks are living the same way? Sharecroppers down South, big city people that work in factories and live like rats in the slimy slums.'"[56] According to this young philosopher, Jesus would say people need to work together to rebuild the country and then to share it with everyone. But even this, the young man acknowledges, would draw criticism: "'Sure, they'll call it a bad ism. Jesus don't care if you call it socialism or communism, or just me and you.'"[57] Too easily some rationalize indifference on ideological and political grounds, just as others do by appeal to religious ones. Adding labels (socialism, communism) becomes an excuse to withhold, a workaround, a way to dismiss more commonsense notions like compassion, generosity, and the simple idea of community, "'just me and you.'"

As noted, Guthrie occasionally shifts to the second person to great effect. After describing the conditions in that makeshift camp near Redding, he does so again and encourages readers to connect the specific individuals and families he describes with others just like them:

> You've *seen* a million people like this already. Maybe you *saw* them down on the crowded side of your big city; the back side, that's jammed and packed, the hard section to drive through. Maybe you wondered where so many of them come from, how they eat, stay alive, what good they do, what makes them live like this? These people have had a house and a home just about like your own, settled down and had a job of work just about like you. Then something hit them and they lost all of that. They've been . . . looking for that home again. Now they're looking, for a while, in your town. Ain't much difference between you and them.[58]

Though Guthrie wrote this nearly a hundred years ago, his words are no less true. We've seen them, too, even well into the twenty-first century and in societies with more social safety nets than were available in the dust bowl '30s and wartime '40s.

---

56 Guthrie, *Bound for Glory*, 251.
57 Guthrie, *Bound for Glory*, 251.
58 Guthrie, *Bound for Glory*, 249. Italics added.

As with Dickens's *Oliver Twist*, reading *Bound for Glory* alongside the teaching about the sheep and goats (Matt 25:31–46) helps us think through the implications of Jesus's remarks. Guthrie refers to *seeing* the needy around us. The damned to whom Jesus speaks plead ignorance: "'Lord, when was it that we *saw* you hungry or thirsty or a stranger or naked or sick or in prison, and did not take care of you?'" (Matt 25:44; italics added). As Jesus and Guthrie make clear, there is no excuse. We've seen a million people like this already. Three times (25:37, 38, 39) the blessed ask Jesus when they *saw* him and cared for him. Jesus and Guthrie, and in his own fashion Charles Dickens, explain it was when they saw the millions on the margins, the millions they chose to help.

CHAPTER TWO

Anne Brontë Confronts Domestic Unrest
Reading Wisdom's Diary

Shew me thy ways, O Lord; teach me thy paths.

—Psalm 25:4

Fiction provides a context to grapple with moral dilemmas. We see this in the opening pages of Khaled Hosseini's 2013 novel *And the Mountains Echoed*, which are achingly bittersweet. A father named Saboor puts his young son, Abdullah, and daughter, Pari, to bed and agrees when asked to tell them a story. But only one, he insists, because he and Pari have a long day of travel ahead. "Once upon a time, in the days when *divs* and *jinns* and giants roamed the land, there lived a farmer named Baba Ayub," he begins. Baba Ayub is hardworking, barely eking out a living for himself and his family in the town of Maidan Sabz, in a region struggling with drought. A happy homelife is Baba Ayub's only refuge, blessed as he is with a loving, companionable wife and as many children "as a hand has fingers."[1] He loves them all but has a "unique fondness" for his youngest, Qais.

Having established the setting of his bedtime story, Saboor momentarily interrupts the narrative by addressing his children: "Alas, Abdullah and Pari, Baba Ayub's days of happiness came to an end."[2] The effect of this interjection

---

1 Khaled Hosseini, *And the Mountains Echoed* (Toronto: Viking, 2013), 2.
2 Hosseini, *And the Mountains Echoed*, 3.

is a weakening of the gap between fiction and the storyteller's young audience. Even before he begins, when Saboor insists, "Listen, both of you, listen well. And don't interrupt," it is clear the tale he is about to relate, however fantastic, carries meaning.[3] There is a lesson here.

The end of the family's happiness occurs when a *div* visits Maidan Sabz, a fearful giant so large its shadow darkens the skies. The villagers hide in their homes, fearing the worst, because if it taps on the roof of a house, the family must "give it one child." If the family refuses, it takes all the children. The *div* would then "toss the child into a sack," Saboor continued, "sling the sack over its shoulder, and go back the way it had come." Of course, the home selected was Baba Ayub's, and on hearing "the *div*'s dreaded tap," the anguished father "let an agonized cry escape from his lips."[4] He gazes at his five children, realizing "a finger had to be cut, to save the hand."[5] Lots are drawn, and Qais is the one Baba Ayub gives the *div*. The monster then carries the boy back to its mountain fortress.

It is not the end of Baba Ayub's suffering. He later goes after the *div* in what he knows is a suicidal quest to fight the giant and reclaim his son. The long journey alone nearly kills him, but when he finally confronts the *div*, he discovers the tales about the creature circulated in Maidan Sabz are untrue. He's allowed to see Qais through a glass window. Behind the glass is a paradise of gardens, pools, and lush grass. Children are playing, Baby Ayub's boy among them. They are well dressed, well fed, and promised an education. The children have no memory of their former homes so feel no sadness for what they've left behind. They want for nothing and once they are adults will be free to leave if they wish. Baba Ayub then faces another difficult test: "I will allow you to take him home with you, the *div* said. If you choose to, he can never return here. If you choose not to, *you* can never return here."[6] It is a perfect conundrum. At home, the child would face poverty and the same life of hardship his father endures. Having another mouth to feed also puts the other four children at risk as there is not enough to sustain the family as it is. But if he leaves the boy, he would never be allowed to see him again. An impossible choice. The heartbroken father returns home without his child. Mercifully, before he turns from the window for the last time, the *div* gives

---

3 Hosseini, *And the Mountains Echoed*, 1.
4 Hosseini, *And the Mountains Echoed*, 4.
5 Hosseini, *And the Mountains Echoed*, 5.
6 Hosseini, *And the Mountains Echoed*, 11. Italics original.

Baba Ayub a potion that erases his memory of the boy. As Saboor explains it, it was the farmer's "reward for passing the *div*'s second test."[7]

The significance of the bedtime story becomes clear as we discover Saboor faces a difficult decision of his own. The ten-year-old Abdullah is very close to his three-year-old sister, Pari, but circumstances conspire to force their separation. Saboor must sell the girl to a wealthy family in Kabul—a finger cut to save the hand. It is interesting to note that partway through the story about the *div*, Pari drifts off, but Saboor continues: "Abdullah. Your sister has fallen asleep. Cover her feet with the blanket. There. Good. Maybe I should stop now. No? You want me to go on? Are you sure, boy? All right."[8] It seems likely it is Abdullah more than Pari who needs to hear the troubling tale about the *div*. Fiction is the vehicle Saboor needs to explain to his son the unexplainable, namely, the need to take his sister away. The boy's world revolves around Pari, and to lose her is devastating. The fiction also provides a space for the father to process a pressing moral dilemma and express his own grief. Saboor faces the loss of both his children unless he takes drastic action.

These few pages from Hosseini's *And the Mountains Echoed* illustrate ways literature is a resource for ethical contemplation. Baba Ayub is an imagined character who helps the "real" Saboor articulate the emotions he feels when facing the decision to give up his daughter. Both Baba Ayub and Saboor are fictional characters Khaled Hosseini creates to present traumas facing families in twentieth-century Afghanistan. (The novel opens in 1952). And the reader of the novel adds yet another layer by reflecting on the moral ambiguities the tale presents, leading them to wonder whether cutting off the finger to save the hand is really the best course of action. Hosseini takes the epigraph for *And the Mountains Echoed* from the thirteenth-century Persian poet Jelaluddin Rumi: "Out beyond ideas / of wrongdoing and rightdoing, / there is a field. / I'll meet you there." Sometimes right and wrong are easily distinguished but not always. Storytelling is a forum for puzzling over the murky grays, an imaginative way to confront predicaments and figure out the best path forward.

Though the characters' circumstances and the setting and style of Khaled Hosseini's *And the Mountains Echoed* are dramatically different than the story we turn to now, both books share in common accounts of a parent desperate to do what is best when distinguishing wrongdoing from "rightdoing" is difficult.

---

7 Hosseini, *And the Mountains Echoed*, 13.
8 Hosseini, *And the Mountains Echoed*, 6.

Furthermore, just as Saboor turns to storytelling for aid in decision-making, so, too, does the diarist and artist Helen Huntingdon in Anne Brontë's *The Tenant of Wildfell Hall* (1848). For Helen, the competing demands of Victorian social expectations for women and wives present an obstacle for doing what she understands to be her moral duty as a parent. Helen's book, her diary, provides the space needed to process her options and confront her fears, much as Saboor's bedtime story does for him.

A MYSTERIOUS NEIGHBOR

Envy thou not the oppressor,
and choose none of his ways.

—Proverbs 3:31, AV

Wisdom is justified of her children.

—Matthew 11:19, AV

Things are not what they appear. When a single mother moves into a home called Wildfell Hall, tongues begin to wag. No husband. A young child. Reluctance to socialize with others. She's clearly hiding something. The house's very name mirrors what neighborhood gossips project on Helen Graham. She must be a wild, fallen woman. But though they are right to suspect she's hiding something, their conclusions miss the mark entirely. One of these neighbors is the reverend Michael Millward, "a man of fixed principles, strong prejudices, and regular habits,—intolerant of dissent in any shape, acting under a firm conviction that *his* opinions were always right, and whoever differed from them, must be, either most deplorably ignorant, or willfully blind."[9] This minor Anne Brontë character models the kind of inhospitality Jesus seems to deplore. *I was a stranger, and you didn't take me in.* When he learns Helen arrived more than a week before, meaning she didn't attend church the previous Sunday, Reverend Millward arranges "'to offer some pastoral advice, which he fears she needs.'"[10] This is the first mention of

---

9 Anne Brontë, *The Tenant of Wildfell Hall*, ed. Lee A. Talley (1848; Peterborough, ON: Broadview, 2009), 48. Italics original.
10 Brontë, *Tenant of Wildfell Hall*, 45.

the man and is consistent with the description above. Before he even meets Helen, he assumes the worst of her. We later read Helen's perspective on the minister's uninvited intrusion. As she reports in her diary, "the vicar has been [to Wildfell Hall] to scold me for my neglect of the ordinances of religion."[11] The irony is that she is more spiritually alive and pious than Millward. She is theologically savvy, self-sacrificing, and genuinely God-fearing. Whereas Millward's religiosity is external—not unlike Dickens's beadle, Mr. Bumble, discussed in chapter 1—her faith is deeply internalized, and it motivates her actions. Her opinions differ from his, but it turns out he is the one deplorably ignorant and willfully blind.

Rumors about her continue to swirl even after living at Wildfell Hall for a time. Neighbors pass along "'shocking reports'" about Helen Graham and reach the erroneous conclusion she is "'scarcely respectable.'"[12] Some suspect an affair between her and Mr. Lawrence and even wonder if he's the child's father, given a perceived resemblance between him and the boy. Things are not what they appear.[13]

Anne Brontë's *The Tenant of Wildfell Hall* begins and ends with letters from Helen's neighbor Gilbert Markham addressed to his friend J. Halford. In the opening set of letters, he expresses his initial curiosity about, and eventual romantic interest in, the beautiful new tenant of that old house. Early on, she is reluctant to reciprocate his love and in time gives Markham her diary so he might understand the circumstances leading to her arrival in the area, her reasons for being so secretive, and the situation making a romantic attachment impossible. The diary constitutes the bulk of the novel, sandwiched between Markham's correspondence with Halford, and it provides a first-person account of her marriage to the debauched Arthur Huntingdon.

The unusual structure of this novel, with a diary at its core—a book within a book—serves to kindle readers' sympathy for Helen and is instructive and illustrative of the approach to fiction considered in the present book. "The novel seems to assert the possibilities of some type of transformation through reading," observes Lee A. Talley, "because reading Helen's testimony in her

---

11 Brontë, *Tenant of Wildfell Hall*, 333.
12 Brontë, *Tenant of Wildfell Hall*, 91, 94.
13 We later discover Mr. Lawrence is Helen's brother. She anticipated the possibility of such a misunderstanding about the nature of their relationship, but despite the risk, she needed her brother's involvement in the scheme to escape her husband, the Lord of Grassdale Manor. Their relationship is kept secret for as long as possible to safeguard against the discovery of her whereabouts. See Brontë, *Tenant of Wildfell Hall*, 331.

diary makes Gilbert Markham more aware of how difficult the patriarchal structure of society could be for Victorian women."[14] A book, the diary, brings deeper understanding of the plight of someone at the margins. Reading the diary chastens Markham, who tells his correspondent the experience led to "joy unspeakable that my adored Helen was all I wished to think her—that through the noisome vapours of the world's aspersions and my own fancied convictions, her character shone bright, and clear, and stainless." Reading also produced "shame and deep remorse for my own conduct."[15] A form of storytelling, a diary, generates deeper understanding and brings injustices and cruelties to light. Like characters within the novel, readers soon come to understand Helen's desperate situation, and the shift to her first-person narration allows the baseless suspicions and ridicule of others to diminish in relevance.[16] When we listen to others tell their own stories, we are more inclined to respect them.

READING HELEN HUNTINGDON'S DIARY ALONGSIDE SOLOMON'S PROVERBS

"'Would you be *very* glad . . . to find that you were mistaken in your conclusions?'"[17] Gilbert Markham is in love with Helen Graham, the name by which he knows her. When the cruel rumors circulate, charging her with improprieties, he is initially immune to them but in time comes to fear they are true. He is even violent toward Mr. Lawrence, the suspected romantic rival.[18] When confronting her with evidence seeming to support the judgment of others, and after admitting he is brokenhearted about it because he is truly in love with her, she asks the above question. Answering yes, he would

---

14 Lee A. Talley, "Introduction," in Brontë, *Tenant of Wildfell Hall*, 19. Arguably, Gilbert does not change enough, she adds. Helen asks him not to share the contents of the diary, but he does anyway. For her request not to share it, see 130.

15 Brontë, *Tenant of Wildfell Hall*, 335.

16 One example of ridicule concerns Helen's odd strategy for keeping her son away from alcohol. Though only a boy, she gives him some wine with vomit-inducing tartar-emetic to foster a negative association with alcohol. She also gives him wine without tartar-emetic when he is ill. See Brontë, *Tenant of Wildfell Hall*, 57 ("Everybody laughed"), 66–67, 313–314. Her objective: "I wish this aversion to be so deeply grounded in his nature that nothing in after life may be able to overcome it" (314).

17 Brontë, *Tenant of Wildfell Hall*, 130. Italics original.

18 Brontë, *Tenant of Wildfell Hall*, 120.

be glad to discover the truth about her, "she flew to her desk ... snatching thence what seemed a thick album or manuscript volume ... and thrust [it] into [his] hand."[19] It is her diary, with its tragic tale. It answers all the questions he has about her, including the troubling details about her marriage to a loathsome man and the reasons she needed to escape him.

This moment in Anne Brontë's *Tenant of Wildfell Hall* illustrates well the capacity of stories to awaken fellow feeling, to inspire empathy where before there was only disdain or indifference. As noted, the circumstances leading to her reclusive life are not known to her new neighbors, so they fill in the gaps with gossip and baseless speculations. She must be a fallen woman and her child born out of wedlock. She must be irreligious, and she must be having an affair with Mr. Lawrence. What the diary reveals to Gilbert is that they are all mistaken in their conclusions. Helen Graham is a woman of deep faith and a victim of the bad behavior of others.

Arthur Huntingdon is alcoholic, abusive, and unfaithful, but most concerning to Helen is his contaminating influence on her son. The boy's well-being is her highest priority, and it stems from an understanding of motherhood derived from the Bible. When first mentioning her son in the diary, she writes, "I am a mother. . . . God has sent me a soul to educate for heaven," and again later, when planning their escape from Grassdale Manor and her husband, she anticipates being "quite contented to spend my life in obscurity, devoting myself to the training up of my child, and teaching him to avoid the errors of both his parents."[20] She alludes here to Proverbs 22:6, AV: "Train up a child in the way he should go: and when he is old, he will not depart from it." Additionally, Helen recognizes a mother's God-given responsibility to "guide him along the perilous path of youth, and train him to be God's servant." Here again, Proverbs in the King James Version appears to account both for her views on child-rearing and her choice of terms (underlined), as a few passages illustrate:

> My son ... forsake not the law of thy mother. . . . My son, if sinners entice thee, consent thou not. . . . My son, walk not thou in the way with them; refrain thy foot from their path (1:8, 10, 15).
>
> Discretion shall preserve thee. . . . To deliver thee from the way of the evil man. . . . Who leave the paths of uprightness. . . . Whose ways are crooked, and they froward in their paths: To deliver thee from the strange woman . . . Which

---

19 Brontë, *Tenant of Wildfell Hall*, 130.
20 Brontë, *Tenant of Wildfell Hall*, 216, 327.

forsaketh the guide of her youth, and forgetteth the covenant of her God. For her house inclineth unto death, and her paths unto the dead. None that go unto her return again, neither take they hold of the paths of life (2:11–13, 15–18).

I have taught thee in the way of wisdom; I have led thee in right paths. . . . Enter not into the path of the wicked, and go not in the way of evil men (4:11, 14).

My son . . . forsake not the law of thy mother (6:20).

I discerned among the youths, a young man void of understanding (7:7).

Let not thine heart decline to her ways, go not astray in her paths (7:25).

Helen leaves her husband to protect the boy from corruption, and given her religious views—namely, that there are eternal consequences for choices made in this life—this is no small matter. The urgency of the issue is evident in various remarks: "So the little fellow came down every evening," she confides to her diary when home life was at its worst, "in spite of his cross mamma, and learnt to tipple wine like papa, to swear like Mr. Hattersley, and to have his own way like a man, and sent mamma to the devil when she tried to prevent him"; "it would be better that he should die with me, than that he should live with his father."[21]

As discussed below, Arthur is the very embodiment of the Proverbs fool, of one who does not choose the right "path." He is both "a young man void of understanding" and also, as the boy's father, "the evil man" whose "ways are crooked" and is therefore in a position to lead the child astray. How shall I teach my son, Helen muses, "'to respect his father, and yet to avoid his example?'"[22] She has good reasons to leave her husband and is right to do so for her child's sake, though the decision is a hard one to make. Like Saboor, she faces a moral quandary. In addition to societal and ecclesial expectations regarding the duties of wives, Helen is also desperate to rescue Arthur from temporal and eternal destruction.[23] This creates an ethical predicament. Is it better to cut the finger to save the hand? She wrestles with this question constantly.

---

21 Brontë, *Tenant of Wildfell Hall*, 298, 332.

22 Brontë, *Tenant of Wildfell Hall*, 222. Arthur Huntingdon draws on the book of Proverbs himself on one occasion. On his deathbed, he interprets Helen's efforts to comfort him as a form of revenge: "'I suppose you're heaping coals of fire on my head—you think'" (360), a clear allusion to Prov 25:21–22 (cf. Rom 12:20).

23 This, too, is a biblical value, so Helen's patient efforts to reform Arthur, evident throughout the account of their relationship, is comprehensible: "wives, be in subjection to your own husbands; that, if any obey not the word, they also may without the word be won by the conversation of the wives" (1 Pet 3:1, AV).

If Arthur is the Proverbs fool, Helen is Lady Wisdom, both of which are personifications given voice in the Solomonic dictums. The diary she gives Gilbert helps him ignore the gossipy neighbors and recognize their whisperings for what they are. This woman deserves kindness, not criticism. She's a model of decency and piety, not degeneracy and profligacy. As the passages listed above show, Brontë is attentive to the practical advice of biblical wisdom. In her preface to the second edition of the novel, she explains her reasons for including what some reviewers considered the book's coarse subject matter: "Is it better to reveal the *snares and pitfalls* of life to the young and thoughtless traveller, or to cover them with branches and flowers? Oh, reader! if there were less of this delicate concealment of facts—this whispering, 'Peace, peace,' when there is no peace, there would be less of sin and misery to the young of both sexes who are left to wring their bitter knowledge from experience."[24]

The image of sin as a snare is repeated throughout Proverbs in the Authorized Version as well (6:2; 7:23; 12:13; 13:14; 14:27; 18:7; 20:25; 22:5, 25; 29:6, 8, 25), and the author's concern about spiritual dangers informs her character's views and actions. We find Helen stressing the need to warn children of the "'snares of life,'" and explaining, "'I would not send a poor girl into the world, unarmed against her foes, and ignorant of the snare that beset her path.'"[25] Helen admits being "weary of this life," at one point but realizes she must persevere and not "leave my darling [son] in this dark and wicked world alone, without a friend to guide him through its weary mazes, to warn him of its thousand snares, and guard him from the perils that beset him on every hand."[26]

To achieve her pedagogical end, Brontë sets before readers a positive role model, in the person of Helen, and an archetypical "thoughtless traveller" in Arthur Huntingdon, characters owing much, as said, to the biblical book of Proverbs. The fear of the Lord is the beginning of wisdom (Prov 9:10), but there is no such humility in Arthur Huntingdon. Instead of fearing God, he views God as a rival claimant to Helen's affection and challenges her loyalty to a "'higher authority,'" ironically complaining, "'You don't love me with all your heart,'" which twists biblical teaching about directing all love to God

---

24 Brontë, *Tenant of Wildfell Hall*, 39–40. Italics added. She alludes to Jer 6:14 in these remarks.
25 Brontë, *Tenant of Wildfell Hall*, 59, 60–61.
26 Brontë, *Tenant of Wildfell Hall*, 281.

(see Deut 6:5; Matt 22:37; Mark 12:30; Luke 10:27).[27] He complains she is too "'absorbed in . . . devotions'" during a church service and not sufficiently attentive to him. She is "'too religious'" in his opinion, and it is enough to "'make one jealous of one's Maker.'"[28] This argument occurs early in their marriage and sets the tone for all that follows, with Helen clinging to her religious faith and Arthur mocking her for it. He himself descends into excess and irreverence.

There are other ways Arthur aligns with the fool described in biblical wisdom. Brontë presents him as an alcoholic, for one thing, and Proverbs tells us, "Wine is a mocker, strong drink is raging: and whosoever is deceived thereby is not wise" (Prov 20:1, AV). The progression of Huntingdon's alcoholism is often mentioned: "His appetite for the stimulus of wine had increased upon him, as I had too well foreseen. It was now something more to him than an accessory to social enjoyment: it was an important source of enjoyment in itself."[29]

Soon after their marriage, Helen also learns the man's finances are in disarray, and she observes in her diary, "Nearly the whole of the income of my fortune is devoted, for years to come, to the paying off of his debts, and the money he contrives to squander away in London is incomprehensible."[30] Within biblical literature, Proverbs has more to say about prudent financial dealings than other texts (e.g., 5:8–10; 6:1–5; 17:18; 22:7, 26–27). Related to this, Proverbs also warns against idleness (e.g., 6:6; 12:24; 19:15; 24:30–34), and this, too, is clearly marked in the novel as one of Huntingdon's many shortcomings:

> I wish he had something to do, some useful trade, or profession, or employment—anything to occupy his head or his hands for a few hours a day, and give him something besides his own pleasure to think about. If he would play the country gentleman, and attend to the farm—but that he knows nothing about, and won't give his mind to consider,—or if he would take up with some literary study, or learn to draw or to play—as he is so fond of music, I often try to persuade him to learn the piano, but he is far too idle for such an undertaking: he has no more idea of exerting himself to overcome obstacles than he has of restraining his natural appetites.[31]

---

27 Brontë, *Tenant of Wildfell Hall*, 189, 190.
28 Brontë, *Tenant of Wildfell Hall*, 190.
29 Brontë, *Tenant of Wildfell Hall*, 233.
30 Brontë, *Tenant of Wildfell Hall*, 222.
31 Brontë, *Tenant of Wildfell Hall*, 206–207.

Arthur's discontent is understandable viewed through Solomon's wisdom: "The soul of the sluggard desireth, and hath nothing: but the soul of the diligent shall be made fat" (Prov 13:4, AV).

One of the disturbing parallels between the Proverbs fool and Arthur Huntingdon is the man's abusive treatment of animals. Whereas "a righteous man regardeth the life of his beast," Arthur Huntingdon, perhaps as his surname hints (i.e., hunting), disregards the well-being of nonhuman animals: "The tender mercies of the wicked are cruel" (Prov 12:10, AV). Brontë illustrates both sides of that proverb in one telling episode, which has Helen aligned with wisdom and righteousness and Arthur with foolishness and cruelty. Arthur is lying on a couch after taking "an unusual quantity of wine" when "his favourite cocker, Dash, that had been lying at my feet, took the liberty of jumping upon him and beginning to lick his face. He struck it off with a smart blow; and the poor dog squeaked, and ran cowering back to me."[32]

This incident with Dash is troubling on a further level as well because it seems the violence directed at the cocker is also code for spousal abuse. When Arthur calls the dog back, "Dash only looked sheepish and wagged the tip of his tail. He called again, more sharply, but Dash only clung the closer to me [Helen], and licked my hand as if imploring protection. Enraged at this, his master snatched up a heavy book and hurled it at his head. The poor dog set up a piteous outcry and ran to the door."[33] The book misses Dash but hits Helen ("my hand, that had . . . been struck . . . was rather severely grazed"[34]), which suggests domestic assault. In fact, Helen asks if he intended to hit her, which serves to turn the reader's mind in the direction of that interpretation. A remark by Rev. Millward has a similar effect. After learning some of Helen's true history, he still finds reasons to fault her. She should never have left her husband, he insists, "and nothing short of bodily ill-usage (and that of no trifling nature) could excuse such a step—nor even that, for in such a case she ought to appeal to the laws for protection."[35] That it is Millward who makes this remark is important. We are aware by this point that everything he claims to know about Helen is incorrect, so presumably his assumption that there *was not* bodily ill-usage is also mistaken.

---

32 Brontë, *Tenant of Wildfell Hall*, 196.
33 Brontë, *Tenant of Wildfell Hall*, 196.
34 Brontë, *Tenant of Wildfell Hall*, 196.
35 Brontë, *Tenant of Wildfell Hall*, 385.

It is not reading too much into their relationship to conclude there is physical abuse alongside the obvious psychological distress Arthur causes Helen. That Huntingdon's friend Ralph Hattersley is physically abusive to his wife, Milicent, is unambiguous and probably a clue to Arthur's behavior toward Helen. We often read of Hattersley's habit of assaulting his wife:

> He attempted to extort the confession by shaking her and remorselessly crushing her slight arm in the grip of his powerful fingers.[36]
> "Tell me now!" said he with another shake and a squeeze that made her draw in her breath and bite her lip to suppress a cry of pain.[37]
> ... throwing her from him with such violence that she fell on her side[38]
> He clutched a handful of her light brown ringlets and appeared to twist them unmercifully.[39]
> [He brought] her to him by another tug at her hair.[40]
> [Milicent's] silent fretting and constant anxiety on your account [Hattersley], mingled I suspect, with something of bodily fear on her own.[41]

Hattersley is a minor character in the story, but it seems Brontë includes him and these remarks about his violence as another way to fill out the portrait of Arthur Huntingdon. Arthur is especially vile when with him, and yet, when Helen queries Hattersley about her husband's behavior, he observes, "'It's very bad indeed.... [He is] as great a reprobate as ever was d—d." Their mutual friend Hargrave agrees: "'I must say, I thank God I am not such another [as Arthur].'"[42] Hattersley treats his wife badly. Arthur's treatment of Helen, according to the consensus of his circle of friends, is worse. Domestic abuse and other forms of family dysfunction tend to be hidden behind closed doors. It is, for this reason, a problem many do not encounter directly. Stories about it offer at least some indirect knowledge of a category of those who are vulnerable about which many know very little. Here again, fiction offers a kind of education that potentially deepens empathetic connection.

---

36 Brontë, *Tenant of Wildfell Hall*, 246.
37 Brontë, *Tenant of Wildfell Hall*, 246.
38 Brontë, *Tenant of Wildfell Hall*, 247.
39 Brontë, *Tenant of Wildfell Hall*, 253.
40 Brontë, *Tenant of Wildfell Hall*, 254.
41 Brontë, *Tenant of Wildfell Hall*, 321.
42 Brontë, *Tenant of Wildfell Hall*, 256. Hattersley later tells Helen he is "'downright weary'" of Huntingdon and contemplating "'washing my hands of him entirely'" (319). For another depiction of spousal abuse and heavy drinking in fiction of the period, see remarks in chap. 6 about Daniel Quilp, the villain in Dickens's *The Old Curiosity Shop* (1841).

Anne Brontë's *The Tenant of Wildfell Hall* is a difficult story to read owing to its subject matter, and topics like spousal abuse and infidelity are rather unlikely ones for this writer. She remained unmarried and had no children of her own. Furthermore, as Brontë family friend Elizabeth Gaskell observed a few years after its publication, *The Tenant of Wildfell Hall* "is little known; the subject—the deterioration of a character, whose profligacy and ruin took their rise in habits of intemperance, so slight as to be only considered 'good fellowship'—was painfully discordant to one [Anne] who would fain have sheltered herself from all but peaceful and religious ideas."[43] It is a story putting the plight of Victorian women in broken marriages in sharp relief. A wife and mother in such a situation had few legal protections, despite what Mr. Millward thinks, or options to pursue a self-sufficient and independent life. So why did Anne write such a story?

"The pillar of cloud glided constantly before her eyes," wrote sister Charlotte Brontë of the younger Anne: "She ever waited at the foot of a secret Sinai, listening in her head to the voice of a trumpet sounding long and waxing louder."[44] Elsewhere, Charlotte describes Anne as "a very sincere and practical Christian, but the tinge of religious melancholy communicated a sad shade to her brief, blameless life."[45] We find justification for Charlotte's assessments in *The Tenant of Wildfell Hall*, published in June 1848, not long before its author's death at age twenty-nine, in May 1849. If its subject matter seems discordant given Anne's piety and temperament, there is a personal connection that goes some way toward explaining her reasons. Anne's brother Patrick Branwell died in 1848 at the age of thirty-one, the same year the novel was published. Like the dissolute Arthur Huntingdon in *The Tenant of Wildfell Hall*, Branwell was an alcoholic and had an affair with a married woman. Branwell was employed for a time as a private tutor in the same home where Anne was governess, and as a result, as Gaskell notes, she was "a miserable witness to her brother's deterioration of character at this period." Gaskell goes

---

43 Elizabeth Gaskell, *The Life of Charlotte Brontë*, Oxford World's Classics, ed. Angus Easson (1857; Oxford: Oxford University Press, 1996), 280–281.

44 Currer Bell [Charlotte Brontë], "Poems by Acton Bell," in *Wuthering Heights and Agnes Grey*, by Ellis and Acton Bell [Emily and Anne Brontë], new and rev ed. (London: Smith, Elder, 1850), 490–491. In Brontë, *Tenant of Wildfell Hall*, 417.

45 From Charlotte Brontë's "Biographical Notice of Ellis and Acton Bell," in *Wuthering Heights and Agnes Grey* (in Brontë, *Tenant of Wildfell Hall*, 415). Anne uses the phrase "religious melancholy" herself in *Agnes Grey*, ed. Robin L. Inboden (1847; Peterborough, ON: Broadview, 2020), 115.

on to describe the aftermath of his decline, which involved an "irritability of disposition bordering on insanity."[46] There seems to be a lot of Branwell's sad story in Arthur Huntingdon, and the novel is very much a cautionary tale. One interesting feature of *The Tenant of Wildfell Hall* is the way Brontë goes about addressing the debauchery depicted in the story. She turns to the authoritative source that mattered most to her—namely, the Bible. It serves as the basis for Helen's assessment of Arthur's behavior.

Lady Wisdom and Lady Folly

> Say unto wisdom, Thou art my sister; and call understanding thy kinswoman: That they may keep thee from the strange woman, from the stranger which flattereth with her words. For at the window of my house I looked through my casement, And beheld among the simple ones, I discerned among the youths, a young man void of understanding, Passing through the street near her corner; and he went the way to her house, In the twilight, in the evening, in the black and dark night: And, behold, there met him a woman with the attire of an harlot, and subtil of heart. (She is loud and stubborn; her feet abide not in her house: Now is she without, now in the streets, and lieth in wait at every corner.) So she caught him, and kissed him, and with an impudent face said unto him, I have peace offerings with me; this day have I payed my vows. Therefore came I forth to meet thee, diligently to seek thy face, and I have found thee. I have decked my bed with coverings of tapestry, with carved works, with fine linen of Egypt. I have perfumed my bed with myrrh, aloes, and cinnamon. Come, let us take our fill of love until the morning: let us solace ourselves with loves. For the goodman is not at home, he is gone a long journey: He hath taken a bag of money with him, and will come home at the day appointed. With her much fair speech she caused him to yield, with the flattering of her lips she forced him. He goeth after her straightway, as an ox goeth to the slaughter, or as a fool to the correction of the stocks; Till a dart strike through his liver; as a bird hasteth to the snare, and knoweth not that it is for his life. Hearken unto me now therefore, O ye children, and attend to the words of my mouth. Let not thine heart decline to her ways, go not astray in her paths. For she hath cast down many wounded: yea, many strong men have been slain by her. Her house is the way to hell, going down to the chambers of death. (Prov 7:4–27, AV)

Soon after her marriage to Arthur, Helen reports in her diary details about a quarrel with her husband: "Arthur had told me, at different intervals, the

---

[46] Gaskell, *Life of Charlotte Brontë*, 218. For further details on connections between Branwell's behavior and Anne's novel, see, e.g., Talley's editorial note in Brontë, *Tenant of Wildfell Hall*, 356n. 1; and Edward Chitham, *A Life of Anne Brontë* (Oxford: Blackwell, 1991), 12–13, 100–117, etc.

whole story of his intrigue with Lady F—, which I would not believe before. It was some consolation, however, to find that, in this instance, the lady had been more to blame than he; for he was very young at the time, and she had decidedly made the first advances, if what he said was true."[47] This lack of precision in providing the woman's full name, using instead only a capitalized letter and dash, is intriguing. Withholding the full name suggests broad applicability, perhaps a universal meaning that resists reduction to a specific circumstance. Indeed, as seen, this is something important to Brontë, who states her intention in writing *The Tenant of Wildfell Hall* as educating readers and warning them against certain behaviors.[48] In her first and only other novel, *Agnes Grey*, Brontë's narrator also identifies pedagogy as the principal reason for telling the story: "My design, in writing the last few pages, was not to amuse, but to benefit those whom it might concern: he that has no interest in such matters will doubtless have skipped them over with a cursory glance, and, perhaps, a malediction against the prolixity of the writer; but, if a parent has, therefrom, gathered any useful hint, or an unfortunate governess received thereby the slightest benefit, I am well rewarded for my pains."[49] It follows that the nameless woman with whom Arthur had an affair, Lady F—, serves as a model of infamy, a paradigm of villainy whose specific location in time and place is of secondary importance. She is a classic *femme fatale*.

Despite Brontë's lack of precision in naming this woman, there is yet a way to identify her further. Given the author's clear interest in Proverbs, it seems probable she bases her account of Arthur's affair with Lady F— on the template found in 7:4–27, cited above. Arthur is a "young man void of understanding" (7:7, AV), and as Helen describes it in her diary, this woman "caught him, and kissed him" (7:13, AV). It was not the other way around. Furthermore, Lady F— is married (7:19) when she draws this simple youth away from the path of wisdom, ultimately leading him to the "chambers of death" (7:27, AV). The nameless Lady F— in *The Tenant of Wildfell Hall* is

---

47 Brontë, *Tenant of Wildfell Hall*, 194.

48 She is explicit about this in her preface to the second edition (Brontë, *Tenant of Wildfell Hall*, 39–40). This is not the only time she uses a dash this way: "My father, as you know, was a sort of gentleman farmer in —shire" (42); "We had met several times since the —Bay excursion" (88); "'You may go to the d —l if you choose'" (122). See, too, examples pp. 70, 82 (2X), 88, 119 (2X), 238, 328, 330, 355, 367, 381, 382, 387, 388, 391, 393, etc.

49 Brontë, *Agnes Grey*, 68.

Lady Folly, or the Strange Woman, as the Authorized Version refers to her (see 2:16; 5:3, 20; 6:24; 7:5; 23:27), another of Proverbs' personifications, found throughout Proverbs 1-9 especially, and contrasted with Lady Wisdom, the other prominent feminine voice heard throughout these chapters: "Doth not wisdom cry? and understanding put forth her voice? She standeth in the top of high places, by the way in the places of the paths. She crieth at the gates, at the entry of the city, at the coming in at the doors. Unto you, O men, I call; and my voice is to the sons of man" (8:1-4, AV).

The incident where Helen introduces the shorthand Lady F— is brief, and only occasionally does she refer to it later. However, a much longer story appearing in her diary concerns another of Arthur Huntingdon's affairs, one occurring after his marriage to Helen. His friend Lord Lowborough marries Annabella, and soon the new Lady Lowborough begins flirting with and eventually seduces Arthur.[50] Lady Lowborough is the only other titled female in the novel apart from Lady F—, something suggesting a link between the two. Lady Lowborough is also a Lady F—, a Lady Folly, a Strange Woman.

What makes Helen Huntingdon intriguing for readers interested in the Bible is how unlike many Bible-quoting contemporaries she really is. We might reasonably expect a Christian ethicist like her to sprinkle random proof texts throughout her conversations and diary, which comprises the bulk of the novel, with little serious reflection. Casual and highly formulaic appeals to Scripture are familiar to us in literature of the period; think, for instance, of Mrs. Clennam in Charles Dickens's *Little Dorrit*; Charlotte Brontë's reverend Mr. Brocklehurst and the missionary St. John Rivers, both in *Jane Eyre*; the heartless Mr. Hatfield in Anne Brontë's *Agnes Grey* and, as seen, Mr. Millward in *The Tenant of Wildfell Hall*. Instead, Brontë's heroine Helen (Graham) Huntingdon is more complex. She is not beholden to the parish and its values, not afraid to challenge the views of clergymen, and is quite ready to argue the proper interpretation of Scripture, as she understands it, even when it differs from traditional readings. This is most evident when she defends her belief in universal salvation, a conclusion she reaches only after thoughtful reflection of biblical evidence and a position she articulates in defiance to both family and church authorities. On one occasion, she presents this doctrine to her aunt in a spirited conversation, insisting she finds justification for it in the Bible: "'I have searched it through, and found nearly

---

50 Brontë, *Tenant of Wildfell Hall*, 265, etc.

thirty passages, all tending to support the same theory.'"[51] This was Anne Brontë's own theological position, something she wrote about elsewhere, as in the poem "A Word to the Elect," first published in *Poems by Currer, Ellis, and Acton Bell* in 1846.

Anne Brontë's education accounts in part for this thoughtful approach to religion. The Brontë sisters, it comes as no surprise, were voracious readers from early childhood, and their clergyman father ensured this included spiritual works like the Bible and John Bunyan's *Pilgrim's Progress*. To some extent, as with Charles Dickens's *The Old Curiosity Shop* (cf. chap. 6), Bunyan's allegory lies behind the construction of the villainous Arthur Huntingdon, Helen's boorish husband. He is "Mr. Worldly-Wiseman and Beelzebub all rolled into one," according to John Maynard, and his "outrageous vanity of drinking, revelling and adultery lead only down the slippery slope."[52] However, the novel's primary source for Arthur Huntingdon is not Bunyan's *Progress*, I suggest, but rather the book of Proverbs. We find citations of and allusions to Scripture throughout, but Proverbs especially informs and motivates Helen's actions and conversations. Almost everything she does concerns the moral formation of her son and husband. She believes her God-given reason to exist is to "educate [her son] for heaven," which requires keeping the boy from his father's poisonous example, what she calls his "contaminating influence."[53] Her language alludes to and her actions live out the Proverbs 22:6 mandate to train a child in the way he should go.[54] She defines motherhood as being the boy's "instructor, friend—to guide him along the perilous path of youth, and train him to be God's servant while on earth."[55] As seen, her ideas and language are consistent with teachings found in biblical wisdom: "In all thy ways acknowledge him, and he shall direct thy paths" (Prov 3:6); "I have taught thee in the way of wisdom; I have led thee in right paths" (Prov 4:11). Similarly, she frequently speaks of her marriage as an opportunity to reform her husband, to "lead him back to the path of virtue," again using a metaphor familiar from Proverbs.[56] In Helen's first-person diary, she is a

---

51 Brontë, *Tenant of Wildfell Hall*, 169. See full conversation, 167–169.
52 John Maynard, "The Brontës and Religion," in *The Cambridge Companion to the Brontës*, ed. Heather Glen (Cambridge, UK: Cambridge University Press, 2002), 197.
53 Brontë, *Tenant of Wildfell Hall*, 216, 280; cf. 217, 222, etc.
54 See, too, Brontë, *Tenant of Wildfell Hall*, 216–217, 327.
55 Brontë, *Tenant of Wildfell Hall*, 217.
56 Brontë, *Tenant of Wildfell Hall*, 280. Cf. e.g., Prov 2:19–21.

moral authority desperate to save her husband from his dissipations and their child from those destructive influences.[57]

Brontë is explicit about her motives for writing this novel, which is "not simply to amuse the Reader, neither ... to gratify my own taste, nor yet to ingratiate myself with the Press and the Public." Instead, her aim is "to tell the truth, for truth always conveys its own moral to those who are able to receive it." Specifically, she has in mind young readers who might make the same mistakes as characters in the story. This is a novel of warning, with the author motivated by a religiously informed sense of pedagogical duty. Her understanding of the religious writer's role resembles the pedagogical intent of Proverbs, which opens with a call to "hear the instruction of thy father, and forsake not the law of thy mother," who warn youths not to "walk ... in the way of [sinners]; refrain thy foot from their path" (1:8, 15). In her preface, Brontë writes, "I know that [profligate characters like those depicted in my novel] do exist, and if I have warned one rash youth from following in their steps, or prevented one thoughtless girl from falling into the very natural error of my heroine, the book has not been written in vain."[58]

Like the fool of Proverbs, Arthur Huntingdon's decisions destroy him, a victim of Lady Folly. He goes down to what Proverbs calls "the chambers of death," never able to embrace Lady Wisdom even though Helen invites him to do so right up until his last breath. Wisdom is proved right by her actions in this Brontë tale.

---

57 Helen has good reason to fear Arthur's destructive influence on the boy, something made clear in a long section recounting his role in the downward spiral of Lord Lowborough (Brontë, *Tenant of Wildfell Hall*, 175–186). Lowborough loses everything owing to his compulsion for gambling and, in despair, sinks into dependence on laudanum and alcohol. He even contemplates suicide. A series of keywords and actions in the scene present Arthur and his other friends as diabolical in nature and complicit in Lowborough's fall. Arthur and the others are demons (177; cf. 293, 324), devils (183, two times), and tempters (179; cf. 241, 294). They encourage the struggling man to keep drinking (180), and Arthur even places Lowborough's favorite spirit before him when he's trying to stop (179). Arthur later tells Helen, "'I set them [glasses of alcohol] before him'" (181); said "'Take the bottle, man!'" (181); and recommended he take a little wine (182), thus quoting the Bible (see 1 Tim 5:23) for nefarious purposes, much as Satan does in the temptation narratives (Matt 4:1–11; Luke 4:1–13). Lowborough accuses Huntingdon and his friends of playing the devil's part and enticing him to the devil's den (their London club). He shrinks from Arthur's company, fearing, as Huntingdon puts it, "'lest I should wile him back to destruction'" (183). The word *wile* suits the context, plausibly alluding to the warning against "the wiles of the devil" in Eph 6:11, AV.

58 Brontë, *Tenant of Wildfell Hall*, 40.

CHAPTER THREE

Daniel Defoe's Shipwrecked Bible and Jean Rhys's Cardboard World

*The Spirit of the Lord is upon me, because he hath
anointed me to preach the gospel to the poor; he hath sent me
to heal the brokenhearted, to preach deliverance to the captives.*
—Luke 4:18, AV

Inhospitality takes other forms than closed and locked church doors like those Woody Guthrie encountered in Tucson, Arizona. Sometimes welcome is denied to whole categories of people. With our studies in these chapters loosely organized around Jesus's teachings, attention to the dark side of religion suits because he spoke about that too. Biblical authors often discuss forms of marginalization and abuse couched in the appearance of piety. In the Sermon on the Mount, Jesus refers to many who call him Lord but are dismissed with the chilling words, "'I never knew you'" (Matt 7:21–23). He warns of wolves in sheep's clothing and trees not producing good fruit in the near context (7:15–20). Not all that calls itself godly is godly. You "'cross sea and land to make a single convert, and you make the new convert twice as much a child of hell as yourselves,'" he tells some religious authorities (23:15). In the sheep and goats lesson, those Jesus sends away with the stark rejection "'depart from me'" (25:41) seem to think they are on the side of the right when in fact they are not. Their plea in defense, "'Lord, when was it that we saw you?'" (25:44), is insufficient.

It is tempting to read Scripture with a generous disposition toward our own conduct. To recognize that sometimes *we* are the oppressor rather than the oppressed, the sinner rather than the saint, is difficult, and it is for this reason I include this short chapter. Stories, fictional and nonfictional, of religious figures guilty of shameful conduct are common enough. Sexual abuse perpetrated by ministers and priests, financial misdealing, charlatanism, exploitation—all are common headlines. And even this presents a tempting form of evasion for those seeking to be faithful to the call of Christ. At least I'm not *that* bad. But we need to resist that platitude as well: "'God, I thank you that I am not like other people: thieves, rogues, adulterers, or even like this tax collector'" (Luke 18:11). The one speaking these words is certainly *not* the hero of that story.

Here again, I find value in turning to creative writers to further grasp the spirit of gospel ideals. The fact is, I *do* thank God I am not like the thieves and rogues and adulterers I see on the news. And am I as repentant and humble as that tax collector Luke describes? Maybe sometimes. Not always. That man is so broken he doesn't even look up to heaven but only beats his chest, saying, "'God, be merciful to me, a sinner!'" (Luke 18:13). Stories depicting the shortcomings of Christians are instructive in that they highlight, among many other things, ways individuals and communities of faith fail to love their neighbors as themselves. What does inhospitable Christianity look like?

EMPIRE, SLAVERY, AND A VICIOUS CHRISTIAN

There is a lot of religious content in Daniel Defoe's 1719 novel *Robinson Crusoe*; Defoe presents its titular character as a reformed and devoted beneficiary of divine grace. At the same time, however, the man's assumptions and actions are often irreconcilable with contemporary values. We wonder at the violence, arrogance, condescension, greed, and sense of entitlement he displays. Much that he does in the name of religion is repugnant. But for this very reason, there is a lot to learn from this book. The point of this chapter is not so much to critique early eighteenth-century English Protestantism as to consider the capacity of stories from other places and times to instruct. Defoe's Robinson Crusoe is a man of his times, and three hundred years on, we recognize his ethical blind spots. But therein lies one of its potential lessons. We have blind spots too. Twenty-first-century Christianity at its best may think differently about slavery and race and empire compared with Defoe, but we still only see through a glass darkly (cf. 1 Cor 13:12, AV). Our understanding is always only partial.

The basic plot of the novel is familiar to most. The character's name evokes mental images of the lone Tom Hanks-like castaway surviving against all odds. Even before writing the book, Defoe and his seafaring contemporaries were familiar with that storyline from accounts of actual marooned sailors, among them the harrowing adventures of Scottish sailor Alexander Selkirk (1676–1721), who survived nearly five years on the island of Juan Fernandez off the coast of Chile before his rescue in 1709. Defoe knew of Selkirk's adventures from various versions of the story then in circulation, and it is a key source for the novel, though his castaway's island is off the coast of Venezuela. Less familiar perhaps is the religious storyline that is a central part of *Robinson Crusoe*. The book relates a sailor's adventures but is much more than an entertaining yarn, as Defoe explains in his preface: "*The Story is told with Modesty, with Seriousness, and with a religious Application of Events to the Uses to which wise Men always apply them (viz.) to the Instruction of others by this Example, and to justify and honour the Wisdom of Providence in all the Variety of our Circumstances, let them happen how they will.*"[1] Defoe, Anne Brontë (see chap. 2), and John Bunyan (see chap. 6) are alike in announcing their intent to use art for pedagogical ends.

After the shipwreck that results in Crusoe's isolation, he salvages, among other things, three Bibles and "two or three Popish Prayer-Books" from the debris and later begins reading them.[2] He eventually undergoes a conversion, and this is not too strong a term. Though he is clearly Christian in a cultural or social sense all along (note, for instance, his preference not to work on Sundays), he admits to being irreligious many times over: "I had hitherto acted upon no religious Foundation at all, indeed I had very few Notions of Religion in my Head."[3] Even in earlier moments of crisis, he admits occasional cries to God for help were only temporary moments of reform, not wholehearted transformations. One example of this occurs after a series of earthquakes disheartens him, threatening to destroy his shelter and limited resources:

---

[1] Daniel Defoe, *Robinson Crusoe*, ed. Evan R. Davis (Peterborough, ON: Broadview, 2010), 45. Italics original.

[2] Defoe, *Robinson Crusoe*, 100.

[3] Defoe, *Robinson Crusoe*, 112. Regarding Sundays, see 107.

"All this while I had not the least serious religious Thought, nothing but the common, *Lord ha' Mercy upon me*; and when it was over, that went away too."[4]

It was a serious illness that proved to be the final calamity leading to his repentance. Fearing death, he emphasizes how the crisis motivated his first earnest attempts at prayer.[5] While in a feverish delirium, he has a terrifying dream of "a Man descend[ing] from a great black Cloud, in a bright Flame of Fire," who approaches Crusoe with a weapon. The figure then says to him, "*Seeing all these Things have not brought thee to Repentance, now thou shalt die.*"[6] Once awake, Crusoe begins a process of serious self-reflection. He finally acknowledges that the rejection of his father's wise counsel years before, his headstrong and self-interested seafaring, and his dissolute living brought about the series of calamities now befalling him. To this point, he admits, "I never had so much as one Thought of it being the Hand of God, or that it was a just Punishment for my Sin." He is, as he puts it, "wicked and prophane to the last Degree."[7]

So begins Crusoe's religious awakening. The character's entire first-person narrative is thus a spiritual autobiography, reflecting a Puritan theology with its emphasis on such themes as divine providence, human depravity, confession, prayer, and personal moral responsibility: "What is this Earth and Sea of which I have seen so much, whence is it produc'd, and what am I, and all the other Creatures, wild and tame, humane and brutal, whence are we? . . . It is God that has made it all . . . and if nothing happens without his Appointment, he has appointed all this to befal me."[8] From these reflections, he turns immediately to his own moral culpability. He is, to use a recurring term in the story, a wretch who failed to acknowledge the grace of God in preserving his life and consequently deserves the hardships he endures.

Protestant Calvinism stresses the importance of the Bible as God's Word, and indeed it is central to Crusoe's conversion experience. After the shift in perspective just mentioned, he decides to use some tobacco, recalling medicinal qualities attributed to it. In the same chest with the tobacco are the long-forgotten rescued Bibles, and for the first time he takes one to read. The experience is revelatory: "Only having open'd the Book casually, the first

---

4 Defoe, *Robinson Crusoe*, 114. Italics original.
5 Defoe, *Robinson Crusoe*, 119, 123.
6 Defoe, *Robinson Crusoe*, 120.
7 Defoe, *Robinson Crusoe*, 121, 120.
8 Defoe, *Robinson Crusoe*, 124.

Words that occurr'd to me were these, *Call on me in the Day of Trouble, and I will deliver, and thou shalt glorify me.*"⁹ The passage fits his circumstances, and it leads him to wonder, with the Israelites, "*Can God spread a Table in the Wilderness?*"¹⁰ He later marvels at heaven's provisions for one "in such a Wilderness," when years later he secures a ship, allowing him to get off the island.¹¹

With his recovery from illness underway, Crusoe begins reading the Bible regularly, beginning with the New Testament. This, combined with his recollection of the terrifying dream, culminates in his final surrender to God: "I was earnestly begging of God to give me Repentance [in keeping with the dream], when it happen'd providentially the very Day that reading the Scripture, I came to these Words, *He is exalted a Prince and a Saviour, to give Repentance, and to give Remission.*"¹²

Crusoe then prays what he describes as the first real prayer in his life because it is based on a biblical view of hope. An important shift in his thinking occurs at this point. Now when he prays Psalm 50:15—*call on me and I will deliver you*—its meaning shifts. Crusoe no longer sees his present circumstances, being marooned on an isolated island and the daily struggle to survive, as the primary concern. Prior to reaching this spiritual understanding of deliverance, Crusoe thought of his island as "a Prison" from which he needed rescue, but his perceptions shift from his literal plight to his spiritual poverty:

> Now I look'd back upon my past Life with such Horrour, and my Sins appear'd so dreadful, that my Soul sought nothing of God, but Deliverance from the Load of Guilt that bore down all my Comfort: As for my solitary Life it was nothing; I did not so much as pray to be deliver'd from it, or think of it; It was all of no Consideration in Comparison to this: And I add this Part here, to hint to whoever shall read it, that whenever they come to a true Sense of things, they will find Deliverance from Sin a much greater Blessing, than Deliverance from Affliction.¹³

---

9 Defoe, *Robinson Crusoe*, 125. Italics original, citing Ps 50:15. Cf. 179.

10 Defoe, *Robinson Crusoe*, 125–126. Italics original, citing Ps 78:19. He recalls the moment later (156).

11 Defoe, *Robinson Crusoe*, 277. For a description of the island, complete with a map, see Alberto Manguel and Gianni Guadalupi, *The Dictionary of Imaginary Places* (Toronto: Vintage, 2001), 148–149.

12 Defoe, *Robinson Crusoe*, 127. Italics original, citing Acts 5:31.

13 Defoe, *Robinson Crusoe*, 128. Cf. 125 for the quotation of Ps 50:15.

As the book is a spiritual autobiography, readers naturally see Defoe's island as a metaphor, as a spiritual captivity, or, as St. Paul puts it, death as the wages of sin (Rom 6:23). Crusoe discovers there is grace even in that remote location. Ultimately, Crusoe's physical circumstances reflect the spiritual recovery he describes. He escapes the island many years later and prospers, just as Job escapes his sufferings to see happier days. The resemblance between him and Job is one Crusoe himself recognizes.[14]

For those approaching the book from a Christian perspective, especially from Protestant traditions with an emphasis on personal religious experience, *Robinson Crusoe* is a narrative of spiritual progress. But it is a difficult book for other reasons. Prior to conversion, Crusoe was a slave trader, but little changes in this respect after his religious turn. Though not by design, *Robinson Crusoe* serves to illustrate how moral blind spots are possible despite sincere religious commitments (cf. Jesus's warning, "Thou hypocrite, first cast out the beam out of thine own eye; and then shalt thou see clearly to cast out the mote out of thy brother's eye" [Matt 7:5, AV]). For Defoe (1660–1731) and many of his first readers, it was possible to reconcile empire-building and slavery with Christian faith. This is not the case anymore.

Crusoe and Racism

Robinson Crusoe is a racist and measures other people against a supposed English ideal—white, Christian, Protestant, English-speaking—though there is perhaps some irony here given he is himself an outsider in terms of the family's history, his father "being a Foreigner." It is a minor point, however, since the name Crusoe, he explains, is an English corruption of *Kreutznaer*, which suggests "nearer the cross" or "to cruise, to journey," both definitions that suit the titular character.[15]

There is further irony in Crusoe's early career because this slave owner himself experiences the indignities of being enslaved. A Turkish pirate ship overtakes his vessel early in the novel, and its captain forces Crusoe into service at the Moroccan seaport Sallee for about two years, during which

---

14 In remarks about his own circumstances, referring to Job 42:12–17: "I might well say, now indeed, That the latter End of *Job* was better than the Beginning" (Defoe, *Robinson Crusoe*, 286; italics original).

15 Defoe, *Robinson Crusoe*, 47. See, too, Davis's editorial note, Defoe, *Robinson Crusoe*, 47n. 1.

time he plans his escape.[16] When an opportunity comes to steal away in one of his master's boats while fishing, he casts a man overboard and forces a Moorish boy named Xury to promise allegiance or face the ocean waters. The boy chooses to stay and is a good friend and helpmate to Crusoe as they flee south along the African coast. They escape the slave owner and survive rough sailing conditions as well as dangerous beasts and people at every stop on shore for water and food.

Crusoe's relationship with the African child foreshadows that with Friday in years to come. Xury and Friday are both Crusoe's slaves, and there is a dark inference of European supremacy in the fact that Crusoe escapes his slavery, whereas these two do not. Crusoe eventually "sell[s] the poor Boy's Liberty" to a Portuguese ship captain.[17] The paralleling of Xury and Friday's fates rules out a pre-conversion/post-conversion distinction in his treatment of other humans, as though Crusoe's cruel betrayal of the boy was nothing more than evidence of his unregenerate state. He acts the same way after the "Deliverance from Sin" he so piously proclaims. Crusoe uses these non-Europeans as tools, as resources to aid survival and further his colonizing ambitions and pursuit of wealth. We see this also in his purchase of a Black slave, left nameless, made to work on his Brazilian tobacco plantation.[18] There is no consideration of the well-being of any of these people. At one point, Xury even offers to sacrifice himself if "wild Mans" were to attack them, thus allowing Crusoe to "go wey," an offer made with "so much Affection that made [Crusoe] love him ever after." But this is a hollow sentiment. He soon after trades the boy for "60 Pieces of Eight."[19]

It is the pursuit of slaves that is ultimately the cause of Crusoe's famous crisis. Not content with his slow accumulation of wealth at the Brazilian plantation, he plans with other landowners an expedition to Africa to bring back slaves to expand production in their operations. Looking back, Defoe puts the scheme in a negative light: "I that was born to be my own Destroyer, could no more resist the Offer than I could restrain my first rambling Designs, when my Father's good Counsel was lost upon me."[20] However, it's the pursuit of yet greater riches and Crusoe's lack of contentment, not slavery, that are the

---

16 Defoe, *Robinson Crusoe*, 60–64.
17 Defoe, *Robinson Crusoe*, 74.
18 Defoe, *Robinson Crusoe*, 77.
19 Defoe, *Robinson Crusoe*, 67, 74.
20 Defoe, *Robinson Crusoe*, 79.

problems in his view.[21] Crusoe's commentary on this ambition shortly before describing the African plan makes this clear: "As I had once done thus in my breaking away from my Parents, so I could not be content now, but I must go and leave the happy View I had of being a rich and thriving Man in my new Plantation, only to pursue a rash and immoderate Desire of rising faster than the Nature of the Thing admitted; and thus I cast my self [sic] down again into the deepest Gulph of human Misery that ever Man fell into."[22]

It needs to be remembered that the narrator is looking back at all the adventures related in the novel, so it is the retrospective, post-conversion Crusoe who offers the commentary on this expedition to get more slaves. For the Christian narrator Crusoe, greed, not slavery, is the cause of his downfall. The pursuit of African slaves does not figure into his moral calculations, and so it is the post-conversion Crusoe later plans to make "Slaves" of any of the cannibals he captures when marooned on his island. This comes to pass. When he sees a man fleeing the cannibals who visit his island, he thinks that now is "my Time to get me a Servant." He rescues that man, assigns him the name Friday, and refers to him as "my Slave" and "my Savage."[23]

Crusoe's Dominion over the Earth

The last stormy moments of the voyage that leaves Crusoe marooned recall the opening chapters of Genesis. Occasional remarks in his narrative do the same, such as the observation that his is the first gun fired there since "the Creation of the World."[24] What these allusions do is sanction Crusoe's lordship over the land. It begins when Crusoe and the crew take to a small boat after the ship runs aground on a sandbar. A huge wave, "Mountain-like," overwhelms it and Crusoe's shipmates, but he struggles on alone to reach

---

21 Crusoe's obsession with wealth is another moral blind spot. It is true he experiences a chastening about his pursuit of riches, as is evident in his acknowledgment that for a castaway, the tools found in a "Carpenter's Chest" are of greater value than gold, a single knife worth more than money. But the overall arc of the story suggests wealth is evidence of a proper Christian faith and God's blessing (88, 94; cf. 155–156 on the worthlessness of money). When he finally returns to Europe, he discovers he is a wealthy man owing to the success of his Brazilian plantation (280, 286). He is wealthy, at least in part, because of the use of slave labor on that plantation (283, 286).
22 Defoe, *Robinson Crusoe*, 78.
23 Defoe, *Robinson Crusoe*, 215, 217, 220, 218.
24 Defoe, *Robinson Crusoe*, 90.

shore.[25] Enormous swells catch him up, and he nearly drowns in each, but the water gradually grows shallower. His feet touch land before the next rise in the surf carries him up again, and then, "I strook forward against the Return of the Waves," he writes, "and felt Ground again with my Feet."[26] The pattern repeats, and the alternation hints at the gradual separation of water from dry land described in the first Genesis creation account (1:9). Significantly that account asserts humanity's dominion over the earth (1:26–28), and this is what we see Crusoe do throughout the rest of the story. He sets about tilling the soil like Adam in Eden (Gen 2:15) and ruling all the creatures he encounters. This loose correspondence with Genesis presents the marooned sailor as a god himself. Crusoe creates a new world. He causes vegetation to grow (cf. Gen 1:29–30) and flocks to increase through his skills in husbandry (1:24–25). He is lord of the land.

Adam meets God in the garden of Eden, and Crusoe meets God on the island. Both stories stress the importance of human nurturing of vegetation and interaction with animals (2:20). But one way Crusoe is clearly un-Adamic is in the treatment of those animals. Like Xury and Friday, they, too, are mere tools and playthings and nuisances and threats over which Crusoe asserts dominion. Crusoe's conquest of and mastery over agriculture, birds, fish, and animals is a recurring subject in the novel. The Genesis picture of Adam, however, is very different from Defoe's story, with its titular character constantly demanding submission from all, his ever-present gun in hand. Animals approach Adam peacefully in Eden, and plants alone are Adam and Eve's food (Gen 2:19; 1:29–30). Crusoe, in sharp contrast, is gratuitously violent. We see this even before he is a castaway, with Crusoe killing a sleeping lion for sport when sailing along the African coast: "This was Game indeed to us, but this was no Food."[27] A later example involves the killing of a parrot merely to show Friday his superior power: "To let *Friday* understand a little what I would do, I call'd him to me . . . pointed at the Fowl which was indeed a Parrot . . . accordingly I fir'd and bad him look, and immediately he saw the Parrot fall, he stood like one frighted. . . . [He] thought that there must be some wonderful Fund of Death and Destruction in that Thing, able to kill Man, Beast, Bird or any Thing near, or far off."[28]

---

25 Defoe, *Robinson Crusoe*, 83.
26 Defoe, *Robinson Crusoe*, 84.
27 Defoe, *Robinson Crusoe*, 69.
28 Defoe, *Robinson Crusoe*, 224–225. Italics original.

A further episode of such purposeless violence occurs toward the end of the story when Friday kills a bear merely to make Crusoe and his comrades laugh. Though the bear "was walking softly on, and offer'd to meddle with no Body," Friday first taunts and torments the animal before shooting it.[29] Though these actions are Friday's, the whole episode begins with Crusoe giving him permission to engage in sport with the bear.[30] The frequency of such senseless destruction is conspicuous; it is a way to demonstrate the greater power of European technology and Crusoe's invincibility. There are occasional moments when he appreciates animals, as in a friendly encounter with a catlike creature, which, if read through a Genesis lens, evokes the animals approaching Adam without fear.[31] Resembling this scene in attitude is Crusoe's rescue of two cats from the ship and his mention of a dog who survived the wreck and remained a constant companion for years to come. But even this appreciation for the dog's support is dominative in tone as Crusoe refers to the animal as "a trusty Servant."[32] Far more frequent, however, are his various references to killing, which begin soon after he lands. Crusoe's power over animals, through hunting, taming, and breeding when on the island and surviving attacks by wild wolves when back in Europe, serves to prove his mastery over nature.[33] He even masters the weather by planning how best to manage rainy seasons and storms, organizing his crops accordingly. The episodes with the bear and wolves occur while Crusoe and others trek across Europe from Lisbon to Dover during a particularly bad winter with heavy snows. Nothing defeats him.

After Crusoe salvages all he can from the wreck, sets up a shelter, and attends to his basic needs, there is time for reflection, which, as seen, takes a decidedly religious turn. Here, too, there is a vague resemblance to themes and language found in Genesis. With his immediate needs met, Crusoe turns to a description of his state of mind: "And now being to enter into a melancholy Relation of a Scene of silent Life, such perhaps as was never heard of in the World before, I shall take it from its Beginning, and continue it in

---

29 Defoe, *Robinson Crusoe*, 294, 296.
30 Defoe, *Robinson Crusoe*, 294.
31 Defoe, *Robinson Crusoe*, 92.
32 Defoe, *Robinson Crusoe*, 100.
33 Defoe, *Robinson Crusoe*, 297–301.

its Order."[34] Opening his record with these words echoes the Bible's "in the beginning God created the heaven and the earth" (Gen 1:1, AV). So, too, does his scheme for keeping track of days, months, and years and his explanation of his rudimentary calendar. This includes distinguishing "the Sabbath Days from the working Days."[35] Genesis 1 has a similar organizational structure, with the counting of six workdays followed by a seventh-day Sabbath rest (2:2–3). Crusoe uses a knife to etch his calendar onto "a great Cross," which makes explicit the religious overtones of the scene and serves to reinforce the hand of Providence in all Crusoe's activities. With the great cross serving as the literal foundation of Crusoe's calendar, it implies all that happens to him, all that he achieves during this time, has the blessing of heaven. Significantly, it is after his description of the cross-calendar that he reports having rescued the three Bibles from the wrecked ship.[36] This is sacred time and so a record of activities arranged and approved by God.

Much of the first half of the novel focuses on Crusoe's struggle to overcome obstacles and secure a comfortable, safe existence on the island. In time, he reaches a point where he is satisfied with his efforts: "It would have made a Stoick smile to have seen, me and my little Family [domesticated animals] sit down to Dinner; there was my Majesty the Prince and Lord of the whole Island; I had the Lives of all my Subjects at my absolute Command. I could hang, draw, give Liberty, and take it away, and no Rebels among all my Subjects."[37] He then goes on to recapitulate his various achievements as they concern his mastery of such things as shelter, clothing, agriculture, animal husbandry, and travel (i.e., a canoe he made).[38] He has absolute "dominion over the fish of the sea, and over the fowl of the air, and over every living thing that moveth upon the earth" (Gen 1:28, AV; cf. 1:26). It is at this point in the story he finds, after several years, the first evidence of another human on the island. He comes upon "the Print of a Man's naked Foot on the Shore."[39] This begins a long sequence of events, dominating the second half of the book, demonstrating Crusoe's skill in mastering human beings in addition to nature. His gun, his cunning, and his assertion of that "absolute Command" present

---

34 Defoe, *Robinson Crusoe*, 99.
35 Defoe, *Robinson Crusoe*, 100.
36 Defoe, *Robinson Crusoe*, 100.
37 Defoe, *Robinson Crusoe*, 171.
38 Defoe, *Robinson Crusoe*, 172–175.
39 Defoe, *Robinson Crusoe*, 176.

a picture of European conquest that in a contemporary postcolonial context disturbs far more than it impresses.[40]

Crusoe eventually rescues a man from certain death and then, in effect, enslaves him. He changes the man's name, forces him to learn English, and urges his conversion to Christianity.[41] The last involves a long theological discourse that begins with Crusoe laying "a Foundation of religious Knowledge" and concludes with the self-satisfied announcement, "The Savage was now a good Christian... a Christian, as I have known few equal to him in my Life."[42] Of course, Friday's embrace of Crusoe's religion is, from one way of looking at it, coerced. What choice did he have? The episode resembles Xury's situation. Crusoe sells that boy to a Portuguese ship captain, who promises to set him free after ten years "if he turn'd Christian."[43] Like Friday, what choice does Xury have?

LITERARY RESISTANCE TO EMPIRE

Sometimes those who are colonized fight back. Jean Rhys's 1966 novel *Wide Sargasso Sea* is a prequel to Charlotte Brontë's *Jane Eyre* (1847) and a response to the Victorian novelist's depiction of the non-English Bertha Mason. Bertha is Edward Rochester's insane first wife, locked away in the attic of Thornfield Hall. Brontë's novel enjoys canonical status as a European myth of the happily ever-after ending, culminating as it does in the marriage of its titular English heroine and the brooding Rochester. Rhys's *Wide Sargasso Sea* (1966) presents readers with the backstory of the Caribbean-born Bertha and in doing so, challenges the earlier depiction of that hapless woman. On reading Brontë's novel, "Rhys became outraged by the caricature of the Creole she found in the murky background," notes Andrea Ashworth. Bertha Mason is

---

40 "After building his world, he realizes he is not alone. First a single human footprint on the beach, then a scene of natives of the islands that terrifies him, then his violent attack on them and acquisition from among them of his 'man' and friend, Friday: all this has served as a parable of British colonialism and encounters with indigenous peoples" (editorial introduction to Daniel Defoe, in Stephen Greenblatt et al., eds., *The Norton Anthology of English Literature*, vol. C. 10th ed. [New York: Norton, 2018], 567). The story shows low regard for other-than-white-European-Christian human lives.
41 Defoe, *Robinson Crusoe*, 220, 231–232.
42 Defoe, *Robinson Crusoe*, 228, 233.
43 Defoe, *Robinson Crusoe*, 74.

"faceless, voiceless and sacrificed to the success story of the famous English heroine. 'That's only one side,' Rhys protested: 'the English side.' Indignant and inspired, she responded to the story with sensitive zeal, determined to paint her vision of the other side."[44]

In Rhys's novel, we first meet that Brontë character in childhood, when she is Antoinette Cosway. Her widowed mother remarries a man named Alexander Mason. When she herself marries, Antoinette's husband assigns her the name Bertha against her wishes.[45] She is angry he does so, insisting it is not her name, and she accuses him of trying to make her into someone else.[46] It is a form of erasure not unlike that experienced by the man captured by Crusoe; he, too, loses his name and must leave his home for Europe. Antoinette's English husband rejects her identity, and so it is she sees herself drift away each time he calls her Bertha. Why? Because, as she notes, "Names matter."[47] This is not the only way we see her husband stifle her true self. His tendency to think of her as a doll or marionette suggests much the same thing.[48] He controls her. This is most obvious when he takes her away from Jamaica and Dominica, where she grew up, to live in England. Her story ends as she leaps to her death from the battlements of Thornfield Hall.

Brontë's depiction of the vulnerable, mentally unstable female from the colonies is entirely unsympathetic. She is largely dehumanized in *Jane Eyre*. "'It seemed, sir, a woman, tall and large,'" says a terrified Jane Eyre to Mr. Rochester. Her features were "'fearful and ghastly to me—oh sir, I never saw a face like it! It was a discoloured face—it was a savage face. I wish I could forget the roll of the red eyes and the fearful blackened inflation of the lineaments.' 'Ghosts are usually pale, Jane.' 'This, sir, was purple; the lips were swelled and dark; the brow furrowed: the black eyebrows widely raised over the bloodshot eyes. Shall I tell you of what it remined me? . . . Of the

---

44 Andrea Ashworth, "Afterword," in Jean Rhys, *Wide Sargasso Sea* (London: Penguin, 2019), 152-153.

45 See Jean Rhys, *Wide Sargasso Sea*, Norton Critical Edition, ed. Judith L. Raiskin (1966; New York: Norton, 1999), 68, 81-82. Rhys does not follow Brontë rigidly with respect to "Bertha's" family. In *Jane Eyre*, Mr. Mason is her biological father and Richard Mason, who visits Thornfield, her biological brother. See, e.g., Raiskin, ed., *Wide Sargasso Sea*, 16n. 8.

46 Rhys, *Wide Sargasso Sea*, 88.

47 Rhys, *Wide Sargasso Sea*, 106-107. Those who come to *Wide Sargasso Sea* already familiar with Brontë's novel recognize her husband to be Edward Rochester. Rhys, however, never identifies him that way so in effect steals his name just as he steals Antoinette's.

48 Rhys, *Wide Sargasso Sea*, e.g., 90, 92-93, 95, 102, 103.

foul German spectre—the Vampyre.'"[49] In Brontë's novel, she is a "mocking demon," a "hideous demon," directing a "demon-hate" toward her husband, and she lives in a "goblin's cell."[50]

In addition to imagery of the monstrous, Brontë further degrades Rochester's wife with a range of animal descriptors: "Whether beast or human being, one could not, at first sight, tell: it grovelled, seemingly, on all fours"; "it . . . growled like some strange wild animal"; "grizzled hair, wild as a mane"; "her wolfish cries."[51] When she assaults Rochester after his failed first attempt to marry Jane, Bertha attacks him in ways suggesting a predatory animal: "grappled his throat viciously, and laid her teeth to his cheek."[52]

As Jane contemplates Bertha, this dehumanizing tendency continues: "I had to listen as well as watch: to listen for the movements of the wild beast or the fiend in yonder side den. . . . What creature was it, that, masked in an ordinary woman's face and shape, uttered the voice, now of a mocking demon, and anon of a carrion-seeking bird of prey?"[53] After Bertha attacks her brother, the language used to describe her also associates her with the bestial and monstrous: "'She bit me,' he murmured. 'She worried me like a tigress, when Rochester got the knife from her.' . . . 'She sucked the blood: she said she'd drain my heart,' said Mason."[54]

Jean Rhys's *Wide Sargasso Sea* defies Brontë's characterization of the bestial, monstrous, mad woman in the attic. Much of the later story is told from Antoinette's (Bertha's) point of view (parts 1 and 3), and in various ways we see her as a victim of circumstances and cruel manipulations. She is a sympathetic character. Her marriage is arranged, her husband doesn't love her, and because of British law, she loses her fortune to him.[55] Rhys's prequel proved influential for subsequent adaptations of the Brontë classic and certainly shapes the experience for those returning to *Jane Eyre* after reading *Wide Sargasso Sea*. Patsy Stonemen touches on this when observing that Rhys's novel "had an immediate impact on popular

---

49 Charlotte Brontë, *Jane Eyre*, ed. Richard Nemesvari, 2nd ed. (1847; Peterborough, ON: Broadview, 2021), 356.
50 Brontë, *Jane Eyre*, 285, 390, 383, 384.
51 Brontë, *Jane Eyre*, 365, 383.
52 Brontë, *Jane Eyre*, 365.
53 Brontë, *Jane Eyre*, 285.
54 Brontë, *Jane Eyre*, 287.
55 Rhys, *Wide Sargasso Sea*, 65, 66. He even receives payment for marrying her (41).

perceptions of *Jane Eyre*." She gives the example of Delbert Mann's 1970 film that "replaces the raging maniac of earlier representations with a sweet-faced, vacant young woman."[56] The same is arguably the case with Cary Fukunaga's 2011 film.

Though a vividly drawn villainess in some respects, Brontë's "mad woman in the attic" is maddeningly incomplete. Just as there are many rooms in the sprawling Thornfield Hall Brontë does not describe, so, too, this character is a blank page in the text. Bertha is an absence. Her full story a gap or an erasure. Rhys "rescues the disposable, barking-mad woman from the 'cardboard world' of the attic of Thornfield Hall. The Englishman's Creole wife is lifted off all-fours and thrust into the literary limelight as the thinking, feeling, talking heroine at the heart of a vividly realized Caribbean world."[57] The cardboard world is how the mad, dreaming Antoinette/Bertha defines her situation late in Rhys's prequel: "[I] take the keys. . . . Then I open the door and walk into their world. It is, as I always knew, made of cardboard. I have seen it before somewhere, this cardboard world. . . . As I walk along the passages [of *Jane Eyre*'s Thornfield Hall] I wish I could see what is behind the cardboard."[58] She is trapped in this cardboard world, which is to say trapped between the covers of Brontë's book:

> It is now, at the very end of the book, that Antoinette/Bertha can say: "Now at last I know why I was brought here and what I have to do." . . . We can read this as her having been brought into the England of Brontë's novel: "This cardboard house"—a book between cardboard covers—"where I walk at night is not England" . . .. In this fictive England, she must play out her role, act out the transformation of her "self" into that fictive Other, set fire to the house and kill herself, so that Jane Eyre can become the feminist individualist heroine of British fiction.[59]

Rhys's *Wide Sargasso Sea* releases her, "redressing the indignity and injustice of the wiped-out woman's situation," and it "offers, with 'a deep curtsey' to Brontë, a moving post-colonial account that colours in the pre-history of the Creole. Her story makes amends for the sins of omission committed by the

---

56 Patsy Stoneman, "The Brontë Myth," in *The Cambridge Companion to the Brontës*, ed. Heather Glen (Cambridge, UK: Cambridge University Press 2002), 236–237.
57 Ashworth, "Afterword," 153.
58 Rhys, *Wide Sargasso Sea*, 107.
59 Gayatri Chakravorty Spivak, "Three Women's Texts and a Critique of Imperialism," *Critical Inquiry* 12, no. 1 (1988): 250–251. Full article 243–261.

Victorian writer, and by that era's literature and history in general."⁶⁰ Books in conversation with books, worldviews confronting worldviews. Art can be combative and a form of redress for historic wrongs.

This brief recital of the Rhys-Brontë stories does justice to neither but hopefully illustrates the idea of literature as a form of resistance to empire.⁶¹ As John Marx observes, it is commonplace to treat writings from Europe's former colonies "as the antithesis of canonical writing and as an instrumental component in efforts to recover oral and print traditions that imperialism threatened to obliterate." Furthermore, "postcolonial literature has been shown to *revise* canonical texts and concepts." Such literature not only critiques Western literary traditions but involves "the rewriting of specific works . . . and the appropriation of entire genres."⁶² Defoe and Brontë and hundreds of others like them don't have the last word.

Jesus's mention of nakedness when describing the "least of these" in the sheep and goats passage emphasizes their vulnerability. To speak comforting words to the hungry and naked without attending to their needs, James tells us, is evidence of meaningless religiosity: "If a brother or sister is naked and lacks daily food, and one of you says to them, 'Go in peace; keep warm and eat your fill,' and yet you do not supply their bodily needs, what is the good of that?" Faith without care for others is dead (2:15–17). What is needed is a willingness to serve and protect like that evidenced by the pious Tobit: "I would give my food to the hungry and my clothing to the naked" (Tob 1:17). Pairing the same terms, Paul teaches that nothing separates us from the love of God, not even famine or nakedness (Rom 8:35). He knew this firsthand as he outlines challenges faced during his ministry: "in toil and hardship, through many a sleepless night, hungry and thirsty, often without food, cold and naked" (2 Cor 11:27). The term for nakedness used by Matthew, James, Tobit, and Paul suggests complete exposure (cf. Heb 4:13), and, by extension, defenselessness.

These stories put before us such exposed and defenseless characters. As noted with reference to Robinson Crusoe's slaves Xury and Friday, and with

---

60 Ashworth, "Afterword," 153.

61 Jean Rhys herself was born and raised in Dominica, which is a Caribbean Island nation first colonized by the British in 1763.

62 John Marx, "Postcolonial Literature and the Western Literary Canon," in *The Cambridge Companion to Postcolonial Literary Studies*, ed. Neil Lazarus (Cambridge, UK: Cambridge University Press, 2004), 83. Italics original.

reference to Antoinette Cosway, the powerlessness of some makes them easy targets for exploitation and abuse by the powerful. Robinson Crusoe is an embodiment of European expansionist ambition, so the character himself and the broader attitude toward colonization he reflects illustrate a profound disregard for the Other. Similarly, the Creole Antoinette's husband erases her identity and locks her up in what amounts to a tragic enactment of subjugation by a European power. Both fail to care for the least of these.

CHAPTER FOUR

Joy Kogawa and Salman Rushdie "Verses" Racism

I was a stranger, and ye took me not in.

—Matthew 25:43, AV

Post-Pearl Harbor America was not kind to Japanese residents. Near the end of Woody Guthrie's *Bound for Glory*, he tells of an incident occurring in Los Angeles's Skid Row. Guthrie and Cisco Houston are singing for tips in a small Chinese-owned bar, next door to a Japanese-owned saloon. They hear shattered glass as they sing, and going outside, they discover a mob across the street threatening to attack the Japanese business. Woody, Cisco, and others stand in front of the saloon, ready to defend their neighbors, trading arguments with those confronting them. The mob seeks vengeance for Pearl Harbor, and their language is troubling, with epithets like "Jap rats" hurled around, along with baseless accusations about these saloon keepers spying in support of the Japanese war effort.[1] Guthrie and the others reject their lies and stand up to the bullies, fully prepared to protect the innocent. Fortunately, the vigilantes stand down and disperse without recourse to violence.

Not all the brutalities of wartime occurred on battlefields. Another manifestation of such race-based hostilities in the United States was the imprisonment of Japanese Americans in the 1940s. Perhaps the most famous of these interns was *Star Trek*'s George Takei, who writes about the experience in his children's book, *They Called Us Enemy* (2019). On the Canadian side of

---

1 Guthrie, *Bound for Glory*, 265.

the border, the situation facing Japanese residents during World War II was similar. There, the most famous among those displaced and subjected to cruel racist government policies was the renowned author Joy Kogawa.

Unwell and incarcerated individuals are often out of sight. We do not see them. Sickbeds and cells tend to be hidden places, off limits to most. An inclination to avoid both is all too familiar. To visit the seriously ill in a hospital is to be reminded of our own mortality. Prisons likely stir other revulsions. A fear of confinement. A dread of proximity to society's worst. Of course, not all who are imprisoned deserve to be there, but does a duty to care not extend also to those who do? *I was in prison, and you came to visit me.* As mentioned more than once, fiction takes us places we rarely if ever see. It has the capacity to concretize verses like Matthew 25:36, 39, 44, 45. I am not likely ever to visit a prison. Few do outside of enforcement personnel, family members, social workers, and other support services. The reality is, thanks be to God, I am unlikely to be incarcerated myself. I know little of those who are.

Joy Kogawa's 1981 novel, *Obasan*, is a story about hidden traumas. For an epigraph, she cites Revelation 2:17 in the King James Version and spaces the lines as follows:

> To him that overcometh
> will I give to eat
> of the hidden manna
> and will give him
> a white stone
> and in the stone
> a new name written . . .
>
> —The Bible[2]

In the context of the letter to the church in Pergamum, where Jesus speaks these words, feeding on the hidden manna is an elegant way of referring to the destiny of the faithful, their participation in the kingdom of God. This bread or manna comes down from heaven to sustain the Israelites during their desert wandering (Exod 16:4; cf. Neh 9:15). In later times, they celebrated this provision from heaven in song (Ps 105:40). With explicit reference to this ancient story, Jesus refers to himself as the bread from heaven and the

---

2 Joy Kogawa, *Obasan* (1981; Toronto: Penguin, 2003), front matter.

bread of life (John 6:30–35). The manna once provided literal sustenance for the beleaguered Israelites during their liberation from captivity and journey toward the promised land. Jesus now provides believers in Pergamum with the resources they need as they struggle toward their own promised land. It is striking that we first read of the biblical manna in the context of a liberation narrative. The imprisoned and enslaved Israelites escape their oppressors in Egypt, and God sustains them during their long journey toward a land flowing with milk and honey. The reference to that story likely resonated with the Pergamum church addressed in Revelation because they, too, understood oppression. They live "where Satan lives," and at least one of their number already died as the result of religious persecution (his name is Antipas; see Rev 2:13). The inhospitality experienced by Christians in late first-century Pergamum presents a fitting introduction to Kogawa's novel because it, too, is about inhospitality toward an identifiable subsection of the community who also endured various forms of oppression and imprisonment.

The next key image in the Revelation 2:17 epigraph is a stone inscribed with a new name. This is deeply suggestive as well. It gets at the idea of one's *real* identity and *true* worth. The despised minority who worshipped Christ in the communities of Asia Minor to whom John the Seer wrote likely experienced a cognitive dissonance. On the one hand, they were unwelcome in their own homes and societies because of their religious beliefs, but on the other, they understood themselves to be—or, at least, John wanted them to see themselves as—favored and blessed beyond all imagining. Their real identity and value are known to Christ alone: "He that hath an ear, let him hear what the Spirit saith unto the churches; To him that overcometh will I give . . . a white stone, and in the stone a new name written, which no man knoweth saving he that receiveth it" (AV). Their true selves remain unseen by those who treat them with disdain. Perhaps like the characters in Kogawa's *Obasan*, those ancient Christians also lacked an appreciation of their own worth and beauty, despising themselves and listening too readily to the insults of intolerant neighbors. Jesus's letter to the Pergamum church, and indeed the whole of John the Seer's book of Revelation, reminds readers of their inestimable value in the eyes of God.

When we pick up Kogawa's novel, the word *hidden* in the epigraph is among the first we read. It is also worth noting she does not cite the last clause of Revelation 2:17: "which no man knoweth saving he that receiveth it" (AV). What Kogawa leaves *unwritten* is a crucial part of Jesus's message to that church. Awareness of that community's real identity, which is to say their true significance in the eyes of God, potentially goes unrecognized ("no man knoweth"). If not embraced ("receiveth it"), it remains a story untold. It is hidden. Kogawa's novel concerns an untold story, an *unwritten* and *unspoken* family history and a largely ignored dark chapter in Canadian history. Across generations of this family's experiences, the silencing of hard truths—a strategy to protect children—has heartbreaking consequences. There is a silence that cannot and will not speak, says the narrator, Naomi Nakane, in the book's second epigraph: "*The word is stone. / I admit it. / I hate the stillness. I hate the stone.*" The term *stone*, of course, echoes the language of the first epigraph, Revelation 2:17. Without the opportunity to fully embrace one's identity ("receiveth it"), unless, as she puts it, the stone "*bursts with telling*," there is "*no living word.*" There is only silence.[3] Some treasure remains hidden, but like Woody Guthrie's family story, that city on a hill (see chap. 1), Naomi's story and that of her family and community need to be told.

Naomi was a child during World War II, and her family lived on the Canadian west coast. The fear of a post-Pearl Harbor Japanese attack resulted in government policies that displaced Japanese residents in British Columbia, moving them farther inland, detaining some and forcing others to work. When parents were incarcerated, older relatives did what they could to protect the children from the horrors of the situation. The novel relates one family's displacements and hardships during wartime as Naomi experienced it, as well as her discovery of long-hidden secrets many years later. Details about this child's vulnerability are disturbing, and to an extent, her individual experiences are metonymic of abuses directed at the whole communality.

For our purposes here, I highlight just one brief scene in this beautiful book. Joy Kogawa's integration of religious references in *Obasan* invites Christians to confront their collective failure to show hospitality to strangers in wartime Canada. When Naomi's family is told they must leave Slocan, British Columbia, their Japanese minister holds a prayer service in their home, using the Anglican *Book of Common Prayer*.[4] Ironically, the prayers include the following words: "'Amen,' everyone says at the end of the prayer and Sensei addresses them. 'Hear what our Lord Jesus Christ saith. Thou shalt love the Lord thy God with all thy heart, and with all thy soul, and with all thy mind. This is the first and great commandment, and the second is like unto it: Thou

---

3 Kogawa, *Obasan*, front matter. Italics original.
4 Kogawa, *Obasan*, 159.

shalt love thy neighbour as thyself'."⁵ The assembled community utters this prayer at the very moment their own inhospitable neighbors turn them away.

In addition, Kogawa subtly aligns the persecuted family and community with Jesus, who, as noted already, identifies with those who are vulnerable mentioned in the sheep and goats passage (*I was hungry*, etc.) and with children (*whoever welcomes them welcomes me*). During the prayer service, Naomi's brother "had been kneeling but shifts and sits on the edge of an open box. There is a muffled crack like the noise of a twig breaking under a pile of needles."⁶ It is their mother's favorite record. Naomi and Stephen's mother is in Japan, and with chaos resulting from the war, all contact with her was lost. "One small piece" of that record, Naomi observes, "is *broken* off like a bite off a giant cookie."⁷ This all occurs at the very moment the priest leads the Eucharist prayers. "He [the priest, Sensei] raises the *broken* wafer" and then recites the Gospel words as part of the ritual: "In the same night that He was *betrayed* He took Bread; and when He had given thanks, He *brake* it, and gave it to his disciples, saying, 'Take, eat.'"⁸ Kogawa deftly holds Jesus's story in parallel with that of the children's mother. Her favorite record *breaks*, a small piece "is broken off like a bite off a giant cookie." Jesus's body breaks, and the Eucharist involves taking and eating the bread that represents that body. Also like Jesus, Naomi, the Nakane family, and the Canadian Japanese community are all betrayed, Judas-like, by neighbors who ought to have shown love, in keeping with their own prayers about loving their neighbors as themselves. The children only learn the tragic story of their mother's Christ-like brokenness much later.

There are two contrasting visions in *Obasan*, both marked with biblical language, that invite comparison. Later in life, before learning the truth about her mother's tragedy, Naomi's view is to let the dead bury their own dead (cf. Matt 8:22; Luke 9:60).⁹ Leave history to history, deal with today, and forget about the past. Her aunt Emily thinks differently: "Aunt Emily's writing is as wispy and hard to decipher as the marks of a speed skater on ice. 'Write the vision and make it plain. Habakkuk 2:2.'"¹⁰ She

---

5 Kogawa, *Obasan*, 160. Cf. Mark 12:30–31.
6 Kogawa, *Obasan*, 160.
7 Kogawa, *Obasan*, 161. Italics added.
8 Kogawa, *Obasan*, 161. Italics added.
9 Kogawa, *Obasan*, 42.
10 Kogawa, *Obasan*, 32.

wants to uncover the past, to confront it. The story of cruelties directed at Japanese Canadians is one that must be told. Like Naomi, it is tempting to respond with a glib "let the dead bury their own dead." What is past is past. Let's everyone move on. But to do so is to silence victims of atrocities and personal traumas, to keep such things hidden. Systemic racism is an all too familiar reality in many societies, and sometimes creative writers make important contributions to the struggle for justice, as Kerri Sakamoto observes in her introduction to the Penguin edition of the novel: "When *Obasan* was published in 1981, it touched a nation's conscience and gave a voice to a movement to redress the injustices perpetrated against Japanese Canadians during World War II. The book served as a literary companion to the redress struggle that culminated in the 1988 Redress Settlement Agreement."[11]

THE ADAPTABLE BIBLE

Since the late 1980s, the public has invariably associated novelist Salman Rushdie with the outrageous *fatwa* calling for his death following the publication of *The Satanic Verses* (1988). The terrible attack on the author in the summer of 2022 only reinforces the connection. Rushdie's defiance of the enemies of free speech despite the hate is courageous and never so eloquent as in *Joseph Anton: A Memoir* (2012), which recounts his experiences in the years following the *fatwa*, and in a very different form in his children's novel *Haroun and the Sea of Stories* (1990), published soon after the terrors unleashed by extremists began. Despite the tendency to connect Rushdie with the events of 1989 and 2022, his work, including *The Satanic Verses*, involves more than representations of Islam. One of the most important takeaways from this contentious novel, with respect to the present context, is what Rushdie has to say about racism and the dislocation and disdain experienced by immigrants and migrant workers. As with the Kogawa novel and other works considered throughout, engagement with this work of fiction provides an opportunity for readers to visit the margins, to view the circumstances of vulnerable people from a different perspective.

---

11 Kerri Sakamoto, "Introduction," in Kogawa, *Obasan*, viii.

One technique Rushdie employs in this confrontation with racism and systemic abuse involves the adaptation of biblical texts. Linda Hutcheon defines *adaptation* as "repetition without replication," "repetition with difference," "derivation that is not derivative," paraphrase, and translation.[12] She adds that residual traces of an earlier text in a later one provide degrees of pleasure for readers. The mixture of repetition with variation offers the satisfaction of familiarity and the delight of discovery as audiences and readers recognize ways that artists reshape sources for new settings.[13] As she puts it, we enjoy adaptations because they blend "the comfort of ritual . . . with the piquancy of surprise."[14] These are useful observations as we consider adaptations of the Bible in later cultural artifacts, such as the works of literature considered throughout the present volume.

Canonical writings lend themselves to this kind of repetition and paraphrase, according to Robert Alter. He defines *canon* as a "transhistorical textual community" involving received writings on the one hand and readers appealing to those texts for meaning and authority on the other, but this dynamic does not limit their elasticity. In the case of the biblical canon, even among communities of traditional believers, the Bible "has been imagined to endorse as a matter of divine revelation rationalism, sensualism, determinism, free will, and a good deal else." The concept of canon lacks fixity, he argues; there is no "singular, authoritative meaning, however much the established spokesmen for the canon at any given moment may claim that is the case."[15] From this, Alter goes on to observe that creative writers using the Bible are similarly flexible: "Modern writers merely push to the next step this process of extending the range of meanings of the textual community in which they participate when they use the biblical canon [referring here to the specific writers he examines] to express vitalistic pantheism, or an individual fate of hapless victimhood, or a vision of cosmic pitilessness, or a notion of eternal

---

12 Linda Hutcheon, *A Theory of Adaptation* (New York: Routledge, 2006), xvi, 142, 9, 17. See, too, 4, 7, 149, 173, 176. An earlier version of the following argument appeared as "Some Novel Remarks about Popular Culture and Religion: Salman Rushdie and the Adaptation of Sacred Texts," in *The Bible in/and Popular Culture: A Creative Encounter*, Semeia Studies, ed. Philip Culbertson and Elaine Wainwright (Atlanta: SBL, 2010), 13–25. It appears here, adapted, with permission.

13 Hutcheon, *A Theory of Adaptation*, 173.

14 Hutcheon, *A Theory of Adaptation*, 5.

15 Robert Alter, *Canon and Creativity: Modern Writing and the Authority of Scripture* (New Haven, CT: Yale University Press, 2000), 4.

recurrence."[16] He further argues that the imaginative response to the Bible by "writers in a wide variety of languages bears witness to a power of canonicity that is not limited to doctrine or strictly contingent on belief in the inspired character of the texts invoked."[17]

Theorists are not the only ones who reflect on the complexities, subtleties, and ubiquity of literary influence. Salman Rushdie imagines all the stories of the world as waters swirling around a vast sea, "a thousand thousand thousand and one different currents," he adds, with a nod to Scheherazade and the *Arabian Nights* tales, "each one a different colour, weaving in and out of one another like a liquid tapestry of breathtaking complexity." This ocean of stories already told, and those yet to be told, is "in fact the biggest library in the universe."[18] This instructive image from *Haroun and the Sea of Stories* illustrates why, even though artists continually adapt earlier materials (Hutcheon), including canonical stories (Alter), attempts to track the Christian Bible's influence on the arts are always partial and selective. A thousand colored currents, crisscrossing and mingling with one another, will perpetually create new combinations, and while biblical stories, themes, and imagery are frequently part of the mix, they do not stand alone in this intertextual soup. We cannot drink all the colored currents composing this ocean, but we can, like Haroun Khalifa, who floats along the surface of Rushdie's magical ocean on the moon Kahani, dip a golden cup into the waters and take the occasional sip.[19] Even a small taste permits some insights into the qualities of this ocean as a whole. Said differently, exploring instances of influence helps readers appreciate aspects of the phenomenon, reminding us that all stories are intertextual in nature—byproducts and rewritings of, and contributions to, other stories.

For the remainder of this chapter, I dip a cup into one specific story to observe ways that a biblically rooted image morphs into something very unlike itself as it appears in its canonical setting and, in doing so, consider another instance of fiction drawing attention to those overlooked and vulnerable. Rushdie's novel *The Satanic Verses* is an unusual choice for this exercise, to be

---

16 Alter, *Canon and Creativity*, 5–6. By *modern* in this context, Alter means literary modernism. His study includes chapters on Franz Kafka's *Amerika* (1927), Haim Nahman Bialik's *The Dead of the Desert* (1902), and James Joyce's *Ulysses* (1922).
17 Alter, *Canon and Creativity*, 60.
18 Salman Rushdie, *Haroun and the Sea of Stories* (London: Granta, 1990), 72.
19 Rushdie, *Haroun and the Sea of Stories*, 72.

sure, since most readers associate this novel with creative reflections on the Qur'an and Islamic theology, but this is precisely one of the points I wish to make. As stories migrate from one context to another—from sacred text to the arts—they inevitably bump into other stories. In the example that follows, Rushdie stirs what amounts to a footnote in the Christian Bible with other religious and mythological material, and as his liquid metaphor suggests, these story waters mingle to produce something entirely new.

I focus on Rushdie's rewriting of the story of Lucifer's fall, a myth originating in the biblical text and adapted by, and widely disseminated in English through, such imaginative works as John Milton's *Paradise Lost* (1667, 1674). The name Lucifer is Latin and so obviously does not originate in the Hebrew and Greek Scriptures. The adjective *lucifer* means "light bringing," combining the feminine noun *lux* (light, brightness) with the verb *ferō* (to bear, carry), and is used substantively to render the Hebrew phrase "son of dawn" in Isaiah 14:12: "How you are fallen from heaven, O Day Star, son of Dawn!" Though the wider context of this verse refers to an earthly ruler ("you will take up this taunt against the king of Babylon" [Isa 14:4; see also Ezek 28:11–19]), many Christian readers, especially since the publication of *Paradise Lost*, assume the Isaiah passage refers to the fall of the angel Lucifer. In this received tradition, the name Lucifer is synonymous with the Hebrew *satan* (Satan; accuser) and the Greek *diabolos* (devil).

Several biblical passages inform the popular imagination concerning the Lucifer/Satan/devil figure. He is the adversary in the book of Job, the *satan* who questions the protagonist's integrity before God (1:6–2:7), and in the New Testament, he tempts the fasting Jesus (Matt 4:1–11; Mark 1:12–13; Luke 4:1–13). In the Christian Scriptures, the term *devil* (*diabolos*) is interchangeable with the transliterated *satan* (e.g., Matt 4:1; cf. Matt 4:10). The devil's fall from heaven is mentioned in Revelation 12:9: "The great dragon was thrown down, that ancient serpent, who is called the Devil and Satan, the deceiver of the whole world—he was thrown down to earth, and his angels were thrown down with him." In Luke 10:18, Jesus watches "Satan fall from heaven like a flash of lightning."

A radical adaptation of this myth in Rushdie's novel illustrates some of the ideas mentioned above. We find that mix of familiarity and surprise noted by Hutcheon in this retelling of a well-known story. We see the elasticity of the biblical canon Alter describes, as a story rooted in Scripture becomes a disturbing statement about systemic injustices. It is yet another instance of a creative writer pushing "to the next step this process of extending the range of meanings"—in Rushdie's world, the fallen, devilish angel is a victim, not a villain.[20] Like other works considered here, a creative engagement with biblical texts startles readers and turns their attention to those who are marginalized.

BIBLICAL CONTENT IN SALMAN RUSHDIE'S *THE SATANIC VERSES* (1988)

In the tradition of such diverse storytellers as Ovid and Franz Kafka, Salman Rushdie often imagines the plight of characters who transform into nonhuman creatures. One of the more striking examples of this occurs in *The Satanic Verses*, in which an individual named Saladin Chamcha becomes a goat-like devil. There are, in fact, two interrelated stories of transformation in this novel. One describes the alteration of the human Gibreel Farishta into the archangel Gibreel/Gabriel. In his transformed state, Gibreel transcends time and space and is simultaneously a spectator of and participant in events happening in both modern London and the world of the sixth- and seventh-century prophet Mahound/Mohammed. Much of Rushdie's sharpest religious

---

20 For another adaptation of the Lucifer myth that highlights the plight of marginalized people, see Timothy Findley's 1984 novel *Not Wanted on the Voyage*, a retelling of the Genesis flood story. To "survive the holocaust in heaven" (cf. Rev 12:7–9), Lucy (= Lucifer, the traditional Christian devil) joins humanity ([1984; Toronto: Penguin, 1996], 110). There is an earlier foreshadowing of this moment when the stargazing Ham observes, "The morning star had fallen all the way to the earth" (22, 108; cf. Job 38:6–7 with Isa 34:4 and Rev 12:9). The story loosely recounts the Miltonian version of Lucifer's fall, and Lucy's crimes in the heavenly realm are said to include a "damned and damnable pride" (108). In *Paradise Lost*, Satan admits the same: "I fell, how glorious once above thy sphere, / Till pride and worse ambition threw me down" (4.39–40). Findley's Luc(y)ifer also has an insatiable curiosity. Michael Archangelis says to him, "*Why?* All you ever said [to God] was *why?* Why this and why that and why everything. How dare you. How *dare* you" (108; italics original). Obviously, Findley's presentation of Lucy and "her" marriage to Ham involves various levels of irony; it implies that Satan (→ Lucifer→ Lucy) is a positive image of independent thought, and what is more, "she" is someone who has compassion for those who are weak and innocent. Ham and Lucy are marginalized in another sense as well, as suggested by use of "her" above. This cross-dressing, homosexual angel marries Noah's son Ham (107). Since this son of Doctor Noyes "never so much as looked at a woman," he is clearly gay, though this is concealed from everyone except Mottyl the cat, who alone knows Lucy's actual identity (male, angelic; see 119). Here we find the story exploring the vulnerability of those who are marginalized. Openness about one's sexuality and gender identity is not an option under the tyrannical rule of Dr. Noyes.

critique involves the angelic Gibreel. For instance, Gibreel's mobility and constantly changing perspective suggest flaws in the processes of communicating the divine word because this character alternates among so many roles, including auditor, prophet/speaker, divine source, and stand-in for the deaf masses.[21] Furthermore, Gibreel makes dubious contributions to Mahound's new religion because of the ambiguities of his prophetic role; Gibreel tends to "reduce prophecy to prescription" and serves as both prophet and fulfiller of prophecy in a tyrannical way.[22] While Gibreel's story is a central one to the novel and closely tied to Saladin Chamcha's, I focus here on the latter because of its more explicit adaptation of a biblical precursor.

That transformation of an Indian migrant into a monstrous devil begins in the opening pages of the novel, which describe its two principal characters— Saladin Chamcha and Gibreel Farishta— falling from the sky to the shores of England after their plane explodes. Farishta interprets their survival, this miracle of a second chance at life, as a rebirth, a "second period of gestation."[23] As he puts it, "Born again, Spoono, you and me," "To be born again . . . first you have to die" (cf. John 3:3).[24] Birthing imagery is explicit in the moments following the explosion of the jumbo jet *Bostan*, Flight AI-420. Chamcha falls headfirst, the "recommended position for babies entering the birth canal." At the very moment the bomb is detonated, the narrator observes this is "not death: birth."[25] In the days before the explosion, when Gibreel and Saladin are hostages aboard the *Bostan*, Gibreel names a long list of stories and mythologies involving different kinds of metamorphoses or "eccentric reincarnation theories."[26] Each represents a form of rebirth: phoenix from ashes, the resurrection of Christ, the transmigration of the soul at death, the soul of the Dalai Lama in the body of a newborn baby, and the metamorphosis of Jupiter into a bull (imitating Vishnu). Gibreel also comments on Hindu beliefs concerning the progress of humans through successive cycles of life, "now as cockroaches, now as kings, toward the bliss of no-more-returns."[27]

---

21 Christine Cavanaugh, "Auguries of Power: Prophecy and Violence in *The Satanic Verses*," *Studies in the Novel* 36 (2004): 395.

22 Cavanaugh, "Auguries of Power," 403.

23 Salman Rushdie, *The Satanic Verses* (New York: Picador, 1988), 85.

24 Rushdie, *Satanic Verses*, 11, 3. The latter are the opening words of the novel, which appear again on p. 86.

25 Rushdie, *Satanic Verses*, 5, 89.

26 Rushdie, *Satanic Verses*, 85.

27 Rushdie, *Satanic Verses*, 86.

Collectively, these stories anticipate the metamorphoses of the novel's two principal characters. Since Gibreel draws most of his examples of transformation from religious myths, it is appropriate that he and his friend become the embodiment of religious figures, resembling ones from the Abrahamic traditions of Judaism, Christianity, and Islam, namely, the archangel Gabriel and the fallen angel Lucifer.

The explosion and birth that propel the narrative from its opening pages defy conventional notions of time and space, suggested not least by the biblical language of "falling stars" (cf. Isa 34:4, cited by Jesus in Mark 13:24–25).[28] There is a pun involved in Rushdie's imagery since both men are actors, celebrities, and therefore "falling stars" in a literal sense, but there is more. The narrator of *The Satanic Verses* speaks of "a big bang.... A universal beginning, a miniature echo of the birth of time."[29] Such language appears to anticipate the angelic presence of the novel (the transformed Gibreel) because it alludes to the divine speaker in the book of Job, who indicates that angels ("morning stars") attended the creation of the universe (38:4–7).

There is also a devilish presence in the story, a satanic narrator lurking through the pages of the book.[30] To give but one example, there is a moment when Gibreel Farishta, transformed into the angel Gibreel, finds another entity speaking through him to the prophet Mahound: "The dragging again the dragging and now the miracle starts in his my our guts, he is straining with all his might at something, forcing something, and Gibreel begins to feel that strength that force, here it is at my own jaw working it, opening shutting; and the power, starting within Mahound, reaching up to my vocal cords and the voice comes. Not my voice I'd never know such words I'm no classy speaker never was never will be but this isn't my voice it's a Voice."[31] The scene suggests the machinations of a puppeteer controlling characters in the novel, including the angelic Gibreel. He and Saladin are in some sense possessed during their rebirth, following the universal beginning represented by the exploding plane. While falling, these characters experience trans/mutation, they tumble into Alice's Wonderland, and they

---

28 Rushdie, *Satanic Verses*, 4.
29 Rushdie, *Satanic Verses*, 4.
30 Rushdie, *Satanic Verses*, 4, 95–97, 114, 137.
31 Rushdie, *Satanic Verses*, 114.

experience, as seen, "birth."³² As they undergo these transformations, both men become intertwined, both literally, as they hold on to each other while dropping from the sky, and more profoundly at the moment when their "transmutation began": "Gibreelsaladin Farishtachamcha, condemned to this endless but also ending angelicdevilish fall."³³ This blending of names and the nature of their possessions/rebirths introduces the inevitability of their combined fates in a way recalling the close ties and ongoing battles between the fallen and the loyal angels of the biblical and Miltonian stories (see table below).³⁴

There is a further allusion to this angelic battle in the description of a Christian fundamentalist early in the novel, a fellow passenger on the doomed *Bostan*. This American creationist appears to represent the archangel Michael, described in martial terms in the Bible (e.g., in Dan 12:1, Michael is "the great prince, the protector of your people"; in Jude 9, he battles Satan). The war this passenger wages is against Darwinism. Indeed, he finds the name "Mr. Darwin" as distasteful as "any other forktail fiend, Beelzebub, Asmodeus or Lucifer himself."³⁵ He also has "a pair of Chinese dragons" that are "writhed and intertwined" on his shirt, which seems to echo the battles between Michael and Satan described in Revelation and Jude, as well as the closely linked Saladin Chamcha and Gibreel Farishta. Gibreel eventually takes this passenger's seat beside Saladin, thus bringing together the angelic and satanic characters who, soon after, battle in the sky just as the archangel and the devil do in the Apocalypse of John (see Rev 12:7).³⁶

The satanic figure taking hold of Saladin Chamcha makes his presence known early, asking the reader "Who am I? Who else is there?"³⁷ The phrasing echoes the Rolling Stones' song "Sympathy for the Devil" (*Beggars Banquet*,

---

32 Rushdie, *Satanic Verses*, 5, 7, 9. See also 137.

33 Rushdie, *Satanic Verses*, 5. Saladin Chamcha appears physically devilish but is still distinct from this satanic narrator. The relationship is one of possession. Saladin is not himself satanic.

34 The close connection between Saladin and Gibreel is evident in other ways too. For instance, Gibreel Farishta's legendary bad breath (*Satanic Verses*, 13) becomes sweet, and his halitosis transfers to Saladin Chamcha (137).

35 Rushdie, *Satanic Verses*, 77.

36 Rushdie, *Satanic Verses*, 81.

37 Rushdie, *Satanic Verses*, 4.

1968): "Pleased to meet you, can you guess my name?"[38] As Chamcha falls after the plane's explosion, he feels "his heart being gripped by a force so implacable that he understood it was impossible for him to die." After his "feet were once more firmly planted on the ground," he is overtaken by "a will to live."[39] Note the echo of Revelation 12:18 (included in the table below). This possession transforms Chamcha, and he quickly loses all sense of independence. He feels like a bystander watching his metamorphosis as his blood changes to iron, his flesh to steel. Soon this "will to live" conquers him so completely, it "could work his mouth, his fingers, whatever it chose, and once it was sure of its dominion it spread outward from his body and grabbed Gibreel Farishta by the balls."[40]

The story of Saladin Chamcha, a star (celebrity) falling from the sky to earth like the morning star (angel) Lucifer, with physical attributes traditionally linked to the devil (horns, hooves, tail), echoes biblical, literary, and popular discourses dealing with Christian notions of the great enemy of God. To illustrate, the following table highlights some of the connections among Rushdie's novel, the Christian Bible, and John Milton's *Paradise Lost*.[41]

---

38 This connection is plausible given Rushdie's love of rock music generally (see esp. his novel *The Ground Beneath Her Feet*, [Toronto: Vintage, 1999]) and the Rolling Stones specifically. For his glowing review of a Rolling Stones performance, see Rushdie, *Step across This Line: Collected Nonfiction, 1992–2002* (Toronto: Knopf, 2002), 87–91. Other rock music connections include various allusions to the Beatles (e.g., a character called the Walrus) in *Haroun and the Sea of Stories* and Rushdie's appearance in U2's video for the song "Ground Beneath Her Feet" (2000). The lyrics for this song come from a poem in Rushdie's novel of the same name. Regarding Rushdie's admiration of Bob Dylan, see chap. 8 below.

39 Rushdie, *Satanic Verses*, 9.

40 Rushdie, *Satanic Verses*, 9.

41 Salman Rushdie's novel *The Moor's Last Sigh* (Toronto: Vintage, 1996) also draws connections between characters and Milton's *Paradise Lost*. When the narrator, Moraes (Moor) Zogoiby, tells his tale, he aligns himself with Milton's Satan through various allusions, describing himself as the offspring of a demonic woman and therefore "a modern Lucifer" (5). Moor tells his readers, "Mine is the story of the fall from grace of a high-born cross-breed . . . my banishment from what I had every right to think of as my natural life" (5). Tales about his great-grandparents are "the first of my story's four sequestered, serpented, Edenic-infernal private universes" (15).

The Satanic Verses	*Paradise Lost* (1667, 1674)[42]	The Christian Bible
"Out of thin air: a big bang, followed by falling stars.... Who am I? Who else is there?"[43]	"'Art thou that traitor angel, art thou he, / Who first broke peace in Heav'n and faith, till then / Unbroken, and in proud rebellious arms / Drew after him the third part of Heav'n's sons?'" (2.689–92)	"the morning stars sang together" (Job 38:7; often interpreted as angels) "A great red dragon [i.e., Satan].... His tail swept down a third of the stars of heaven and threw them to the earth" (Rev 12:3–4)
"Saladin nosedived"[44] "When Mr. Saladin Chamcha fell out of the clouds over the English Channel he felt his heart being gripped by a force so implacable that he understood it was impossible for him to die"[45] "You think they fell a long way? In the matter of tumbles, I yield pride of place to no personage, whether mortal or im-. From clouds to ashes, down the chimney you might say, from heavenlight to hellfire"[46]	"[Satan was] Hurled headlong flaming from th' ethereal sky / With hideous ruin and combustion down / To bottomless perdition" (1.45–47); "Satan . . . / Took leave, and toward the coast of earth beneath, / Down" (3.736–40); "'Of Tartarus, which ready opens wide / His fiery chaos to receive their fall'" (6.54–55)	"There was no longer any place for [Satan and his angels] in heaven. The great dragon was thrown down, that ancient serpent, who is called the Devil and Satan, the deceiver of the whole world—he was thrown down to the earth, and his angels were thrown down with him" (Rev 12:8–9)
"[Chamcha's] feet were once more firmly planted on the ground"[47]	"Nathless he so endured, till on the beach / Of that inflamed sea, he stood and called / His legions, angel forms" (1.299–301)	"the dragon [i.e., Satan] took his stand on the sand of the seashore" (Rev 12:18)

(*Cont.*)

---

42 I take citations of John Milton's *Paradise Lost* here and throughout from Stephen Greenblatt et al., eds., *The Norton Anthology of English Literature*, vol. B, 10th ed. (New York: W. W. Norton, 2018), 1496–1727. The poem first appeared in ten books in 1667 and in twelve books in 1674. This Norton edition uses the latter.

43 Rushdie, *Satanic Verses*, 4, indicating the satanic narrator.

44 Rushdie, *Satanic Verses*, 5.

45 Rushdie, *Satanic Verses*, 9, indicating satanic possession.

46 Rushdie, *Satanic Verses*, 137.

47 Rushdie, *Satanic Verses*, 9.

The Satanic Verses	*Paradise Lost* (1667, 1674)[42]	The Christian Bible
"its [i.e., the satanic narrator's] dominion"[48]	"Satan exalted sat, by merit raised / To that bad eminence; and from despair / Thus high uplifted beyond hope, aspires / Beyond thus high, insatiate to pursue / Vain war with Heav'n, and by success untaught / His proud imaginations thus displayed. / 'Powers and Dominions, deities of Heaven, / For since no deep within her gulf can hold / Immortal vigor, though oppressed and fall'n, / I give not Heav'n for lost'" (2.5–14)	"The devil led [Jesus] up and showed him in an instant all the kingdoms of the world. And the devil said to him, 'To you I will give their glory and all authority; for it has been given over to me'" (Luke 4:5–6; cf. Matt 4:8–9)
"it had conquered him totally [i.e., the satanic possession] . . . and [it] grabbed Gibreel Farishta by the balls"[49] "'A humble foot soldier, sir, in the army of Guard Almighty.' . . . 'To do battle with the most pernicious devilment ever got folks' brains by the balls'"[50]	"Go Michael of celestial armies prince, / And thou in military prowess next / Gabriel, lead forth to battle these my sons / Invincible, lead forth my armèd saints / By thousands and millions ranged for fight; / Equal in number to that godless crew" (6.44–49) [an angel and Satan fight in the same way in *The Satanic Verses*; cf. 4.1006–1007: "Satan, I know thy strength, and thou know'st mine, / Neither our own but giv'n" (Gabriel speaking)]	"War broke out in heaven; Michael and his angels fought against the dragon. The dragon and his angels fought back" (Rev 12:7)

These echoes of the Bible and Milton do not stand alone in the novel. Rushdie integrates the narrative of Lucifer's fall with other religious mythologies, such as the Qur'anic story of Iblis's disobedience, and literary villains like Shakespeare's Iago in *Othello*.[51] The stories whirl in and out of one another like so many currents in Rushdie's magical ocean. So what does he do with

---

48 Rushdie, *Satanic Verses*, 9.
49 Rushdie, *Satanic Verses*, 9.
50 Rushdie, *Satanic Verses*, 77.
51 Roger Y. Clark, *Stranger Gods: Salman Rushdie's Other Worlds* (Montreal: McGill-Queens University Press, 2001), chap. 6.

this biblical imagery as it mingles with so many other diverse influences? At this point, I consider how Rushdie politicizes his adaptation of a biblical story (Satan's fall) in this setting, allowing it to function as a vehicle for commentary on racism and the plight of im/migrants.

RECONTEXTUALIZING A BIBLICAL STORY FOR THE PURPOSE OF SOCIAL COMMENTARY

Significantly, the demonic possession of Saladin Chamcha occurs as he moves from East to West, from India to England. Early in the story, Rushdie links Saladin's identification with and affection for England with his struggle to escape India and especially his father's attempts to preserve both the past and the traditional family ways. Like other migrants, Saladin's true self/identity remains hidden beneath disguises when he moves to England.[52] He attempts to deny his familial and ethnic inheritance. His father recognizes this, calling him a "demon up from hell" for doing so, language that anticipates his son's literal transformation into a devil. The father's language equates the desire to Westernize or integrate with the demonic, which to a degree parallels those in England who demonize Saladin—and all immigrants—as invading outsiders. Saladin becomes a devilish figure *when he migrates*, during his encounters with Westerners. At the same time, he is already devilish in the eyes of his Indian father, who condemns his son for moving to London in the first place and so denying his heritage and family roots. Saladin is a borderland character, trapped at the interstices of two very different worlds.

Among other things, Saladin Chamcha's metamorphosis into a fallen devil points to the consequences of racism and systemic abuse. For the most part, it is during his migration from India to the United Kingdom that Chamcha's remarkable transformation from a human being into a devilish monster occurs, a nightmare that commences with the appearance of "two new, goaty, unarguable horns."[53] One telling scene illustrating Saladin Chamcha's profound sense of displacement as an immigrant trying to fit into London society occurs in the back of a police van shortly after his fall from the exploded *Bostan* to the shores of England. Three immigration and five police officers

---

52 Rushdie, *Satanic Verses*, 49.
53 Rushdie, *Satanic Verses*, 145.

brutalize and humiliate him.⁵⁴ The fact that a new immigrant arriving to the West experiences this abuse/transformation while under the control of white, Western authority figures is a sharp critique of British society. Chamcha is not British in their eyes, and therefore he is an Other, treated like, and therefore transformed into, a monster. The brutal treatment and racist slurs directed at him during his captivity coincide with his physical transformation into a devilish goat.

It is revealing that some of the police officers' remarks distinguish cleanliness from filth. This is a recurring trope in discourses relating the immigration experience, according to Katarzyna Marciniak. Those crossing borders represent a threat to the establishment and so are often represented as contamination or the entry of filth into an otherwise clean space.⁵⁵ Rushdie literalizes this notion. When the frightened Chamcha shits himself ("a large number of soft, pellety objects had appeared on the floor") during interrogation, the guards respond with further derision: "'Animal,' Stein cursed him as he administered a series of kicks, and Bruno joined in: 'You're all the same. Can't expect animals to observe civilized standards. Eh?' And Novak took up the thread: 'We're talking about fucking personal hygiene here, you little fuck.'"⁵⁶

If we read this short speech as a kind of colonial discourse and therefore as more than mere trash talk, a significant rhetorical strategy is discernible. Homi Bhabha describes colonial discourse as an apparatus that both recognizes and disavows racial, cultural, and historical differences.⁵⁷ Strategically, it serves to create space for subjugated people by producing knowledge through which "surveillance is exercised and a complex form of pleasure/unpleasure is incited."⁵⁸ This knowledge involves stereotyping both colonizer and colonized but in such a way that the two are positioned antithetically to one another. The police-van scene in *The Satanic Verses* involves repetition of familiar tropes concerning migrants—they are dirty, undignified, and somehow less than human ("'Animal,' Stein cursed him")—and functions for those abusing Saladin as a rhetorical means of distinguishing themselves

---

54 Rushdie, *Satanic Verses*, 162–169.
55 Katarzyna Marciniak, *Alienhood: Citizenship, Exile, and the Logic of Difference* (Minneapolis: University of Minnesota Press, 2006), 39–41, 92, 94.
56 Rushdie, *Satanic Verses*, 164.
57 Homi Bhabha, *The Location of Culture* (London: Routledge, 1994), 100.
58 Bhabha, *Location of Culture* 100–101.

as insiders from Saladin as an outsider. Chamcha becomes a symbol of the migrant experience, at once despised and demonized by the English and ridiculed as an Anglophile by other migrants and those back in India, including his father.

A second episode illustrating Saladin Chamcha's liminal status occurs in the Shaandaar Café. This location is, according to Richard J. Lane, a "nightmarish urban space" that is also "a vision of a dystopian London . . . focused on the migrant cultures that live out their 'indeterminate' identities of belonging and not-belonging through their ongoing redefinition of the situations that they have found themselves in."[59] Lane describes here the rooming house where the now-monstrous Saladin sequesters himself in an effort to hide his literal, devilish disfigurations. The Shaandaar Café is a ghetto where immigrants from India, Pakistan, and Bangladesh—"variegated, transient and particoloured inhabitants"[60]—who cannot assimilate into their new environment find refuge with other, similarly marginalized, dislocated souls. Though he finds temporary shelter here, Saladin insists he does not belong in such a ghetto because, unlike the other residents who do not assimilate well into British society, the Anglophile Saladin embraces the culture and language of the United Kingdom.

Saladin Chamcha is, Shailja Sharma observes, the ideal immigrant; he is upwardly mobile, without accent, wealthy, and thoroughly assimilated.[61] Once the transformation into a devil occurs, he "tries his best to retain the vestiges of his bowler-hatted, English self with his tweedy-voiced wife, but fails."[62] The Anglophile Saladin's metamorphosis is complete when he ends up at the Shaandaar Café, the antithesis of everything he holds dear. Leftist Muhammad Sufyan owns the café, and his establishment is a haven for working-class Asians and illegal immigrants. Chamcha rejects identification with this group by declaring, "I'm not your kind. You're not my people."[63] This sets up two "opposing models of integration in a foreign country."[64] On the one hand, Chamcha is "a determinedly apolitical, upper-class man who wants

---

59 Richard J. Lane, *The Postcolonial Novel*, Themes in 20th Century Literature and Culture (Cambridge, UK: Polity, 2006), 89.
60 Rushdie, *Satanic Verses*, 251.
61 Shailja Sharma, "Salman Rushdie: The Ambivalence of Migrancy," *Twentieth Century Literature* 47 (2001): 607–608.
62 Sharma, "Salman Rushdie," 608.
63 Rushdie, *Satanic Verses*, 253.
64 Sharma, "Salman Rushdie," 608.

to be adopted as part of Britain," and on the other, Sufyan is an "exploiter of fellow immigrants . . . whose sense of community unites in his victimhood and resistance with people of his 'own kind.'"[65] British society rejects and ghettoizes Chamcha. Bhabha observes that when he is at the Shaandaar Café in his transformed, mythic-animal state, his symbolic role is evident: "Chamcha . . . has turned into a Goat and has crawled back to the ghetto, to his despised migrant compatriots. . . . He has become the 'borderline' figure of a massive historical displacement—postcolonial migration."[66]

Saladin Chamcha's story illustrates a widespread pattern in Rushdie's work, namely, his use of bestial imagery at intersections between cultures and in contexts involving violence. Marina Warner argues that "tales of metamorphosis often arose in spaces (temporal, geographical, and mental) that were crossroads, cross-cultural zones, points of interchange on the intricate connective tissue of communications between cultures."[67] These stories can serve numerous functions such as promising change, providing a rationale for the oppression of others, indicating progress, or articulating traumas.

Though *The Satanic Verses* deals with biblical and religious subject matter, and despite the hysteria following its publication and the infamous *fatwa* calling for the author's death, this novel is not concerned primarily with Islam or the biblical and Miltonian story of Lucifer's fall. Indeed, according to Rushdie himself, the "central theme [of *The Satanic Verses*] is that of metamorphosis."[68] Saladin finds himself at the interstices between two worlds as he tries to escape India for the West. His eccentric father recognizes the confusion over Saladin's identity that results: "I have your soul kept safe, my son, here in this walnut tree. The devil has only your body."[69] The first half of this statement points to a failed metamorphosis; like so many others, Saladin is unable to integrate completely into his new world because the British will never accept him fully as one of their own. His soul is not allowed to leave that walnut tree. The second half of this statement prepares readers for the very real metamorphosis that the migrant Saladin undergoes later in the story. Rather than becoming British, Saladin is humiliated, beaten, and rejected. His

---

65 Sharma, "Salman Rushdie," 608.
66 Bhabha, *Location of Culture*, 320.
67 Marina Warner, *Fantastic Metamorphoses, Other Worlds: Ways of Telling the Self* (Oxford: Oxford University Press, 2002), 17.
68 Rushdie, *Step across This Line*, 68.
69 Rushdie, *Satanic Verses*, 48.

father's reference to the devil having Saladin's body not only anticipates the literal transformation of the actor into a goat—the goat traditionally a symbol of the devil's incarnation—it also points to the vulnerability of migrants more generally. As is often the case in Rushdie's novels, he introduces hostility and monstrous/bestial imagery at a moment of encounter with Otherness.

According to Roger Y. Clark, a constant in Rushdie's finest work is "a questioning of fundamental truths as they have been formulated by the great religions and myths of the past." Rushdie's explorations into the nature of the universe "lead him to juxtapose one cosmic system with another, and to question the balance within any one system."[70] Like the individual currents in the sea of stories, narratives—even canonical, biblical narratives—do not stand alone and consequently do not gain preeminence over others. Clearly, there is an element of subversion in Rushdie's fiction, directed specifically at religious extremism. We see this in his depiction of "the bearded and turbaned Imam" who dreams of revolution in *The Satanic Verses*.[71] We see it also in the cult master Khattam-Shud, the villain in *Haroun and the Sea of Stories*, who wants to silence all storytelling and dialogue and believes "The world is for Controlling."[72] By flooding his stories with a seemingly endless mix of voices, reflecting religious and cultural diversity—Jewish, Christian, Islamic, Hindu; Indian, Middle Eastern, Western; high and "low"/popular art—Rushdie seeks to prevent the dominance of any one worldview.

This blending of voices occurs throughout the literary arts, often with the Bible mingling with other stories in ways recalling the intertwining of Gibreel and Saladin in *The Satanic Verses* or the rushing story currents in *Haroun and the Sea of Stories*. As we see in the example just considered, artists repeat but do not replicate.[73] They also extend the range of meanings of canonical writings and take advantage of their enormous flexibility.[74] Additionally, as with Joy Kogawa's *Obasan*, we see this intertextual play in Rushdie's fiction drawing attention to the plight of those who are vulnerable. We learn something about those crossing borders and the gap of compassion many societies and individuals need to close. Exodus warns against wronging or

---

70 Clark, *Stranger Gods*, 18.
71 Rushdie, *Satanic Verses*, 211–212.
72 Rushdie, *Haroun and the Sea of Stories*, 161. Rushdie almost certainly has Iran's Ayatollah Khomeini (1902–1989) in mind with both characters. It was Khomeini who called for Rushdie's death following the publication of *The Satanic Verses*.
73 Hutcheon, *A Theory of Adaptation*, xvi.
74 Alter, *Canon and Creativity*, 5–6.

oppressing resident aliens, what we might call immigrants, refugees, asylum seekers, or migrant workers (22:21). Deuteronomy warns not to "withhold the wages of poor and needy laborers . . . who reside in your land" (24:14–15). In this instance, the often bizarre magical realism of Rushdie's fiction is not so remote from biblical ethics as we might initially suppose. We meet the victims of racism and intolerance, and we discover something of ourselves to the extent we are reluctant to show hospitality to those crossing our own borders.

CHAPTER FIVE

The Lion, the Witch, and the Rock Star
Bob Dylan in Narnia

Lord, I believe; help thou mine unbelief.
—Mark 9:24, AV

The call to align with the values and priorities of the kingdom of God is a recurring topic in the New Testament Gospels. "'My sheep hear my voice,'" says Jesus. "'I know them, and they follow me'" (John 10:27). Responses to hearing that voice vary. When Jesus calls to some fishermen, they leave their professions behind to follow him (Matt 4:18–22; cf. Mark 1:16–20; Luke 5:1–11). "'Sell all that you own and distribute the money to poor,'" Jesus tells another, "'and you will have treasure in heaven; then come, follow me'" (Luke 18:22; cf. Matt 19:21; Mark 10:21). That man goes away sad because the need to sacrifice so much overwhelms him. Jesus demands everything of would-be disciples: "'If any want to become my followers, let them deny themselves and take up their cross and follow me'" (Mark 8:34; cf. Matt 16:24; Luke 9:23). Some struggle with his teaching, and because of it, they turn away (John 6:66). Following is just the first step. Those choosing to do so are then to participate in Jesus's rescue of the world: be light in the darkness (Matt 5:13–16), act toward others as you would have them do to you (Matt 7:12), and so on. All this is hard. Even his closest friends, the Gospel writers tell us, betrayed, abandoned, and denied him in moments of crisis. Responding to Jesus's "'come, follow me'" is no easy matter.

Passages like the Sermon on the Mount's Beatitudes and the sheep and goats discourse, both in Matthew's Gospel (see front matter), define aspects of the kingdom of God and describe those belonging to it. Early in his public ministry, Jesus traveled throughout Galilee, teaching in the synagogues and "proclaiming the good news of the kingdom," and this resulted in his spreading fame and a growing audience: "Great crowds followed him from Galilee, the Decapolis, Jerusalem, Judea, and from beyond the Jordan" (4:23–25). This is the setting of Jesus's Sermon on the Mount, which he addresses to those same "crowds" (5:1). The Sermon begins with what are called Beatitudes, a summary list of those who are part of the kingdom Jesus announces: "'Blessed are the poor in spirit.... Blessed are those who mourn.... Blessed are the meek.... Blessed are those who hunger and thirst for righteousness.... Blessed are the merciful.... Blessed are the pure in heart.... Blessed are the peacemakers.... Blessed are those who are persecuted for righteousness' sake'" (Matt 5:3–10). The last Beatitude (5:11–12) shifts to the second-person plural, making it clear some in the crowd he addresses belong to this kingdom: "'Blessed are you when people revile you and persecute you.... Rejoice and be glad, for your reward is great in heaven'" (5:11–12).

His teaching about the sheep and the goats further defines this community. It is one of three lessons in Matthew 25, which opens with, "the kingdom of heaven will be like this" (Matt 25:1). What does the kingdom of God look like? What characterizes those who belong to it, who choose to follow him? Why are some excluded? The Son of Man addresses both groups in 25:31–46. There is an insider-outsider dynamic in these Matthean passages, and they inevitably promote self-reflection. Am I a sheep or a goat, a peacemaker or a warmonger?

We are considering ways creative writing promotes contemplation of sacred themes and nurtures a worldview that is inclusive, outward-focused, turned away from self and toward the margins. According to Matthew, caring attention to those on the fringes defines in part this vision of a new world. Matthew couples the proclamation of the kingdom with examples of Jesus's actions, noting he cured "every disease and every sickness" among the people (4:23). As his fame spread, people "brought to him all the sick, those who were afflicted with various diseases and pains, demoniacs, epileptics, and paralytics, and he cured them" (4:24). Those who are vulnerable matter. But before this widening of perspective that encompasses "'the least of these'" (25:40, 45), a decentering of the self is necessary. Come, follow me. Take up your cross. Let go of possessions that divide your loyalties. In the language of the Sermon on the Mount, not all actions are consistent with the values of God's reign. As Jesus puts it, "'Not everyone who says to me, "Lord, Lord," will enter the kingdom of heaven, but only the one who does the will of my Father in heaven. On that day many will say to me, "Lord, Lord, did we not . . . do many deeds in your name?" Then I will declare to them, "I never knew you; go away from me"'" (7:21–23). Matthew's presentation invites self-assessment and consideration of whether the whole of one's life is consistent with Jesus's teachings.

My choice of text for exploring the kind of inner dialogue the Gospel invites may seem unusual in this context, but the question of whether Bob Dylan is a serious writer warranting close attention was settled definitively when he received the Nobel Prize for Literature in 2016. Also settled is whether his writing on religion and the Bible deserves notice, at least if the bibliography on these topics is any indication.[1] Furthermore, this consideration of a Dylan album is an example of the main premise of this book, namely, that the arts provide a context to encounter and contemplate religious mysteries. The thesis advanced in this chapter has the singer engaging sacred themes aided by a work of fiction. I opened the book with selections from C. S. Lewis's letters, both before and after his conversion. In those selections, we saw how reading and writing imaginative works provided a lens through which he navigated and interpreted real-life experiences. Here, I propose Bob Dylan did the same, using one of Lewis's own stories.

A LION ON THE ROCK-AND-ROLL STAGE

"When I Paint My Masterpiece" first appeared on *Bob Dylan's Greatest Hits Volume II* in 1971. The song's narrator tells of time spent in Rome's Coliseum "dodging lions." He can hardly stand seeing those mighty kings of the jungle.[2]

---

1 See, e.g., Seth Rogovoy, *Bob Dylan: Prophet, Mystic, Poet* (New York: Scribner, 2009); R. Clifton Spargo and Anne K. Ream, "Bob Dylan and Religion," in *The Cambridge Companion to Bob Dylan*, ed. Kevin J. H. Dettmar (Cambridge, UK: Cambridge University Press, 2009), 87–99; and Stephen H. Webb, *Dylan Redeemed: From* Highway 61 *to* Saved (New York: Continuum, 2006). See too my entry "Bob Dylan's Bible" in *The Oxford Handbook of Reception History of the Bible*, ed. Michael Lieb, Emma Mason, Christopher Rowland, and Jonathan Roberts (Oxford: Oxford University Press, 2010), 355–368.

2 Bob Dylan, *The Lyrics 1961–2012* (New York: Simon & Schuster, 2016), 271.

Jump back twenty-some years to 1950 and C. S. Lewis's children's novel *The Lion, the Witch and the Wardrobe*. There Mr. Beaver speaks to children newly arrived in Narnia about Aslan. He is no man, he assures them; he is rather, "'the King of the wood'" and "'the King of Beasts . . . a lion—*the* Lion, the great Lion.'"[3] Mere mention of the name causes each to react. For Peter, Susan, and Lucy Pevensie, it awakens a sense of awe, even reverence, but for their brother Edmund, dread: "At the name of Aslan each one of the children felt something jump in his inside. Edmund felt a sensation of mysterious horror."[4] Like the narrator of "When I Paint My Masterpiece," Edmund finds himself dodging a lion—*the* Lion—after a fashion.

Back to the 1970s and the release of Bob Dylan's *Street-Legal*.[5] The leonine language returns, this time with a lion lying with a lamb in the song "No Time to Think" and a lion in the road in "Where Are You Tonight? (Journey through Dark Heat)." Dylan does not sing about lions in the plural now, or about the ancient Roman coliseum, as in 1971. It is *a* lion. Both phrases have biblical overtones. The lion lying with a lamb is part of Isaiah's vision of the peaceful kingdom (11:6). The other comes from Proverbs in one of many charges against the sluggard: "The slothful man saith," as the Authorized Version has it, "There is a lion in the way; a lion is in the streets" (26:13). If the first *Street-Legal* lion points to some utopia for which the narrator longs, the other reveals hesitation, a reluctance to do what is necessary to reach that paradise—but I'm getting ahead of myself.

The year 1978 is a remarkable one in the Bob Dylan story, witnessing among other things one of his more spectacular artistic failures in the strange film *Renaldo and Clara* but also one of the decade's musical highlights with the album *Street-Legal*. What is more, Bob Dylan converted to Christianity. This was the beginning of an unambiguously gospel-oriented period of recordings and performances. But we're looking now at 1978's *Street-Legal*, which anticipates that 1979–1981 artistic, philosophical, and spiritual turn. On *Street-Legal*, he writes about a fork in the road, a changing of the guards. As he puts it in "We Better Talk This Over," it is a time of transition. Perhaps

---

3 Lewis, *Lion, the Witch and the Wardrobe*, 79. Italics original.
4 Lewis, *The Lion, the Witch and the Wardrobe*, 68.
5 For the *Street-Legal* songs, see Dylan, *Lyrics*, 380–396, or bobdylan.com. I recommend reading this chapter with the song lyrics at hand.

significantly for the present argument, that same song includes the very Narnian image of a wand-waving magician.

There are several terms, phrases, and, using the term loosely, plotlines in *Street-Legal* that lead me to wonder if *The Lion, the Witch and the Wardrobe* is among Dylan's inspirations for this album's lyrics. If so, it has gone unnoticed as far as I'm aware. I admit at the outset the reading here proposed is highly speculative and must remain so unless and until scholars working their way through the Bob Dylan Archive in Tulsa, Oklahoma, unearth evidence supporting the connection. I am not aware of any explicit link between Dylan and Lewis's writings or of Dylan scholars proposing one. Whether or not such an archival clue appears, it is a question worth asking owing to the extent of shared imagery and especially so for studies of biblical and religious content in his lyrics. The broadly Christian story arc of the Narnia books is potentially a roundabout way the Bible and Christian doctrine inform Dylan's writing. At minimum, reading these texts in parallel presents us with two artistic explorations of self-identity in relation to the Christian story, of the demanding "follow me" storyline of the Gospels.

READING *STREET-LEGAL* THROUGH A NARNIAN LENS: A THOUGHT EXPERIMENT

Whether real or imagined, at several points in the *Street-Legal* songs, I hear an engagement with that familiar children's story. As its title suggests, *The Lion, the Witch and the Wardrobe* relates a struggle of good versus evil, represented by a lion and a witch, respectively. All its major characters, save one, are relatively flat, which is to say aligned unambiguously with one side or the other. For them, there is no narrative exploration of internal struggle. They are either for Aslan or for the witch. The one exception is Edmund Pevensie. Seduced by the wicked, usurping ruler of Narnia, he turns away from friends and family for purely selfish ends. He thus finds himself on the losing side because Aslan has returned and is about to reclaim his lost world. Edmund undergoes a dramatic transformation by the book's end as he acknowledges the errors of his ways and grows to love and serve the great lion, but early on, he is antagonistic. Dylan's *Street-Legal* presents a similar ambivalence with its narrator pulled this way and that, torn between two competing calls. Edmund and the *Street-Legal* narrator both hesitate but ultimately make the difficult decision to turn away from darkness to light. The closing song, "Where Are You Tonight? (Journey through Dark Heat)," refers to a lion standing on the road and an escaped demon. Here in brief, we have the two options. Like Edmund, the song's narrator must choose between Christ / the Christlike lion and the devil / the demon witch. We all gotta serve somebody, as Dylan would soon put it. In the novel, the desperate struggle between these alternatives is Edmund's story. It was also Dylan's struggle in the mid- to late 1970s.

Most agree *Street-Legal* foreshadows Dylan's Christian period, meaning songs on the three albums following.[6] Its last song refers to a train, anticipating the shift to gospel music on *Slow Train Coming* (1979). But for the music we're considering here, the singer/narrator is not there yet. The resemblance between the *Street-Legal* narrator and Edmund is in their agonizing struggle to choose sides. The novel provides Dylan, I propose, with both imagery and a loose narrative frame to express his own ambivalence toward Christ/ianity at this stage of his life. For what it's worth, the Narnia novelist faced a similar struggle. Long an atheist, C. S. Lewis depicted the moment of his own conversion as a kind of defeat: "That which I greatly feared had at last come upon me. In the Trinity Term of 1929 I gave in, and admitted that God was God, and knelt and prayed: perhaps, that night, the most dejected and reluctant convert in all England. I did not then see what is now the most shining and obvious thing; the Divine humility which will accept a convert even on such terms."[7] *Street-Legal* has a similar "dragged in kicking and screaming" feel to it, as in, for instance, the seemingly dejected concession "All right, I'll take a chance, I will fall in love with you" ("Is Your Love in Vain?").

If this connection is correct, it is not all that surprising Dylan knew Lewis's Chronicles of Narnia or at least the first book in the series. It was and is widely read, of course. Passages in his memoir *Chronicles: Volume One* (2004)—note the shared title—and *The Nobel Lecture* (2017), and an entire industry of scholarly source-hunting provide clear evidence of the singer's wide-ranging and eclectic reading habits and his frequent integration of literary sources to

---

6 For instance, Howard Sounes takes "Señor (Tales of Yankee Power)" to be "a signpost to Bob's conversion to Christianity" (*Down the Highway: The Life of Bob Dylan*, updated edition [New York: Grove, 2021], 319). Though "hardly a Christian record," write Spargo and Ream, *Street-Legal* "was a harbinger of things to come" ("Bob Dylan and Religion," 96).

7 C. S. Lewis, *Surprised by Joy: The Shape of My Early Life* (1955; Boston: Houghton Mifflin Harcourt, 2012), 228–229.

lyrics.[8] The Chronicles of Narnia were and are also popular among American evangelicals, a circle with whom Dylan had connections at the time he wrote the album. It is conceivable he came across the book as he moved among them. Again, we don't know any of this for sure, but there are clues suggesting the subtle presence of Lewis's first Narnia novel in the songs. This literary palimpsest is most evident in "Changing of the Guards" (track 1), "No Time to Think" (track 3), and "Where Are You Tonight? (Journey through Dark Heat)" (track 9), but there are hints in the others too. More specifically, the *Street-Legal* songs connect to Edmund's story, that selfish, vengeful, power-hungry betrayer seduced by the evil witch but eventually redeemed by Aslan's self-sacrifice. To explore this connection, I consider these three songs in turn.

Track 1: "Changing of the Guards"

In 1935, C. S. Lewis published a poem titled "The Planets," in which he describes Mercury and its influence this way:

> MERCURY marches;—madcap rover,
> Patron of pilf'rers. . . .
> His flint has struck
> The spark of speech from spirit's tinder,
> Lord of language! He leads forever
> The spangle and splendour, sport that mingles
> Sound with senses, in subtle pattern,
> Words in wedlock, and wedding also
> Of thing with thought.[9]

I cite this because there are references to planets and associated mythologies on *Street-Legal*, Mercury among them (mentioned two times in "No Time to Think," discussed below). In "Changing of the Guards," a maid (stanza three) finds herself pulled in two directions, drawn to / pulled toward both Jupiter

---

8 Bob Dylan, *Chronicles: Volume One* (New York: Simon & Schuster, 2004) and *The Nobel Lecture* (New York: Simon & Schuster, 2017). The scholarly attention given to this subject is enormous, but among recent work, see, e.g., Florence Dore's "American Literature," Anne-Marie Mai's "World Literature," and Steven Belletto's "The Beats," all in *The World of Bob Dylan*, ed. Sean Latham (Cambridge, UK: Cambridge University Press, 2021), 147–157, 158–168, 169–180.

9 C. S. Lewis, *Poems* (1964; New York: HarperOne, 2017), 21–22.

and Apollo (stanza four). Jupiter is king of the Olympian pantheon in classical antiquity, and the ancients associated Apollo with song and eloquence and poetry. As classicist Richard F. Thomas puts it in remarks about this song, "One god is the figure of ultimate authority, the other the divine musician, expert on the lyre—*cithara* (. . . guitar)."[10] The image seems to capture something of the songwriter's philosophical and religious restlessness in the 1970s as he faced the possibility of conversion to Christ—who, like Jupiter, is god of gods—perhaps while considering the implications this would have for his Apollo-like art.[11] However taken, the lyrics suggest an in-betweenness, a moment of (in)decision. The singer feels a change coming on.

That there are autobiographical elements in these songs seems likely, beginning with the album's opening words ("Sixteen years"), which presumably refers to the span of Dylan's recording career up to the release of 1978's *Street-Legal*. His first album, *Bob Dylan*, came out in 1962. The planetary and mythological language returns, as mentioned, in "No Time to Think" with Mercury ruling and somehow connected to destiny (stanza 6). Dylan's birthday is May 24, which makes him a Gemini, a sign ruled by the planet Mercury. A subtle self-reference? Lewis's poetic portrait of Mercury and its influence suits, if so. As Lewis explains, Mercury is the "Lord of language!" How fitting for the Nobel laureate, *cithara*-playing poet, and master of word and song. Mercury (i.e., Dylan as Gemini) is perhaps a circumlocution for "I," as though to say, *This is my story too*.[12]

Christ is clearly in view in "Changing of the Guards," and this has obvious significance for Dylan at this stage of his life and career. The opening lines of the album refer to the good shepherd, which Dylan takes from John 10:11–18. This good shepherd grieves (stanza one), which has possible connections to a few scenes in the Gospels (Lazarus's death, the garden of Gethsemane) and also to the portrait of Aslan in *The Lion, the Witch and the Wardrobe*: "'I am

---

10 Richard F. Thomas, *Why Bob Dylan Matters* (New York: Dey Street, 2017), 82. Thomas's book reveals the surprising (to me, at least) degree to which the ancient Greek and Roman worlds fire Dylan's imagination, an interest Thomas traces back to, among other things, Dylan's participation in his high school's Latin club.

11 Does the call of fortune (second stanza) refer to the goddess of chance, Tyche, or more simply to wealth?

12 Lewis's poem also identifies Mercury as the patron god of thieves ("pilf'rers"), a term Dylan uses in "Changing of the Guards" (stanza two). The presence of thieves in the one song and their patron god in the other invites reading these lyrics together. The album was Dylan's first after renegotiating his contract with Columbia (Sounes, *Down the Highway*, 319). Perhaps "thieves" has something to do with that as well.

sad and lonely,'" he says to Susan and Lucy as they walk together toward the site of his death.[13] The unusual reference to a shaved (female) head in the fourth stanza also echoes that dark scene. Before the witch kills the lion, she shaves his luxurious mane to humiliate him. Only then does she give the lethal dose. Use of the feminine ("shaved her head") is difficult, but as noted below with reference to "Where Are You Tonight? (Journey through Dark Heat)," there are reasons to connect the feminine imagery to Aslan. The one "shaved" in "Changing of the Guards" attracts the narrator, and he cannot help but follow (stanza four).

There are several images in "Changing of the Guards" bringing *The Lion, the Witch and the Wardrobe* to mind. A palace with mirrors (stanza six) captures poetically the most distinctive feature of the witch's palace, namely, its statues. They are reflections of a sort, being all that remains of the once-living creatures she turned to stone. And immediately after mentioning the palace, we learn of "dog soldiers." The witch has wolves at her command who secure the palace and serve as her police force. One of them is even a captain, Fenris Ulf, captain of the secret police and cold-blooded servant of the witch; the term appears in stanza three and in the liner notes of the album, in one of the acknowledgments. There is a tower in the song as well (stanza two), which is another of this palace's conspicuous features: "At last he [Edmund] came to a part where it was more level and the valley opened out. And there, on the other side of the river, quite close to him, in the middle of a little plain between two hills, he saw what must be the White Witch's house. And the moon was shining brighter than ever. The house was really a small castle. It seemed to be all towers; little towers with long pointed spires on them, sharp as needles. They looked like huge dunce's caps or sorcerer's caps."[14]

The word *witches* appears in stanza five, and a king and queen with swords in the song's last stanza, all terms used in the Narnian tale.[15] In the second-to-last stanza, we're told Eden burns. Eden, of course, is a reference to the biblical garden, which we read about in Genesis 2 and 3. We also find there the names Adam and Eve, which appear throughout *The Lion, the Witch and the Wardrobe* with reference to the Pevensie children, referred to as the sons and daughters of Adam and Eve. The Narnian "Eden" faces a destruction of

---

13 Lewis, *The Lion, the Witch and the Wardrobe*, 150.
14 Lewis, *The Lion, the Witch and the Wardrobe*, 92.
15 The credits for Martin Scorsese's film *Rolling Thunder Revue: A Bob Dylan Story* (2019) list the violinist Scarlet Rivera as "The Queen of Swords."

its own during the time of the White Witch's cruel reign. Gardens don't grow in perpetual winter.

The last three stanzas of "Changing of the Guards" include several connections to *The Lion, the Witch and the Wardrobe* as well as the Gospels' accounts of the resurrection of Christ. Significantly, a few details are closer to Lewis's resurrection story than those in the New Testament. The song's reference to one waking up at daybreak after two days corresponds loosely with the story of Christ's three days in the tomb, as does mention of rocks rolling, which recalls the stone rolled in front of and then away from the entrance to Jesus's tomb (Matt 27:60; Mark 15:46; 16:4; Luke 24:2; John 20:1). In the Narnian story, Aslan is dead just one night, and Dylan sings of one waking after two days. Neither author conforms rigidly to the Gospels' timeline. Dylan also sings of broken chains. Jesus is bound before the crucifixion (Matt 27:2; Mark 15:1), and friends wrap his body in linen for burial (John 19:40; cf. Luke 24:12; John 20:5), but there is no equivalent to the binding of the body as a security measure ("chains") after death. This does occur in the Lewis story, however. The witch and her minions tie Aslan's body on the stone table before killing him as a precaution, and once done, *they leave the corpse wrapped in heavy ropes*. Perhaps Dylan's term "broken chains" refers to the mice who chew those ropes to free Aslan's body.[16]

Dylan also sings about a female "clutching" the one who wakes after forty-eight hours, alluding to Jesus's conversation with Mary Magdalene (John 20:17). The shined shoes and moved mountains of stanza eight recall Jesus washing the disciples' feet (John 13:1–17) and speaking of a faith that moves mountains (Mark 11:23; Matt 17:20; 21:21; cf. 1 Cor 13:2). But the one who wakes after forty-eight hours in Dylan's song differs from Jesus in a noteworthy way. Dylan refers to this individual's golden hair (stanza seven), a descriptor not mentioned in the Gospels. It seems possible the Narnian death and resurrection story here overlaps with those in the Gospels. When Lucy and Susan first see the resurrected Aslan, they fear he is a ghost, a term appearing in the last stanza of "Changing of the Guards." Immediately after that dreaded possibility presents itself to their minds, especially to Susan's, "Aslan stooped his *golden* head and licked her forehead."[17] Aslan then invites Susan and Lucy to jump on his

---

16 Lewis, *The Lion, the Witch and the Wardrobe*, 159–160. See, too, Aslan's recollection of the mice's kindness in the later Chronicle, *Prince Caspian*, chap. 15.

17 Lewis, *The Lion, the Witch and the Wardrobe*, 162. Italics added.

back for a journey, and the color of Aslan's fur is again prominent: "He crouched down and the children climbed onto his warm, *golden* back and Susan sat first holding on tightly to his mane and Lucy sat behind holding on tightly to Susan . . . instead of the black or grey or chestnut back of the horse the soft roughness of *golden* fur, and the mane flying back in the wind."[18] Aslan's golden appearance is a recurring feature in the Chronicles' descriptions of the lion.

Another parallel between the song and novel that differs from the Gospels occurs in the same context. In the excerpt just cited, Susan holds Aslan "tightly." Additionally, before Aslan and the girls set off to join their friends, there is a lighthearted moment of play among the three of them that emphasizes physical contact:

> "Oh, children," said the Lion, "I feel my strength coming back to me. Oh, children, catch me if you can!" He stood for a second, his eyes very bright, his limbs quivering, lashing himself with his tail. Then he made a leap high over their heads and landed on the other side of the Table. Laughing, though she didn't know why, Lucy scrambled over it to reach him. Aslan leaped again. A mad chase began. Round and round the hill-top he led them, now hopelessly out of their reach, now letting them almost catch his tail, now diving between them, now tossing them in the air with his huge and beautifully velveted paws and catching them again, and now stopping unexpectedly so that all three of them rolled over together in a happy laughing heap of fur and arms and legs.... when all three finally lay together panting in the sun the girls no longer felt in the least tired or hungry or thirsty.[19]

Nothing in the Gospels corresponds to Dylan's "he's pulling her down" (stanza seven), which is the phrase immediately preceding that about the female "clutching" the resurrected one's golden locks.[20] In fact, the evangelist John makes the opposite point when Jesus tells Mary *not* to hold him (20:17). This scene from the novel comes close to Dylan's language. His version of the resurrection story has a very Narnian quality to it.

---

18 Lewis, *The Lion, the Witch and the Wardrobe*, 164, 165. Italics added. Cf. C. S. Lewis, *Prince Caspian: The Return to Narnia* (New York: HarperCollins, 1994), in which the girls "climbed onto the warm *golden* back as they had done . . . before" (197; italics added).

19 Lewis, *The Lion, the Witch and the Wardrobe*, 163–164.

20 There are also echoes of the Samson and Delilah story in this line about hair. See, e.g., Spargo and Ream, "Bob Dylan and Religion," 96.

Track 3: "No Time to Think"

This song's very title suggests a crisis. The situation is urgent and serious. In the opening line, the narrator addresses someone ("you") who is dead but simultaneously facing life. This is Edmund's position in Lewis's novel. Within the logic of the story, the boy is spiritually dead the moment he sides with the evil witch. He chases the tantalizing rewards she offers—power and riches, a form of revenge against his annoying siblings, and enchanted Turkish delight. He is to be a prince and later king of Narnia, or at least she leads him so to believe, and he finds the idea intoxicating. Later, he faces literal death in the form of the witch's knife. In one terrible scene, she is about to slit the boy's throat, but Aslan's warriors, on his orders, arrive just in time to rescue Edmund.[21] In this moment, he faces life, in the form of his rescuers, while on the cusp of death. *In death you face life.* When the witch later asserts her legal claim to him and all traitors (cf. the album title, *Street-Legal*), Aslan again rescues the boy. Here, too, the boy is "in death" but facing life. This opening line even includes the word *child*.[22]

The next line of "No Time to Think" provides context for this coupling of death and life but is grammatically ambiguous: "In death, you face life with a child and a wife / Who sleep-walks through your dreams into walls." On first reading, the phrase about sleepwalking into walls while dreaming appears to refer to the child *and* wife of the previous line, but if so, the grammar is incorrect. If the reference is to both, it ought to be *who sleepwalk* rather than *who sleepwalks*. The latter suggests just one person sleepwalking. The "who" in this second line must be one or the other, the child or the wife, for the syntax to make sense. The proposed Narnian reading potentially clarifies the meaning. If there is an autobiographical element in the child/wife pairing of the opening line (cf. previous note), the song drifts away from that reality in the second line and into fantasy with the mention of sleepwalking and dreaming. It is here Edmund's story comes into focus.

Like Edmund, Dylan is in a state of spiritual death, as the evangelicals around him in the mid-1970s and he himself in the gospel songs of 1979 through 1981, would think of it. Edmund/Dylan are spiritually dead / facing life; they must let go of the witch/devil to embrace Aslan/Christ and inherit the

---

21 Lewis, *The Lion, the Witch and the Wardrobe*, 137.
22 Dylan released *Street-Legal* a year after divorcing his first wife, Sara Lownds. If there is an autobiographical note here, one imagines family was very much in mind when facing the momentous life-death alternative he sings about.

Narnian kingdom / heaven. Lewis and Dylan both liken this encounter with another world, with spiritual realities beyond the mundane, with dreams. Of the four children in the novel, Lucy is the first to visit Narnia, and when she returns, the others do not believe such a world exists. After a while, she, too, begins to doubt: "By this time she was beginning to wonder herself whether Narnia and the Faun had not been a dream."[23] When the children first hear about Aslan, Lewis uses the term *dream* five times and *nightmare* once, in a short space, stressing the strangeness and otherworldliness of the experience: "Perhaps it has sometimes happened to you in a dream that someone says something which you don't understand but in the dream it feels as if it had some enormous meaning—either a terrifying one which turns the whole dream into a nightmare or else a lovely meaning too lovely to put into words, which makes the dream so beautiful that you remember it all your life and are always wishing you could get into that dream again. It was like that now."[24] However dreamlike, the subject explored in the novel and *Street-Legal* is not illusory. This ain't no dream, sings Dylan in "Señor (Tales of Yankee Power)." It's the real thing.

Returning to the grammatical question mentioned above concerning the second line of the song, I suggest it is the child of the first line rather than the wife who sleepwalks and dreams and more specifically that Edmund is the inspiration here. When we're told in the next line the addressee is a soldier of mercy, perhaps we ought to hear it as *mercenary*, meaning the pursuit of profit at the expense of ethics. This describes Edmund well.[25] It is a lust for power (and candy) that motivates his poor decision to cooperate with the witch. We also learn in the same line that he is cold and cursing, both terms resonating with the portrait of Edmund in *The Lion, the Witch and the Wardrobe*. When he first enters Narnia, it is winter, and "he shivered." He soon meets the witch, and when speaking to her, his "teeth were chattering."[26] Later, he suffers in the cold when he travels alone to her house. The word *cold* appears eight times in chapter 9, which tells of that long, difficult walk. When she takes him prisoner, "the Dwarf whipped up the reindeer and the Witch and Edmund drove out under the archway and on and away into the darkness and

---

23 Lewis, *The Lion, the Witch and the Wardrobe*, 27.
24 Lewis, *The Lion, the Witch and the Wardrobe*, 67–68.
25 By the end of the book, he is a soldier of mercy as well, fighting in Aslan's army in defense of all Narnia's diverse residents.
26 Lewis, *The Lion, the Witch and the Wardrobe*, 30, 35.

the cold. This was a terrible journey for Edmund who had no coat."[27] Edmund is also spiteful and wishes ill on his siblings and Aslan and all enemies of the witch, cursing them in his own way throughout the first half of the book.

In *Lyrics*, the closing line of the opening stanza of "No Time to Think" appears in quotation marks: "You're a soldier of mercy, you're cold and you curse / 'He who cannot be trusted must fall.'" These are the only words in the song presented this way, and of course, the use of quotation marks indicates words spoken or written by another. This cold, cursing mercenary cannot be trusted, and the words in quotation marks declare those who are untrustworthy must fall. This is what we learn about the law governing Narnia as well, namely, that traitors must die. Edmund is untrustworthy. He betrays his siblings, Aslan, and all of Narnia, and so the witch makes her bloody claim on his life:

> "You have a traitor there, Aslan," said the Witch.... "Well," said Aslan. "His offence was not against you." "Have you forgotten the Deep Magic?" asked the Witch. "Let us say I have forgotten it," answered Aslan gravely. "Tell us of this Deep Magic." "Tell you?" said the Witch, her voice growing suddenly shriller. "Tell you what is *written* on that very Table of Stone which stands beside us? Tell you what is *written* in letters deep as a spear is long on the trunk of the World Ash Tree? Tell you what is *engraved* on the sceptre of the Emperor-beyond-the-Sea? You at least know the magic which the Emperor put into Narnia at the very beginning. You know that every traitor belongs to me as my lawful prey and that for every treachery I have a right to a kill."[28]

Edmund must fall. The word *written* appears two times in this exchange, along with *engraved*. Dylan's use of quotation marks, though not directly citing the novel, hints at this fixed edict, this written-down legislation.

Most of the song's eighteen stanzas are in the second person (you, your), but three of the eighteen stanzas (the fifth, seventh, and ninth) include the first person (I, us). This possibly indicates Edmund's story (you, your) and the narrator's (I, us) overlap in some ways. The narrator recognizes something of himself in Edmund's predicament. Again, the boy is caught between a lion and a witch. Both repel and both attract simultaneously, in very different ways. But you gotta serve one or the other, the devil or the lord, so there must be a decision.

The second stanza also aligns neatly with Edmund's story. Dylan writes of "you" (Edmund) *fighting for a throne* and *traveling alone*, which is what

---

27 Lewis, *The Lion, the Witch and the Wardrobe*, 113–114.
28 Lewis, *The Lion, the Witch and the Wardrobe*, 141–142. Italics added.

Edmund does immediately after leaving the Beavers' home, where he first learns of the great lion, parting ways with his siblings and their Aslan-loyal hosts: "You mustn't think that even now [as he set out for the witch's castle] Edmund was quite so bad that he actually wanted his brother and sisters to be turned into stone. He did want Turkish Delight and to be a Prince (and later a King)."[29]

He fights for that promised throne, and the solitary nature of Edmund's journey to the witch's home to claim it corresponds with Dylan's choice of descriptors: "The silence and the *loneliness* were dreadful."[30] Edmund makes the cold journey alone, or *in secret,* as Dylan puts it in the fourth stanza. Dylan's mention of loneliness, high society, and notoriety in this stanza are not random terms chosen simply to accommodate the rhyme scheme, but rather they take us into the snowy forests of Narnia, as Edmund makes his fateful choice to pursue the witch and so gain the power and fame a royal status confers. Dylan captures the reason in the fourth stanza, namely, that the empress (think witch) attracts the one addressed. He commits this secret betrayal for mere "pieces of change" (third stanza), phrasing that recalls Judas's betrayal of Jesus for thirty pieces of silver (Matt 26:15; 27:3, 9). The Judas theme returns in stanza four, woven into Edmund's story, with a betraying kiss on a "cool night," which again reminds us of the snowy, cold (cf. stanza one) Narnian winter in which Edmund travels alone to the witch's castle. There is nothing in the Gospels mentioning it was cold on the dark night of Judas's fateful kiss. Alongside the betrayal on a cool night, Dylan sings of a valley, and the witch's home is in one: "At last he [Edmund] came to a part where it was more level and the valley opened out. And there, on the other side of the river, quite close to him, in the middle of a little plain between two hills, he saw what must be the White Witch's house."[31]

Female characters in the *Street-Legal* songs are dangerous or difficult.[32] In the fifth stanza of "No Time to Think," we hear about judges haunting the

---

29 Lewis, *The Lion, the Witch and the Wardrobe*, 89.
30 Lewis, *The Lion, the Witch and the Wardrobe*, 91. Italics added.
31 Lewis, *The Lion, the Witch and the Wardrobe*, 92.
32 See, e.g., "New Pony." Is there a connection between Narnia's Lucy and the song's mention of Lucifer? Both names indicate light. That Lucifer, the traditional devil, is dangerous makes sense, but how so the Narnian Lucy? It is through her that Edmund and his other siblings, and with them readers, meet Aslan. At least from Edmund's point of view, this is a negative thing. He's torn between the devilish witch and Aslan for the first part of the story.

"you" addressed by the singer, as well as a priestess of the country. This pairing is interesting because Edmund knows what it is to be criticized, judged, by those around him. He finds the witch attractive because she represents a way of getting back at his persecutors (as he sees them), namely, his brother and sisters. That she is a priestess of the *country* also suits. Narnia is referred to often as a country. When Lucy first tells the others of her experiences there, Edmund teases her about her "imaginary country."[33] After a second visit, Lucy announces to the others, "There *is* a country you can get to through the wardrobe."[34] When Edmund finally discovers Narnia, his first encounter is with the story's villainous usurping ruler. Her title in the novel is queen or witch, not priestess as in the song, but the latter suggests authority and power, and she definitely *wants* Edmund, in keeping with the Dylan lyric: "Judges will haunt you, the country priestess will want you / Her worst is better than best." She wants him because it is through the boy she plans to capture all the sons of Adam and daughters of Eve, who, according to a prophecy, threaten her rule.

Edmund's judgmental siblings haunt him, but the priestess/queen of Narnia wants him. To Edmund, she is both terrifying and compelling. What she offers—power, wealth, a means of revenge against his siblings, the enchanted candy—is appealing but dangerous. Edmund doesn't realize it, but the last of these is also deadly: "The Turkish Delight was all finished and Edmund was looking very hard at the empty box and wishing that she would ask him whether he would like some more. Probably the Queen knew quite well what he was thinking; for she knew, though Edmund did not, that this was enchanted Turkish Delight and that anyone who had once tasted it would want more and more of it, and would even, if they were allowed, go on eating it till they killed themselves."[35] But her gifts are all he thinks of. Dylan notes the worst things she offers are better than anything else. That's how Edmund sees it, at least initially. He goes to great lengths to get more of that deadly treat. The narrator of "No Time to Think" then shifts to the first person, indicating he is witness to the experiences of the "you" addressed and presumably sympathetic. There is a recognition here, something familiar.

The reference to "a set of deep turquoise eyes" in the same stanza is both a beautiful line and a further clue the Narnian queen is in view. Her name is

---

33 Lewis, *The Lion, the Witch and the Wardrobe*, 27, 30.
34 Lewis, *The Lion, the Witch and the Wardrobe*, 44. Italics original.
35 Lewis, *The Lion, the Witch and the Wardrobe*, 37–38.

Jadis, which makes one think of jade stone, which is green-blue or turquoise in color. In addition, the witch's box of Turkish delight that so enchants Edmund has a green ribbon.[36] Jadis, the powerful female priestess/queen/witch of the Narnian "country," who lives in a valley, is the *femme fatale* of the story told in "No Time to Think." Seeing Edmund's downfall, and perhaps recognizing something of his own downfall in that story, suggested by the shift to the first-person singular in this stanza and mention of Mercury two times, leaves the narrator depressed.

There are other ideas in "No Time to Think" corresponding to Lewis's *The Lion, the Witch and the Wardrobe*. Stanza seven refers to betrayal, a tyrant, a lion, and a traitor, all words connected to Edmund's story. The eighth includes the terms *magician*, *blood*, and *ink*, which remind us of Aslan dying by the witch's hand in Edmund's place to satisfy the law written (ink) on the stone table. In the eleventh stanza, there are sorrowful warriors and tomorrow's queens. Use of the plural *queens* is unusual, at least if it refers to the simultaneous rule of two or more monarchs as opposed to successive reigns. Such things don't usually happen but in the novel, Lucy and Susan both become queens of Narnia, at the same time, just as Peter and Edmund become kings. The two queens in waiting, Lucy and Susan, are also associated with sorrow in a key scene as they are witnesses to the killing of Aslan: "I hope no one who reads this book has been quite as miserable as Susan and Lucy were that night; but if you have been—if you've been up all night and cried till you have no more tears left in you—you will know that there comes in the end a sort of quietness."[37] This is the darkest moment in Lewis's novel, with the two queens-in-waiting shedding tears. The lyric about sorrowful *queens* is conspicuous.

Track 9: "Where Are You Tonight? (Journey through Dark Heat)"

The album's closing song includes several connections to Lewis's fantasy that pick up the Gospels' redemption storyline. The most direct reference is to a lion and a demon in stanza eight, suggesting Aslan and the witch are the alternatives the narrator has before them. As mentioned, many commentators view the song's opening line—"There's a long-distance train rolling through the rain"—as a segue into Dylan's next album, the first of three with a gospel

---

36 Lewis, *The Lion, the Witch and the Wardrobe*, 58 (the name), 36 (the ribbon).
37 Lewis, *The Lion, the Witch and the Wardrobe*, 158.

focus. Indeed, a journey through rain precedes redemption in the Narnian tale as well. The children's adventures begin, two times, on rainy days that force them to play indoors.

> When next morning came, there was a steady rain falling, so thick that when you looked out of the window you could see neither the mountains nor the woods nor even the stream in the garden.[38]
>
> Lucy could not properly enjoy any of it [the children's outdoor play]. And so things went on until the next wet day. That day, when it came to the afternoon and there was still no sign of a break in the weather, they decided to play hide-and-seek.[39]

Both times it rains, one or more of the children find their way into Narnia during their indoor play. It is because of the rain they discover the wardrobe. All the adventures, including the discovery of a new world and the encounter with Aslan, result from going through the wardrobe on those rainy days.

The opening stanza of "Where Are You Tonight? (Journey through Dark Heat)" also refers to a woman the narrator misses and longs to touch, though she is now out of reach. We learn details about her in the second stanza. For one thing, she is associated with a bell: "a lonesome bell tone in that valley of stone." The first time we meet the White Witch of Narnia, she is in a sled pulled by reindeer with bells on their harnesses. She is the first one Edmund meets, and three times in the span of a few sentences there is mention of those bells.[40] In Lewis's later prequel, *The Magician's Nephew* (1955), we learn it is the ringing of a bell that awakens Jadis from a long-enchanted sleep in the first place (chap. 4). Furthermore, Dylan tells us this woman he longs to touch is in a valley of stone. That describes well the Narnian villain, who also lives in a valley of stone. In *The Lion, the Witch and the Wardrobe*, the evil queen waves her wand and turns those who oppose her to stone, and there are many such victims in her house. As Mr. Beaver says, "'There's not many taken in there that ever comes out again. Statues. All full of statues they say it is—in the courtyard and up the stairs and in the hall. People she's turned—' (he paused and shuddered) 'turned into stone.'"[41] And as mentioned, this house with its stone statues is in a valley: "The little valley . . . the valley opened

---

38 Lewis, *The Lion, the Witch and the Wardrobe*, 5.
39 Lewis, *The Lion, the Witch and the Wardrobe*, 26–27.
40 Lewis, *The Lion, the Witch and the Wardrobe*, 30–31.
41 Lewis, *The Lion, the Witch and the Wardrobe*, 77–78.

out. And there, on the other side of the river . . . he saw what must be the White Witch's house."⁴² When Edmund reaches this castle in the valley, the first thing he notices are the stone victims. Note the stress on the term in this description of the courtyard: "There were dozens of statues all about—standing here and there rather as the pieces stand on a chess board. . . . There were stone satyrs, and stone wolves, and bears and foxes and cat-a-mountains of stone. There were lovely stone shapes that looked like women but who were really the spirits of trees."⁴³

We're also told the woman in Dylan's song bathes in a stream of pure heat in this valley of stone, which picks up on the song's parenthetical subtitle. Biblical writers often use the language of dark/darkness (e.g., Isa 29:25; John 3:19; Eph 5:11) and fire/heat (e.g., Prov 16:27; Isa 33:11; Eph 6:16) with reference to evil. The woman in the first two stanzas of "Where Are You Tonight? (Journey through Dark Heat)" is the escaped demon mentioned in stanza 8, mentioned in the same line alongside the lion. The subtitle's phrasing of a *journey through* darkness and heat picks up on the novel's most familiar device. The children go *through* the dark wardrobe into a new world, a world where they discover a battle between good and evil. In that world, they learn the means of escaping the cruel manifestation of evil that is the witch, and they only discover this and other spiritual realities by taking that strange journey *through*. Dylan's song suggests much the same. The journey *through* dark heat is a journey *away from* the temptress of the valley of stone and all she represents. The picture on the album cover even has Dylan emerging from a staircase/tunnel, looking out from darkness into light, which loosely captures the spatial movement of the children's journey through the wardrobe.

That journey leads to a "sweet paradise" (stanza 12), Dylan sings, but getting there is painful. He misses that woman—letting her go is not easy—and longs to touch her still (stanza 1). The singer despairs (stanza 7) and pays a heavy price when he finally makes the break. Doing so leaves him with scars (stanza 12).⁴⁴ In a 1980 interview, Dylan commented on the struggle conversion involves: "'Being born again is a hard thing. You ever seen a mother give

---

42 Lewis, *The Lion, the Witch and the Wardrobe*, 92.
43 Lewis, *The Lion, the Witch and the Wardrobe*, 96.
44 Once on Aslan's side, Edmund participates in a great battle against the witch and her followers and sustains serious injuries in the fight.

birth to a child? Well it's painful. We don't like to lose those old attitudes and hang-ups."[45]

As the singer puts the lion and demon in parallel in stanza 8 (lion in the road versus escaped demon), so, too, he summarizes the choice before him in stanza 12, in what is, to my mind, one of Dylan's more beautiful and haunting lyrics: "There's a white diamond gloom on the dark side of this room / And a pathway that leads up to the stars."

These are not parallel descriptions of the same thing but rather two alternatives. The villain of Lewis's novel is the *White* Witch—"Her face was white—not merely pale, but white like snow or paper or icing sugar."[46] The terms *diamond* and *gloom* also attach to her at key moments and especially with reference to Edmund. She enchants Edmund early on by pouring a drop from a magic potion on the snow that "shin[es] like a diamond."[47] It produces a hot drink. A second drop produces the enchanted Turkish delight that enslaves him. When Edmund later visits the castle in the valley of stone, he enters "a long gloomy hall."[48] The term only appears three times in the novel and always with reference to the witch's actions. Mr. Tumnus, the faun, speaks "gloomily" to Lucy, explaining how it is always winter in Narnia, adding later how the witch is responsible for this. Mr. Beaver shakes his head in "a very gloomy fashion" as he tells the children she not only turned Mr. Tumnus to stone but took him to her castle in the valley of stone.[49]

Another suggestive pairing of images is the raging woman with a babe in her arms, who is alongside another with golden hair (stanza 4). The witch is constantly angry in *The Lion, the Witch and the Wardrobe*, and Edmund is the child (babe) prisoner she intends to use and then kill. In the novel, as mentioned, Lewis regularly describes Aslan as gold in color: "When they tried to look at Aslan's face they just caught a glimpse of the golden mane and the great, royal, solemn, overwhelming eyes."[50] The witch and Aslan appear side by side in one scene, when discussing Edmund's fate, Edmund the "babe"

---

45 Remarks from his interview with Karen Hughes of *The Dominion* (Wellington, New Zealand), May 21, 1980, in *Bob Dylan: The Essential Interviews*, ed. Jonathan Cott (New York: Wenner, 2006), 276.
46 Lewis, *The Lion, the Witch and the Wardrobe*, 31.
47 Lewis, *The Lion, the Witch and the Wardrobe*, 36.
48 Lewis, *The Lion, the Witch and the Wardrobe*, 98.
49 Lewis, *The Lion, the Witch and the Wardrobe*, 16 and 19 (winter), 77–78 (Mr. Beaver's reaction).
50 Lewis, *The Lion, the Witch and the Wardrobe*, 126.

to whom she insists she has a right: "It was the oddest thing to see those two faces—the golden face and the dead-white face—so close together."[51]

The one with the golden hair Dylan sings about, who contrasts with the raging woman, is said to be a stripper (stanza 4). This beautiful, golden-haired "woman" reappears in stanza 8, the same stanza that puts the terms *lion* and *demon* side by side. The lion / gold-haired stripper and the raging woman / demon represent the extremes, the two alternatives facing the narrator. This makes sense if we keep in view the one other use of "strip" on this album. To "strip and kneel," a phrase appearing in "Señor (Tales of Yankee Power)," suggests submission and letting go of personal attachments. Humorously, the golden-haired stripper of "Where Are You Tonight? (Journey through Dark Heat)" makes us think of an exotic dancer, but reading it with "Señor (Tales of Yankee Power)" in view, the sense is very different.[52] If someone humbly strips and kneels before a higher power, that higher power is the one who strips the kneeler. It is an image of submission—of Edmund's submission to Aslan, of the narrator's/Dylan's submission to Christ.

Stanza eight, with its contrast of a lion and a demon, also refers to the loss of dreams and the destruction of a landscape. In Lewis's novel, the evil witch makes it always winter. She destroys many of Narnia's residents, turning them to stone with her magic wand, and she spreads gloom and fear across that once-happy land. The one with golden hair, however, is beautiful and brings joy and the end of winter (cf. "midsummer's eve, near the tower" in "Changing of the Guards"). But that beauty begins to "fade" in this stanza. The singer wavers. It is perhaps a moment like that experienced by Edmund in the Beavers' house when the talk of Aslan repulses him. Again, whereas Peter, Susan, and Lucy recognize something magical and stirring in Aslan's name, Edmund finds it terrifying. This is the narrator's struggle in "Where Are You Tonight? (Journey through Dark Heat)." Both sides demand the singer's loyalty. Both sides attract. He must choose one or the other, but doing so is not easy.

Truth, the singer recognizes, is somehow beyond us. It is obscure, profound, and pure, and to experience it is to lose something of the self, to "explode" (stanza 5). Submission to it is life-altering. The journey through darkness to light, to the sweet paradise, results in scars. And what is the truth? Dylan

---

51 Lewis, *The Lion, the Witch and the Wardrobe*, 141.
52 These are the only two songs on the album with parenthetical subtitles, which is perhaps a further hint that there is a connection between them.

mentions *sacrifice* in stanza 5 alongside these musings on truth, and this is consistent with the Christian gospel and central to *The Lion, the Witch and the Wardrobe*. Aslan sacrifices himself to rescue Edmund, and this leads to the witch's defeat. If it is correct to connect the golden-haired stripper of stanza 4 with Aslan, it makes sense of the language Dylan uses in the next line: "She [Aslan] winds back the clock and she turns back the page / Of a book that no one can write." Compare this with Aslan's words following his resurrection: "Though the Witch knew the Deep Magic, there is a magic deeper still which she did not know. Her knowledge goes back only to the dawn of Time. But if she could have looked a little further back, into the stillness and the darkness before Time dawned, she would have read there a different incantation. She would have known that when a willing victim who had committed no treachery was killed in a traitor's stead, the Table would crack and Death itself would start working backwards."[53] He, too, turns back the clock. The golden stripper / Aslan does what no other can.

It is interesting to note how the witch emphasizes the law written on the stone table as the basis for her claim on Edmund's life: "Every traitor belongs to me as my lawful prey"; "He knows that unless I have blood as the Law says all Narnia will be overturned and perish in fire and water."[54] In "Señor (Tales of Yankee Power)," the singer calls on the Señor, the Lord, to overturn tables, alluding to the Gospel stories of Jesus overturning the tables of moneychangers in the Jerusalem temple (Matt 21:12; Mark 11:15; John 2:15). It also points to an image prominent in *The Lion, the Witch and the Wardrobe*. Aslan "overturns" the stone table on which the devilish witch takes his life. The table breaks when he rises from death, and in doing so, he undoes the law written on it that is the basis of the witch's claim. Lewis conflates the story of Jesus overturning tables with the tearing of the curtain in the Jerusalem temple when Jesus dies (Matt 27:51; Mark 15:38; Luke 23:45). "Where Are You Tonight? (Journey through Dark Heat)" includes an interesting remark about the law. The singer's horseplay and disease are killing him, but the law in question "looks the other way" (stanza 9). Does this refer to the "deeper" magic Aslan describes? If so, *despite* the horseplay and disease, *despite* what the song narrator and Edmund deserve, the law does not condemn. Aslan dies "in a traitor's stead." He overturns the law written on that table, or, said differently, turns back the pages of a book no one else could write.

---

53 Lewis, *The Lion, the Witch and the Wardrobe*, 163.
54 Lewis, *The Lion, the Witch and the Wardrobe*, 142.

In the last stanza of "Where Are You Tonight? (Journey through Dark Heat)," the album's closing song, the rhyming scheme combines the terms *arrived*, *survived*, and *alive*. Despite the scars, despite the terrifying journey through / out of / away from dark heat (biblical images for evil and separation from God), the narrator reaches the desired but dreaded destination, which he describes as "a new day at dawn." This reference to time (stanza 13) corresponds to the language of Lewis's story (see previous block quote) and to terms used in two of the Lewis novel's chapter titles, which include the phrase "Dawn of Time" (chaps. 13, 15). The album's last stanza also corresponds with the religious orientation of the gospel songs Dylan would sing in the years following the release of *Street-Legal*.

WHAT HAPPENED NEXT? ROCK AND ROLL, AND SCRIPTURE AS SCRIPT

I don't know how many times I've listened to "Is Your Love in Vain?" on *Street-Legal*, always assuming the question posed in the closing stanza—"Can you cook and sew, make flowers grow / Do you understand my pain?"—was a throwaway line and, since presumably directed at a woman, awkwardly patriarchal. But Dylan songs are often more complex than initially supposed. Given the religious turn occurring in his life and music in the late 1970s just reviewed, it should have come as no surprise when I finally recognized the Bible lurking behind those seemingly banal words. *Cook, sew, flowers, understanding my pain*. Jesus's comforting words from the Sermon on the Mount are here, just below the surface of the music, with the same ideas appearing in the same sequence in both:

> Therefore I say unto you, Take no thought for your life, <u>what ye shall eat</u>, or what ye shall drink; nor yet for your body, <u>what ye shall put on</u>. Is not the life more than meat, and the body than raiment? Behold the fowls of the air: for they sow not, neither do they reap, nor gather into barns; yet your heavenly Father feedeth them. Are ye not much better than they? Which of you by taking thought can add one cubit unto his stature? And why take ye thought for raiment? Consider the <u>lilies of the field</u>, how they grow; they toil not, neither do they spin: And yet I say unto you, That even Solomon in all his glory was not arrayed like one of these. Wherefore, if God so clothe the grass of the field, which to day is, and to morrow [*sic*] is cast into the oven, shall he not much more clothe you, O ye of little faith? Therefore take no thought, saying, What shall we eat? or, What shall we drink? or, Wherewithal shall we be clothed? (For after all these things

do the Gentiles seek:) for <u>your heavenly Father knoweth that ye have need of all these things</u>. But seek ye first the kingdom of God, and his righteousness; and all these things shall be added unto you. (Matt 6:25–33, AV)

On some level, the singer is in conversation with Jesus, who made these promises. The title of the song is a question, as is its opening line: "Do you love me, or are you just extending goodwill?" This is fitting, given the *yes or no, do I or don't I, this way or that way* anguish experienced by the album narrators. Is this for real? Does God really care about me? The very idea is hard to fathom, but the singer announces the decision he reaches in the closing stanza: "All right, I'll take a chance, I will fall in love with you." And so begins Bob Dylan's gospel period. What was going on during those tumultuous and, in the opinion of many fans and critics, controversial years?

The evangelists present Jesus retracing Israel's and, more generally, humanity's steps. John baptizes him in the Jordan, the very river Israel crossed to enter the promised land (Matt 3:13–17; Mark 1:9–11; Luke 3:21–22; John 1:29–34; cf. Josh 3:1–17). He spends forty days in the wilderness, corresponding to Israel's forty years there (Matt 4:1–11; Mark 1:12–13; Luke 4:1–13; cf. Num 32:13, etc.). That time in the wilderness recalls Adam and Eve's fate (Gen 3:23). While in that wilderness, animals approach Jesus peacefully just as they approached Adam in the garden of Eden (Mark 1:13 cf. Gen 2:18–20). Jesus's birth occurs in David's city (Luke 2:4, 11), and he delivers a sermon from a mountain, like Moses (Matt 5:1–7:29 cf. Exod 19:17–20:21). The holy family flees with the Bethlehem baby because of an evil king; the episode is reminiscent of another evil king's efforts to kill a different infant deliverer of Israel (Matt 2:13–18 cf. Exod 1:22–2:10). Such echoes in the Gospels suggest a strategic shaping of source material to highlight parallels with key luminaries and places and crucial narrative turns in the story of God's work in the world the Hebrew prophets tell. This palimpsestuous quality of the Gospels, this layering of one story over others, serves to persuade readers of continuities. As the Gospel writers see it, what they present are the next chapters in a long, ancient, and ongoing narrative.

What happens on a literary level with the evangelists presenting Jesus's story in ways recalling Adam, Moses, David, and others happens also in the lives of those who read the Gospels as Scripture. For them, there is a religiously motivated effort to replicate the narratives the evangelists tell in their own actions. Said differently, Jesus's followers define themselves by patterning their lives around an archetypal precursor. They, too, take up their cross, in imitation of Christ (cf. Matt 16:24–28; Mark 8:34–9:1; Luke 9:23–27; John 12:25). Each week, they, too, celebrate a Passover-like sacred meal, like the disciples at the Last Supper (Matt 26:26–29; Mark 14:22–25; Luke 22:15–20). Follow my example, says Saint Paul, as I follow the example of Christ (1 Cor 11:1). This is the broad shape of New Testament religion; it is an alignment of self and community with a master text, with a divine script.

Religious ritual involves performative repetition of central tenets of belief. Within Christianity, as noted, the Eucharist involves reenactment of Jesus's last meal with the disciples. The church calendar, with its celebrations of feast days like Easter and Christmas, guides the faithful through the sacred story each year, allowing them to participate anew in the seminal events around which the church coheres. This is a useful place to begin when thinking of Bob Dylan's gospel material, by which I mean the albums and concerts of 1979–1981 that followed *Street-Legal*. They, too, involve a form of ritual. The 2017 release *Trouble No More—A Musical Film*, part of the deluxe edition of the Bootleg Series, volume 13, *Trouble No More*, a collection of recordings from 1979 to 1981—illustrates the point. The film alternates between concert performances by Dylan and his band and a fiery cross-wearing preacher (played by actor Michael Shannon), whose short King James Version-infused sermonettes bring the viewer, in effect, into the church sanctuary. The expected themes are all there—sin and virtue, God and the devil, hypocrisy, and inescapable judgment. Dylan's banter during concerts of the period did much the same thing, turning theaters and arenas into revival tents and cathedrals. And what do churches do? They recapitulate the gospel story in a variety of ways—preaching sermons, taking communion, calling for repentance, condemning sin, worshipping God, voicing expectation of Christ's return. Dylan's entire gospel oeuvre engages in that kind of retelling, that kind of ritual reenactment, that conforming to a preexisting template.[55]

We even find this kind of mimicry in the language of *Trouble No More: A Musical Film*, produced and directed by Jennifer LeBeau. Lucy Sante wrote the script for the preacher portions of the film, and I asked her what if any

---

55 In a very different kind of study, Andrew McCarron finds something similar across several songs, namely, "a Biblically patterned progression from the Babylonian Exile to Gethsemane to Golgotha predicated on a cycle of struggle, death, and subsequent rebirth. The forms of religious yearning and change present across the songs reflect a defining feature of much of Christian spirituality—that is, it's progressive (as opposed to regressive) nature" (*Light Come Shining: The Transformation of Bob Dylan* [New York: Oxford University Press, 2017], 128–129).

direction she received from the Dylan team and what sources and inspirations informed her writing. She replied as follows:

> The only direction I was given by Dylan via his manager was regarding the subject matter: hypocrisy, virtue, gluttony, temperance, and justice. There were a few other non-binding suggestions, such as that I could include contemporary elements, maybe quote modern writers. For my part I was faced with the fact that my experience of sermons was limited and fairly second-hand; I was raised Catholic, lost my faith at 13 or so, and couldn't remember a single sermon from my churchgoing years. I knew the works of the seventeenth-century Puritans, but they didn't strike the right tone, to say the least. So I drew upon the resource that lay closest at hand, both literally and in terms of Dylan's music: the recorded works of Black, mostly Southern preachers from the 1920s and '30s: Rev. J. M. Gates [1884–1945], Rev. D. C. Rice [ca. 1888–1973], Rev. A. W. Nix [1880–1949], et al. I listened to them over and over to fix a rhythm, as well as to study the sense of intimacy with the congregation those guys project even on recordings. When I started writing I found myself thinking of a more contemporary version of those preachers, a plainspoken, commonsensical, community-minded minister, someone who could give voice to my own ethics without too much theology—I wanted to believe every word. I guess I was thinking of someone along the lines of Rev. William Barber, although here necessarily addressing everyday relationships rather than national affairs. But as far as how they flow with the songs [which is something I asked Sante about in my initial inquiry]—that is marvelous but serendipitous. I didn't know the songs when I was writing, and hadn't seen the [concert] footage.[56]

Dylan's proclamation of the Christian story is idiosyncratic, inimitable, and selective, but the inclusion of Sante's script, rooted as it is in a particular homiletical tradition, suggests the singer sees his work in continuity with others. At some point, Dylan must have approved the Sante script. In that respect, his is not a voice crying in the wilderness but rather one added to a chorus of others. My point is that imitation is at play. We recognize gospel music when we hear it owing to instrumental and lyrical conventions. The rhythms of early twentieth-century revival meetings live on through mimicry, both in the arts and in Sante's script but also in the living church, where similar rhythms are heard each Sunday. On a grander scale, Dylan, those revivalist preachers, and the echo of them in an early twenty-first-century film follow a pattern found in the pages of the New Testament.

A palimpsest is an underlying textual presence such as the faint pencil markings that remain on paper after erasing an earlier text. When we write

---

56 Personal correspondence, February 11, 2021. Cited with permission.

over them, traces of the original markings remain. They show through, so an earlier message continues to "speak" through a later one. Metaphorically, it is a way to think about literary influence. A palimpsest is a presupposed story, one already told, a precursor, over which / on which readers read, writers write, and singers sing. The metaphor is useful as we consider the transition from *Street-Legal* to Dylan's gospel albums. Clearly, Dylan experienced something deeply profound in the late 1970s, and for a brief time (1979–1981), he described a transformed worldview directly through songs and stage sermons and interviews.[57] For details about this, see the biographies. This does not mean there was no interest in religion and spirituality in his earlier albums or an abandonment of the experience afterward, but the albums of this era, meaning *Slow Train Coming* (1979), *Saved* (1980), and *Shot of Love* (1981), naturally stand apart from the others as clear(er) recitals of an identifiable belief system. That the album immediately before anticipates this lyrical emphasis (*Street-Legal*, 1978)[58] and the first album afterward (*Infidels*, 1983) continues with its biblical atmosphere is a reminder that periodization of Dylan's art is never straightforward. The borders assigned are usually porous, with continuations and anticipations, with echoes of what was and foreshadowing of what was yet to be.[59]

The three gospel albums, the *Trouble No More* collection, as well as interviews and concerts with his preachy stage banter, all have a discernible shape, corresponding, broadly speaking, to a biblical model. Dylan and his song narrators and concert persona step into an already told story. There are exceptions and plenty of idiosyncrasies, but still, in what he writes/sings/speaks, there is a

---

57 For transcripts of a selection of Dylan's sermons from the stage, see Clinton Heylin's Appendix II, "Some Alternate Raps," in *Trouble in Mind: Bob Dylan's Gospel Years, What Really Happened* (New York: Lesser Gods, 2017), 301–311. See, too, examples in Heylin's "Saved! Bob Dylan's Conversion to Christianity," in *Wanted Man: In Search of Bob Dylan*, ed. John Bauldie (New York: Citadel, 1991), 128–134.

58 Of course, recognizing a pattern of progression from one album to the next is only possible in hindsight. Robert Shelton: "*Street-Legal* is one of Dylan's most overtly autobiographical albums, telling of loss, searching, estrangement, and exile. It also clearly foreshadows the Christian conversion ahead, but who among us could perceive it at that time?" (*No Direction Home: The Life and Music of Bob Dylan* [1986; London: Penguin, 1987], 478).

59 Dylan's reflections on religion are ongoing: "I'm a religious person. I read the scriptures a lot, meditate and pray, light candles in church. I believe in damnation and salvation, as well as predestination. The Five Books of Moses, Pauline Epistles, Invocation of the Saints, all of it" (interview about his book *The Philosophy of Modern Song* [2022] posted at bobdylan.com).

discernible coherence. It is a repetition of the New Testament portrait of discipleship, of the response of those choosing to heed Jesus's call to "follow me."

The biblical story underlying the gospel trilogy is, to borrow Bunyan's term, that of the pilgrim's progress. It is the oft-told tale of one seeking the celestial city. It begins with that difficult step toward initial faith (as in *Street-Legal*) and proceeds as a journey through life modeled on and mapped out across the New Testament. Jesus's teachings, along with the writings of Saint Paul and others, repeat the story constantly and in different ways, but a consistent, overall story arc is discernible—the wayward come home, repenting, and striving to live in obedience to the commandments. They face temptations and confess their failures. They are joyful, worshipping God and giving thanks for the many blessings they enjoy. There are hardships, too, including persecution and ridicule from unbelievers. They appeal to God for the endurance needed to persevere.

In addition to these widely represented actions and experiences, the New Testament disciple holds to key tenets of the faith: God as creator, humanity's sinfulness, Jesus's death and resurrection as the solution to humanity's alienation from God. There is also acknowledgment of Jesus's call to proclaim the good news of reconciliation with God and an expectation Christ will return in a moment, in the twinkling of an eye. This belief gives urgency to the disciple's efforts to proclaim the gospel and live out its demands. To approach Dylan's gospel songs without attention to this metanarrative has an obscuring effect. Taken individually, the songs of this period are sometimes strange, sometimes incomprehensible, but when plotted along the image of the New Testament disciple as roughly sketched out above, it is possible to view most of them as moments in the pilgrim's journey. Perhaps this is one reason Dylan performed only the new gospel songs in the early stages of the 1979–1981 tours. They belong together. When taken as a whole, a picture emerges, a "biography" of the New Testament disciple.

CHAPTER SIX

An Old Curiosity Shop and an Old Copy of Bunyan's *Progress*

Lead us not into temptation, but deliver us from evil.
—Matthew 6:13, AV

Hospitality is a prized virtue in biblical literature. When a stranger or foreigner resides in your land, "you shall not oppress" that person. Instead, treat them "as the citizen among you; you shall love the alien as yourself." Here again, empathy, the capacity to identify with the struggles of another, is at the core of a biblical mandate to care: "Love the alien as yourself, for you were aliens in the land of Egypt" (Lev 19:33–34). We find appeals for this kind of generous reception of those outside our immediate circles throughout a wide range of texts. What is the purpose for the day on which you fast if not "to share your bread with the hungry, and bring the homeless poor into your house; when you see the naked, to cover them, and not to hide yourself from your own kin?" (Isa 58:7). Jesus appears to echo this text in his sheep and goats lesson (Matt 25:31–46). The hospitable Job is confident he withheld nothing from those who are poor, has seen no one perish for lack of clothing, has not raised his hand against an orphan (31:16–23). We find writers prizing such generosity in early Christian literature as well. Contribute to the saints, writes Paul, but such kindness is not only to be shown to those with whom you identify. You are also to extend "hospitality to strangers" (Rom 12:13). Charity is a hallmark of Christian faithfulness (cf., 1 Tim 5:10; Titus 1:8; 1 Pet 4:9).

Serving those with whom we have natural bonds—family, friends, religious community, those of a shared language group and culture—is much easier than doing so when such connections are lacking. To intervene when a stranger is in crisis perhaps requires an exercise of the imagination because we do not know their backstory or have any firsthand knowledge of what they're going through. To know less about them increases the temptation to pass them by. As a Samaritan, what concern is it of mine to see that injured Jew on the side of the road? If his own people passed him by (a priest, a Levite), why should I stop and help?

Writers build tension by allowing readers to know things fictional characters do not. Sometimes the reverse is true. The latter is common in Charles Dickens's stories, with revealed secrets—there is another will, someone's real identity comes to light, someone thought dead returns—providing unexpected plot twists. My interest as I open this chapter, however, is a little different as I turn to a relatively minor but key character in Dickens's *The Old Curiosity Shop* (1841). It is the poor schoolmaster named Mr. Marton. His name, it deserves notice, appears only three times in the novel, all in chapter 52 and all during a single conversation, subtly suggesting his is a supporting role in this drama that centers on the young girl Nell. She must increase, but he must decrease, to paraphrase another character with an important but comparatively minor part to play (see John 3:30). In this instance, we know more than Mr. Marton.

Nell and her grandfather flee London, forced out of their home by the devilish Daniel Quilp. They are financially destitute and anxious to keep their backstory hidden for fear Quilp or others will track them down. Two times, Nell and the old man meet the poor schoolmaster when they are in desperate need, and both times he rescues them. After the second chance encounter, he takes the ailing girl to an inn for care, and as he converses with the lady of the house, we glimpse the spirit of the biblical call to care for strangers we meet:

> The schoolmaster sat for a long time smoking his pipe by the kitchen fire, which was now deserted, thinking, with a very happy face, on the fortunate chance which had brought him so opportunely to the child's assistance, and parrying, as well as in his simple way he could, the inquisitive cross-examination of the landlady, who had a great curiosity to be made acquainted with every particular of Nell's life and history. The poor schoolmaster was so open-hearted, and so little versed in the most ordinary cunning or deceit, that she could not have failed to succeed in the first five minutes, but that he happened to be unacquainted with what she wished to know; and so he told her.... "I assure you, my good lady,"

said the mild schoolmaster, "that I have told you the plain truth. As I hope to be saved, I have told you the truth."[1]

He knows nothing about the girl he helps. The only thing Mr. Marton knows about her and her grandfather is that they are in need. As readers, we know far more about them by this point and are anxious to see them succeed. What the novel provides is an illustration of kindness unmotivated by an intimate connection. Marton knows nothing about these desperate folks, and he wants nothing in return for his care. *When were you hungry, Lord, and we gave you something to eat?* The schoolmaster teaches us what showing "hospitality to strangers" means. He entertains angels unaware (Heb 13:2; cf. Gen 18:2–15; 19:1–14; Judg 6:11–24; 13:3–23), a fitting image in this context given Nell is regularly associated with angels (about which, see below). My main thesis is that some fiction has a kind of pedagogical function, allowing us to inhabit stories manifesting biblical values. A blunt command to show "hospitality to strangers" ought to be enough for me to act, and for many it is, but it is a call to service I find difficult. To witness a fictional character do it, and for the sake of one (Nell) so deserving of kindness, potentially awakens and nurtures a desire to do the same for those I meet, even those I do not know.

One of Dickens's more terrifying villains is the diminutive Daniel Quilp, who, as mentioned, haunts the pages of *The Old Curiosity Shop*. As the plot unfolds, we learn Quilp feeds the old man's gambling addiction by lending him money and, because of the resulting debts, takes possession of his shop and the home where he lives with his granddaughter, Nell. His cruelty and wickedness manifest in many ways, not least in his domestic relations. To illustrate Quilp's character and willingness to harm females in particular, a few examples help us appreciate the danger from which Nell flees. When speaking to others, the sinister Quilp seems rather proud to describe his wife as, among other things, obedient and timid.[2] For Betsy Quilp, the narrator explains, marriage to the man amounts to the performance of a "practical penance for her folly [in marrying him] every day of her life." She is under the "dominion" of her husband. He is "lord of the creation" in their home

---

1 Charles Dickens, *The Old Curiosity Shop* (1841; London: Arcturus, 2011), 350, 352.
2 Dickens, *Old Curiosity Shop*, 34. Plausibly, the name Quilp combines *quill* and *pen*, which leads some to speculate Dickens was parodying himself or his profession. See, e.g., A. N. Wilson, *The Mystery of Charles Dickens* (New York: HarperCollins, 2020), 128–129, 254.

and Betsy Quilp's "lord."[3] Quilp is not beyond enforcing his rule through physical intimidation and assault. He threatens her, "nipping and pinching her arm" on one occasion, to make her do his bidding, something that leaves bruises, and at another time threatens to scratch her.[4] He even looks around "as if for some weapon with which to inflict condign punishment upon his disobedient wife," and when playing cribbage, he steps on her toes "to see whether she cried out or remained silent under the affliction."[5] The latter occurs with Richard Swiveller in attendance. He muses afterward he will not be the kind of husband "to beat or kill" his wife, an aside making it clear Quilp is.[6]

Betsy is not Quilp's only victim in that sad home. His mother-in-law, Mrs. Jiniwin, lives with them and is no stranger to the man's brutality. In addition to their verbal sparring, Dickens signals this by spatial movement. On one occasion, Quilp moves toward her, forcing her to retreat "as he advanced, and [she] falling back before him." The scene suggests she is familiar with his use of violence to ensure compliance. When he backs her into a room, he proceeds to bolt the door, locking her in for the night. Later, he does not allow Mrs. Jiniwin to play cribbage or have a drink, taking delight in the way it torments her.[7] His nasty behavior toward women occurs outside the home as well, as when he terrorizes Mrs. Nubbles, Kit's mother, when both travel in a stagecoach.[8] He is like Arthur Huntingdon in some respects (cf. chap. 3), both in his cruelty to women and his frequent consumption of strong drink. When a group of Betsy's friends discuss her plight, a remark about the tendency of men to "tyrannise over the weaker sex" and use of the term *dominion* in the near context both recall biblical language.[9] Attaching the vague notion of religious sanction to Quilp's cruelty by inclusion of these biblical echoes is a counterpoint to instances of true piety found throughout the story, particularly evident in Kit, the schoolmaster Mr. Marton, and Nell.

Filling out this portrait of a villain even further is the use of bestial imagery attached to the man. This a common device in Dickens's stories, and in this instance, descriptions of Quilp's body occur in most scenes in

---

3 Dickens, *Old Curiosity Shop*, 38, 39, 46, 47.
4 Dickens, *Old Curiosity Shop*, 58, 111, 511.
5 Dickens, *Old Curiosity Shop*, 58, 184.
6 Dickens, *Old Curiosity Shop*, 186.
7 Dickens, *Old Curiosity Shop*, 44, 47, 184.
8 Dickens, *Old Curiosity Shop*, 370, 371.
9 Dickens, *Old Curiosity Shop*, 39. Cf. 1 Pet 3:7 and Gen 1:26, respectively.

which he appears, serving to distinguish him from others.[10] Use of the terms *dwarf* and *ugly* are common, and so, too, are recurring animal descriptors. In particular, he is often assigned canine qualities, something highlighted by a scene in which he teases a chained dog.[11] He threatens to bite his wife, snarls, and wears a "doglike smile" on his face. His wife and mother-in-law both begin "to doubt if he were really a human creature" when they watch him eat.[12] Quilp is a predator who threatens the well-being of the innocent and vulnerable Nell and her aging, foolish caregiver, forcing them to flee London.

Theirs is a journey from desolation to salvation, and it is the account of their escape and search for refuge I focus on here. The danger of staying home—which is to say, the danger of staying in proximity to Quilp—lends a sense of urgency to their flight. I highlight Quilp's evil because Dickens's *The Old Curiosity Shop* owes much to an older book in which staying home is synonymous with spiritual damnation. As Christian puts it in John Bunyan's *The Pilgrim's Progress* with reference to his own escape from home,

> *O world of wonders! (I can say no less)*
> *That I should be preserv'd in that distress*
> *That I have met with here! Oh, blessed bee*
> *That hand that from it hath delivered me!*
> *Dangers in darkness, Devils, Hell, and Sin,*
> *Did compass me, while I this Vale was in.*[13]

As we'll see, Bunyan's allegory is one of Dickens's inspirations for this novel, so it makes sense that his villain, an expression of the darkness and sin Christian flees in *Pilgrim's Progress*, needs to be over the top, violent, and monstrous, a threat to all that is good.

Charles Dickens believed fiction to be "morally didactic, a powerful force for teaching goodness in the general sense of providing models of moral and

---

10 See, e.g., Michael J. Gilmour, "Animal Imagery in Charles Dickens's *Dombey and Son*," *Bhatter College Journal of Multidisciplinary Studies* 3 (2013): 55–61. Cf. Charlotte Brontë's use of bestial imagery in her portrait of *Jane Eyre*'s Bertha Mason, discussed in chap. 2.
11 Dickens, *Old Curiosity Shop*, 172.
12 Dickens, *Old Curiosity Shop*, 44, 46, 49.
13 Bunyan, *Pilgrim's Progress*, 67.

immoral character and action."[14] In *The Old Curiosity Shop* (1840–1841), he presents models of moral and immoral characters and actions with attention to a well-known literary precursor. We're told the heroine Nell Trent often looked at plates in a copy of *The Pilgrim's Progress* in her childhood home, and she recollects it soon after fleeing London with her grandfather, the site of all their Quilpian troubles. They are resting in a beautiful spot in the countryside early in their travels, and the setting puts her in a reflective mood:

> There had been an old copy of the Pilgrim's Progress, with strange plates, upon a shelf at home, over which she had often pored whole evenings, wondering whether it was true in every word, and where those distant countries with the curious names might be. As she looked back upon the place they had left, one part of it came strongly on her mind. 'Dear grandfather, . . . I feel as if we were both Christian [the main character in the first part of *The Pilgrim's Progress*], and laid down on this grass all the cares and troubles we brought with us; never to take them up again.'[15]

Presumably she has in view the moment in the story when, after Christian's conversion, the narrator sees "his burden loosed from off his Shoulders, and fell from off his back," leaving him "glad and lightsome."[16] In Bunyan's tale, this moment of relief from a heavy burden is the beginning of the pilgrim's adventures, and so it is for the girl and the old man in Dickens's story. They've had their burdens "loosed" by escaping the wicked Quilp, but like Christian, there is still a long way to go, obstacles to overcome, and snares to avoid. After her remark, Nell's grandfather agrees they are in a better place and is emphatic nothing will lure them back to the city. Nell's mention of that seventeenth-century book, along with an illustration in chapter 12 using the term *pilgrimage*, invites reading *The Old Curiosity Shop* alongside Bunyan's allegory.

Throughout his travels in *The Pilgrim's Progress*, Christian sees people and places that either help or hinder his journey toward the Celestial City, and vigilance and cautious discernment are of the utmost importance. The

---

14 Fred Kaplan, *Dickens: A Biography* (Baltimore: The Johns Hopkins University Press, 1998), 26. Cf. remarks by and about Anne Brontë in chap. 2 above.

15 Dickens, *Old Curiosity Shop*, 126.

16 Bunyan, *Pilgrim's Progress*, 37. For brief introductions to Bunyan's religious thought, see, e.g., Cavill et al., *Christian Tradition in English Literature*, 196–199; Prior, *On Reading Well*, chap. 9; and Robert G. Collmer, "John Bunyan," in *The Oxford Handbook of English Literature and Theology*, ed. Andrew W. Haas, David Jasper, and Elisabeth Jay (Oxford: Oxford University Press, 2007), 575–589.

explicit identification of the grandfather and girl with Christian in the excerpt above warns readers to expect similar aids and obstacles as those described by Bunyan, and indeed, their perilous flight from London requires Nell to distinguish friend from foe and to be wary of hazards along the way. In *The Pilgrim's Progress*, Graceless, later named Christian, leaves the City of Destruction (cf. Isa 19:18) to reach Mount Zion, or the Celestial City.[17] It is a symbol of salvation, of God's kingdom (cf. e.g., Heb 12:22), of ultimate rest in this life and beyond. For Dickens's characters, London is the City of Destruction they must leave behind. If readers were to follow the same path out of the city taken by Nell and her grandfather, the narrator tells us, they would see old Saint Paul's Cathedral in the distance, looming through the smoke, and "the Babel out of which it grew."[18] The biblical story of Babel tells of people coming together in defiance of God, which deepens the critique of London and perhaps also Saint Paul's and Anglicanism.[19]

There are biblical resonances throughout the novel, as is often the case with Dickens's writing.[20] The pair's journey begins with their escape from Quilp, who has a hold on Nell's grandfather owing to the old man's gambling debts. After Quilp claims possession of their home, temporarily allowing its former owners to stay, Nell sneaks into Quilp's bedroom to get the "key," which they need to get out in the dead of night. This is an important biblical term (e.g., Isa 22:22; Matt 16:18–19; Rev 1:18), and their Bunyanesque salvation only occurs after obtaining it. The vaguely biblical language continues once they step out of the house. The old man looks "right and left" but does not know which way to turn. In the Bible, these terms distinguish life and death, wisdom and folly, right and wrong (e.g., Eccl 10:2; Matt 25:33), which indicates there are potential perils on the path they choose.[21] Nell thus becomes the "guide and leader" on the dangerous road ahead.[22] She, too, does not know where they need to go, language echoing a description of the Holy Spirit in John 3:8. The allusions make it clear they are right to escape, but just as Christian's journey toward the Celestial City in *The Pilgrim's Progress* is not simple, and

---

17 Bunyan, *Pilgrim's Progress*, 47.
18 Dickens, *Old Curiosity Shop*, 125. An illustration in chap. 15 includes the cathedral.
19 Appropriate, given Bunyan was a nonconformist.
20 On this topic, see Gribble, *Dickens and the Bible*. For her understanding of biblical intertextuality in Dickens's work, see esp. 22–27.
21 Dickens, *Old Curiosity Shop*, 105.
22 Dickens, *Old Curiosity Shop*, 125 cf. 147.

involves temptations and threats at every turn, so it will be for Nell and her elderly companion.[23]

Early in Christian's quest for the Celestial City, he visits the house of the interpreter, where the traveler learns "that which will be profitable," and in this house, a picture hangs on the wall depicting a grave person with eyes lifted to heaven and *"the best of Books in its hands, the Law of Truth was written upon its lips."*[24] This person has his back to the world and pleads with people to embrace the truth he proclaims. He is an image of the faithful preacher of the gospel. That preacher's duty is to "unfold dark things to sinners," and so he assures onlookers of the blessings of the world to come and of the need to turn their own backs to the present one. The reason the interpreter shows Christian the picture is because this is the only person God authorizes to guide travelers through the "difficult places" they encounter. Take heed, the interpreter counsels Christian, "lest in thy Journey, thou meet with some that pretend to lead thee right, but their way goes down to death."[25] The theme repeats in part two of *Progress*. When Christian's wife, Christiana, visits the interpreter, he reminds her "that earthly things when they are with Power upon Mens [sic] minds, quite carry their hearts away from God."[26] Dickens's *Old Curiosity Shop* mimics aspects of the cautionary tale that is *Pilgrim's Progress*, warning through the experiences of Nell and her unnamed grandfather that some sheep are wolves in disguise. Consider some of the friends and enemies Nell meets along the way.

---

23 Like Nell's grandfather, the lure of wealth is a temptation faced by Christian and Hopeful in Bunyan's allegory. As noted at the outset of this section, after escaping London, he and Nell are determined never to take up their old troubles or be lured back. The troubles from which they flee include financial ones. For Christian and Hopeful, the temptation of wealth comes in the form of arguments by "Mony-love" [sic] and an invitation from Demas (see 2 Tim 4:10) to see Silver-Mine (Bunyan, *Pilgrim's Progress*, 101–105). They resist those temptations and immediately afterward come across an old monument, which they discover is the pillar of salt that once was Lot's wife (see Gen 19:26). On it is written the Gospel warning to "'remember Lot's wife'" (Luke 17:32). Throughout *The Old Curiosity Shop*, this dread of a return to the start is emphasized, and like Christian and Hopeful, Nell knows better than to look back.

24 Bunyan, *Pilgrim's Progress*, 29. Italics original.

25 Bunyan, *Pilgrim's Progress*, 30.

26 Bunyan, *Pilgrim's Progress*, 188.

Codlin, Short, and the Punch and Judy Show

Nell and her grandfather meet two different kinds of entertainers during their travels. The first, Codlin and Short, are a pair of Punch and Judy performers and the second, Mrs. Jarley, owns a traveling waxwork show. The first entertainers prove dangerous; the second is a friend along the way who offers timely help.

The episode involving the puppet performers begins the series of encounters recalling John Bunyan's tale. Happening upon them amounts to a temptation, the risk of preferring creature comforts in this world to the blessings of the next. As noted, the grandfather is emphatic in his rejection of the City of Destruction, London: "'No—never to return—never to return'—replied the old man, waving his hand towards the city. 'Thou and I are free of it now, Nell. They shall never lure us back.'"[27] But these words prove hollow because he does indeed fall prey to temptations, more than once mistaking the pleasures of a moment with their goal. Like Lot's wife, he looks back, after turning away from the world.

When they first make the acquaintance of the Punch and Judy actors, their companionship leads to a refreshing stay at an inn by a church. These new friends seem to be allies seeking their best interests, but it is illusory. As the grandfather laughs at the puppets and wants to be with them, the wise, discerning Nell remains alert. She is not deceived into mistaking that moment as the end of their troubles, something evident at the close of day. While he sleeps peacefully in that inn by the church, she sews their one gold coin into her dress as a safeguard.[28]

The Punch and Judy episode is at first a pleasant reprieve to the weary wanderers but is not the destination they seek on their "pilgrimage." Given *Pilgrim's Progress* is a Christian allegory, it is noteworthy the bottler, "the misanthrope" Mr. Thomas Codlin, blows "the Pan's pipe" at the performance that so enthralls the grandfather.[29] This mention of a pagan deity within a scene marked by its Christian setting—the church in London and the church by the inn, as well as the reference to *The Pilgrim's Progress*—apparently hints that danger lurks amid otherwise charming moments. Readers also need to be on their guard. After making our way through the gloomy opening chapters

---

27 Dickens, *Old Curiosity Shop*, 126.
28 Dickens, *Old Curiosity Shop*, 136.
29 Dickens, *Old Curiosity Shop*, 136. A bottler is someone who draws crowds and collects money at open-air shows.

of the novel, which emphasize the pair's precarious financial situation and especially Nell's vulnerability as a child responsible for the care of an ailing, foolish, elderly relative, with only occasional moments of relief, *we* feel, for the first time, some lightness as we read about the Punch and Judy actors. Just as it is a kind of trap for the grandfather, it is also a kind of trap Dickens lays for his unwary readers.

Sure enough, the pair of entertainers proves to be a snare for the grandfather and child. The puppeteer Short wonders why they are on their own, apparently running from someone or something. Recognizing the old man's mind wanders and wanting to protect the girl from "'falling into bad hands,'" he concludes he must not let them go their own way. He decides to "'take measures for detainin' of 'em, and restoring 'em to their friends, who I dare say have had their disconsolation pasted up on every wall in London by this time.'" The notion of missing-persons notices plants a thought in Codlin's mind. There might be a reward for their safe return.[30] And so it is that even an initially friendly meeting of strangers poses a threat to the pilgrims. Codlin urges the girl to stay close and be wary of his partner, Short, who, though kind, is not a true friend. This raises Nell's suspicions further, and after looking for an opportune moment during the bustling festival atmosphere of a horse race, she escapes the showmen with her grandfather.[31]

The description of those races, with its games and entertainments, recalls Bunyan's town named Vanity with its year-round fair. The devils Beelzebub, Apollyon, and Legion use the fair to distract pilgrims on their way through the town, distractions that include "Cheats, Games, Plays, Fools . . . and Rogues," among much more.[32] The horse races and merchants, Codlin and Short's puppet play, and their interest in exploiting the travelers all loosely parallel the descriptions of Vanity Fair. Like Christian and his companion Faithful, the attractions of the fair / horse races do not fool Nell, who flees when opportunity presents itself.[33]

---

30 Dickens, *Old Curiosity Shop*, 147, 148.
31 Dickens, *Old Curiosity Shop*, 155, 157.
32 Bunyan, *Pilgrim's Progress*, 86.
33 Unwittingly, Codlin and Short later aid the desperate travelers by providing "the single gentleman" clues to their whereabouts. This gentleman is the estranged younger brother of Nell's grandfather, who seeks to help his kin. The kind Mrs. Jarley's negative assessment of the Punch and Judy actors, and, by extension, activities that go on at horse racing festivals, reinforces the notion that it is a risky place for Nell to be (e.g., Dickens, *Old Curiosity Shop*, 203, 210).

The Arbor and the Schoolmaster

Hints of *The Pilgrim's Progress* continue in other encounters with strangers during Nell and her grandfather's travels. A scene involving the pair stopping to rest in beautiful woods in chapter 24 seems to allude to one of Christian's experiences in that earlier novel. When Christian climbs the hill called Difficulty, he, like Nell, comes across "a pleasant *Arbour*, made by the Lord of the Hill, for the refreshing of weary Travailers," but unlike her, he makes a grievous error by falling into "a slumber" at that spot. It turns out this is serious because it amounts to losing the way of salvation temporarily and results in a terrible delay in his travels.[34] By the time he realizes his mistake and resumes his journey, nightfall approaches. It is now dangerous because beasts "range in the night for their prey."[35] The grandfather is poised to make the same mistake but not so Nell; she finds comfort in the woods, too, but is reluctant to stay: "'while the sun shines above our heads, and everything is bright and happy, we are sitting sadly down, and losing time.'"[36] They must continue, however tired they are. That she "lured the old man on" from that place recalls Christian, who foolishly stayed in the arbor even though it was not intended as a place for sleep. The main parallels and contrasts between *The Pilgrim's Progress* and *The Old Curiosity Shop* at this point are as follows:

The Pilgrim's Progress	*The Old Curiosity Shop*
Mistrust and Timorous are dangerous; Christian does not follow them when they turn back from the difficult road, returning to where they came from instead of persisting in their quest for the Celestial City.[37]	Short and Codlin are dangerous; Nell and her grandfather wisely proceed alone, escaping the actors, who want to end their journey and return them to where they started, namely, "their friends" in London.[38]
Christian finds an "Arbour" for refreshment as he proceeds up the hill called Difficulty.[39]	Nell and her grandfather come to a wood where everything is "bright and happy," a moment of refreshment along the way.[40]

(*Cont.*)

---

34 Bunyan, *Pilgrim's Progress*, 43, 42.
35 Bunyan, *Pilgrim's Progress*, 45.
36 Dickens, *Old Curiosity Shop*, 188.
37 Timorous explains that "they were going to the City of *Zion*, and had got up that *difficult* place; but, said he, the further we go, the more danger we meet with, wherefore we turned, and are going back again" (Bunyan, *Pilgrim's Progress*, 42; italics original).
38 Dickens, *Old Curiosity Shop*, 157, 160.
39 Bunyan, *Pilgrim's Progress*, 42.
40 Dickens, *Old Curiosity Shop*, 188.

The Pilgrim's Progress	*The Old Curiosity Shop*
Christian "fell into a slumber" while in the "Arbour" rather than just resting temporarily.[41]	Unlike Christian and unlike her grandfather, who must be "lured" on, Nell insists they continue, for they are "losing time."[42]
Christian's delay causes distress and puts him in danger; when he continues, he is "made to tread those steps with sorrow, which I might have trod with delight."[43]	Unlike Bunyan's pilgrim, Nell and her grandfather escape despair thanks to their persistence, and they experience the kind of delight Christian missed by slumbering: "The further they passed into the deep green shade, the more they felt the tranquil mind of God was there, and shed its peace on them."[44]
Christian fears the coming of darkness, "for the day is almost spent."[45]	Nell asks a man for assistance because "it would soon be dark."[46]
Christian reaches the palace called Beautiful, "built by the Lord of the Hill; and he built it for the relief and security of Pilgrims."[47]	An old man provides Nell and her grandfather with a safe place to stay the night.[48]
The palace is an allegory for communities of like-minded pilgrims, congregating for encouragement and instruction; they appoint "*Piety* and *Prudence* and *Charity* to discourse with him."[49]	Their host is a schoolmaster, and his home is the school; while there, he teaches Nell an important "lesson."[50]
After providing Christian shelter for the night, the friends in the palace support him as he resumes his journey.	The old teacher supports Nell and her grandfather when they resume their journey.[51]

The encounter with the schoolmaster in the village is a godsend for the desperate pair, and later he again saves their lives and eventually provides a permanent home for them.

---

41 Bunyan, *Pilgrim's Progress*, 42.
42 Dickens, *Old Curiosity Shop*, 188.
43 Bunyan, *Pilgrim's Progress*, 44.
44 Dickens, *Old Curiosity Shop*, 188.
45 Bunyan, *Pilgrim's Progress*, 44.
46 Dickens, *Old Curiosity Shop*, 189.
47 Bunyan, *Pilgrim's Progress*, 47.
48 Dickens, *Old Curiosity Shop*, 189.
49 Bunyan, *Pilgrim's Progress*, 48. Italics original. See, too, W. R. Owens's editorial note, 297.
50 Dickens, *Old Curiosity Shop*, 201.
51 Dickens, *Old Curiosity Shop*, 201–202.

After arriving at the village where the old schoolmaster lives, they learn their kind host is grieving for a dying student. He asks his new friends to stay another day before continuing their "journey," a term used two times in the immediate context of the request.[52] Readers may suspect this is another snare, but unlike the urging of the Punch performers who wish to disrupt their travels, this invitation is no trap. This first episode with the schoolmaster begins in "the deep green shade," where they feel "the tranquil mind of God," and it closes with his final words at their eventual departure—"'God bless you!'"—which serve, in effect, as a benediction.[53] It is a rest along the way, comparable with times of refreshment experienced by Christian during his travels. It is an equivalent to Bunyan's palace called Beautiful, where there is opportunity to be in fellowship with other pilgrims seeking the kingdom of God.

It is also significant the schoolmaster's home is the school itself, and in that place, Nell learns the "lesson of content and gratitude."[54] Having just witnessed the death of young Harry while supporting the schoolmaster during his final visit with the boy, her grief mingles with thankfulness for what little she has—health, freedom, and the company of the one relative she loves. The love between the young dying student—also a grandchild with only a grandparent to mourn his death—and the elderly schoolmaster parallels that between Nell and her own grandfather and foreshadows their ultimate separation. When she dreams of the young scholar "not coffined and covered up" but rather "mingling with angels" and happy, she unwittingly glimpses her own fate.[55]

If Bunyan informs the episode to some extent, a biblical source also contributes to Dickens's portrait of the schoolmaster. When Nell and her grandfather again meet the kindly teacher, the scene recalls one of Jesus's more familiar parables. As that story goes,

> He asked Jesus, "And who is my neighbor?" Jesus replied, "A man was going down from Jerusalem to Jericho and fell into the hands of robbers, who stripped him, beat him, and took off, leaving him half dead. Now by chance a priest was going down that road, and when he saw him he passed by on the other side. So likewise a Levite, when he came to the place and saw him, passed by on the

---

52 Dickens, *Old Curiosity Shop*, 193.
53 Dickens, *Old Curiosity Shop*, 188, 202.
54 Dickens, *Old Curiosity Shop*, 201.
55 Dickens, *Old Curiosity Shop*, 201.

other side. But a Samaritan while traveling came upon him, and when he saw him he was moved with compassion. He went to him and bandaged his wounds, treating them with oil and wine. Then he put him on his own animal, brought him to an inn, and took care of him. The next day he took out two denarii, gave them to the innkeeper, and said, 'Take care of him, and when I come back I will repay you whatever more you spend.'" (Luke 10:30–35)

Nell is desperate at this moment to get her grandfather away from thieving gamblers, who not only conspire to take what little money the old man has in games of chance but who further tempt him to steal so those games might continue. It is because he fell into the hands of robbers, like the victim of the parable, that Nell and her grandfather are left "half dead" on the road they travel. Amid early signs of Nell's illness, and when the situation is dire, the girl dreams of "the little scholar," the boy who died when they were first with the kind schoolmaster, a dream that anticipates their second encounter with that man soon after.[56] On recognizing her, he immediately sees she is gravely ill and takes Nell to an inn for care, asking the innkeeper to provide what they need on the assurance he will pay for it: "'please to take care of her . . . and to understand that I am paymaster for the three'" (i.e., himself, Nell, and the grandfather).[57] The echo of Jesus's parable is hard to miss, especially given that this generous act follows the explicit refusal of others to help the girl: "'Do you think I have charity to bestow, or a morsel of bread to spare?' The child recoiled from the door, and it closed upon her" and, again, Nell "humbly asking for relief at some few doors, and being repulsed."[58] They are Victorian equivalents to Jesus's priest and Levite. Or Woody Guthrie's three churches.

Mrs. Jarley's Waxwork and a Pair of Gamblers

When grandfather and granddaughter leave the schoolmaster after their first meeting, they happen upon another stranger on the road. This time it is the lady of the caravan, Mrs. Jarley. She is having tea on the side of the road when the hungry, tired travelers pass alongside her beautiful wagon. It is clean and pretty, complete with a bright "brass knocker."[59] The narrator specifies she is "a Christian lady" (cf. the association of the Punch and Judy

---

56 Dickens, *Old Curiosity Shop*, 343, 345, 349–350.
57 Dickens, *Old Curiosity Shop*, 359; cf. 349.
58 Dickens, *Old Curiosity Shop*, 348.
59 Dickens, *Old Curiosity Shop*, 202; cf. 205, 207.

actors with the god Pan), but the descriptor is a playful one, considering a few other things we learn about her. Among the tea things is "a bottle of rather suspicious character," and the tea itself possibly accompanied with "just the slightest dash or gleam of something out of the suspicious bottle."[60] Nor is that the last we hear of it. In addition, when she asks her carter, George, about his cold pie and stone bottle of beer, she appears more interested in the latter than the former.[61] Also conspicuous is the lady's pride. She takes great delight in her beautiful caravan, is condescending about performers in Punch and Judy shows, tries to impress Nell with her purported renown as a collector of waxwork, and sits at the window of her caravan "in all the pride and poetry of the musical instruments" hanging on the walls.[62] If we allow the Puritan Bunyan's allegory is an interpretive clue, we may wonder if these subtle mentions of alcohol and pride frame Mrs. Jarley as a threat to pilgrims on a sacred journey, but it turns out she is a friend. She is a Christian *but maybe not as straightforwardly so as we may expect*. She is the flip side of the coin of many of Dickens's portrayals of overt religiosity. The villain Quilp, for instance, attends the Bethel church Kit's mother visits, all the while chuckling to himself "over the joke of his being there at all."[63] As with Guthrie's traveling companions, distinguishing the saints from the sinners is tricky.

Mrs. Jarley eventually offers Nell employment, and the opportunity provides them with temporary reprieve from their difficulties. But it also provides the backdrop for another dangerous encounter. We learn more about the grandfather's deep obsession with gambling at this point in the story. While still with the waxwork show, he and Nell go for a walk when a storm overtakes them. They seek shelter in a public house called the Valiant Soldier and while there overhear some men discussing games of chance. Nell watches alarmed as the old man's appearance changes when he hears it, and he presses Nell to give him whatever money they have so he can play. There are even hints

---

60 Dickens, *Old Curiosity Shop*, 202, 203; see too 205, 208, 222, 247.
61 Dickens, *Old Curiosity Shop*, 206.
62 Dickens, *Old Curiosity Shop*, 208. See, too, 205 (regarding the beautiful caravan), 203, 210 (condescension toward Punch and Judy actors), 209–210 (reputation as a collector of waxwork).
63 Dickens, *Old Curiosity Shop*, 369; cf. 316. The hypocrisy implied by the presence of such a villain amid the flock is consistent with what Wilson refers to as Dickens's "sustained and repeated invective and satire" against "chapel ranters" (*Mystery of Charles Dickens*, 164, cf. 167), the moralizing and fire-and-brimstone type of evangelicals Kit's mother falls in with.

of violence in the description of their interaction: "The hand he laid upon her arm trembled so violently that she shook beneath its grasp.... 'Give [the money] to me, I say,' returned the old man fiercely.... He seized it with the same rapid impatience.... The trembling child followed close behind."[64] His obsession proves so disturbing to the child, she thought it would be better to see him dead than in this state of fixation on gambling.[65] The setting of these games contributes to the atmosphere of this disturbing turn of events. That it was a dangerously stormy night that required them to take refuge in this public house lends a certain foreboding to the scene, as does mention of the devil in the same context.[66] The moral character of the other players is not in question as descriptors like "sinister" and "villainous" and "cunning" attach to them, and though the old man insists the "means of happiness are on the cards and dice," the opposite is clearly the case, marked in the story by the grandfather's neglect of the girl as he plays: "The anxious child was quite forgotten."[67]

Nell later overhears her grandfather conversing with the gamblers Joe Jowl and Isaac List, described in this context as "tempters."[68] They suggest he steal money from Mrs. Jarley's waxwork show so he can continue to play games of chance and potentially recover his losses. Significantly, as though highlighting the threat, one of the men claims to have been brought up "religiously," suggesting he is another wolf in sheep's clothing.[69] The grandfather decides he will steal the money the next day. Nell is so upset knowing her grandfather is about to sink to the level of thievery that she wakes the old man in the night and insists they flee immediately, urging him to pray.[70] The language at this point suggests supernatural intervention breaks the hold gambling has on him; it is the answer to the very prayers for which Nell calls. He looks up at her "as if she were a spirit," and then the old man "rose from his bed ... and, bending before the child as if she had been an angel messenger sent to lead

---

64 Dickens, *Old Curiosity Shop*, 228.
65 Dickens, *Old Curiosity Shop*, 231. For another, near-contemporary depiction of a gambling obsession, see Anne Brontë's *The Tenant of Wildfell Hall*, discussed in chap. 3. It includes a grim account of Lord Lowborough's ruin as he loses his fortune in games of chance and struggles with addiction to laudanum and alcohol (175–186).
66 Dickens, *Old Curiosity Shop*, 226 (storm), 228 (devil).
67 Dickens, *Old Curiosity Shop*, 229, 231.
68 Dickens, *Old Curiosity Shop*, 327. Cf. "temptation" on the same page.
69 Dickens, *Old Curiosity Shop*, 325.
70 Dickens, *Old Curiosity Shop*, 326, 328.

him where she would, made ready to follow her." He then crouches before her "as if in the presence of some superior creature."[71] The resumption of their journey through the "straight streets, and narrow crooked outskirts" recalls Jesus's instruction to take the narrow road (Matt 7:13–14).[72] That the pair "had not once looked behind" and "looked back no more" after their departure is also vaguely biblical (Luke 17:32 with Gen 19:16–17, 26). The old man takes "his staff," recalling Christian, who carries his stave throughout Bunyan's allegory.[73]

Nell is the grandfather's spirit guide and in one sense inhabits a space outside the narrative. She reflects, "'I have saved him,'" phrasing suggesting a spiritual otherness in relation to him.[74] She is not vulnerable to temptations the way he is. He is an "everyman" character, which is presumably one reason Dickens leaves him nameless. As such, he is subject to the bodily and mental decline so often highlighted in the story, as well as temptations to greed and anger and despair. Nell is otherworldly, associated with the angels, who ultimately receive her in death and who are often referenced in comments about her beauty and innocence.

Biographers usually highlight connections between the death of Little Nell at the end of *The Old Curiosity Shop* and Dickens's grief at the death in 1837 of his seventeen-year-old sister-in-law, Mary Hogarth, who lived with her sister and the writer. He was close to her, and she, like Nell, died "Young, Beautiful And Good," and God "Numbered Her With His Angels," which are the words Dickens composed for her London gravestone. In addition to this autobiographical connection, there is also a literary and theological purpose in closing the novel with Nell's death. In *The Pilgrim's Progress*, Christian and Hopeful "left their *Mortal* garments behind them" at the close of the first part of the book.[75] In keeping with this, language throughout *The Old Curiosity Shop* associates Nell with angels: may angels guard her bed, prays her grandfather, a sentiment remembered by a friendly stranger. She dreams of the dead boy Harry "mingling with angels," and she hears angels' wings in her dreams. A boy who loves Nell fears her death and dreads her becoming an angel. Her friend Kit thinks of her as an angel and believes she talks

---

71 Dickens, *Old Curiosity Shop*, 328, 329.
72 Dickens, *Old Curiosity Shop*, 328.
73 Dickens, *Old Curiosity Shop*, 328, 329.
74 Dickens, *Old Curiosity Shop*, 329.
75 Bunyan, *Pilgrim's Progress*, 149.

to them.⁷⁶ The closing illustration in the novel depicts the dead Nell in the company of angels as they escort her to heaven.

That Bunyan describes the culmination of Christian's journey with repeated references to angels accounts for Dickens associating Nell with them. In the earlier book, Christian and Hopeful must pass through the River of Death to reach the Celestial City, something explained to them by "two men [angels], in Raiment that shone like Gold," and once they pass through death, reaching the other side of that terrifying River, "they saw the two shining men again" and soon after "the inumerable [sic] company of Angels."⁷⁷

---

76 Dickens, *Old Curiosity Shop*, 21, 22 (prayers), 201 (dead boy), 397 (wings in dreams), 419 (becoming an angel), 525 (Kit), 549 (talking to angels).

77 Bunyan, *Pilgrim's Progress*, 147, 149.

CHAPTER SEVEN

The Meek Shall Inherit the Earth
Richard Adams's Rabbit Theologians

O Ananias, Azarias, and Misael, bless ye the Lord: praise and exalt him above all for ever: for he hath delivered us from hell, and saved us from the hand of death, and delivered us out of the midst of the furnace and burning flame: even out of the midst of the fire hath he delivered us.
—The Song of the Three Holy Children 1:66 (Dan 3:88), AV[1]

I read the Flannery O'Connor short story "A Circle in the Fire," first published in the *Kenyon Review* in 1954, as a parable of the disruptive nature of reading.[2] Three boys appear at a woman's comfortable farm. One of them

---

1 Taken from Gerald Hammond and Austin Busch, eds., *The English Bible: King James Version*, vol. 2, *The New Testament and the Apocrypha*, Norton Critical Edition (New York: Norton, 2012), 870–871.

2 Flannery O'Connor is a controversial figure. Timothy P. Caron discusses a clear divide between those who focus on theological dimensions of her work while overlooking or excusing the racism that pervades the stories and others who point out this "blind spot" in their criticism ("'The Bottom Rail Is on the Top': Race and 'Theological Whiteness' in Flannery O'Connor's Short Fiction," in *Inside the Church of Flannery O'Connor: Sacrament, Sacramental, and the Sacred in Her Fiction*, ed. Joanne Halleran McMullen and Jon Parrish Peele [Macon, GA: Mercer University Press, 2007], 139; whole chapter 138–164). Caron's point is well taken, and though I don't address O'Connor's troubling views in these few paragraphs, I do discuss racism in chaps. 3 and 4. For further perspectives on O'Connor, race, and theology, see Stanley Hauerwas and Ralph C. Wood, "How the Church Became Invisible: A Christian Reading of American Literary Tradition," in *Invisible Conversations: Religion in the Literature of America*, ed. Roger Lundin (Waco, TX: Baylor University Press, 2009), esp. 171–177. Also instructive is Wood, *Literature and Theology*, chap. 1: "The Scandalous Baptism of Harry Ashfield in Flannery O'Connor's 'The River.'"

previously lived there, his parents being former employees. The boys' presence is mysterious, both unexpected and disconcerting. They refuse to leave, and they are destructive and mischievous. A growing frustration leads Mrs. Cope, who owns the farm, to assert her authority and insist they obey: "'After all,' she said in a suddenly high voice, 'this is my place.'"[3] They ignore her and linger on the property for days, disrupting the orderly rhythms of life there. When the three children set fire to the nearby woods, the story closes with the boys' "wild high shrieks of joy as if the prophets were dancing in the fiery furnace, in the circle the angel had cleared for them."[4] O'Connor refers here to Daniel's three friends, who not only survive when thrown into a furnace by a tyrant but celebrate their God within it.

When Daniel announces Nebuchadnezzar's judgment (4:19–27), he says the king's dominion extends to the distant parts of the earth, a claim echoed in Mrs. Cope's remark about her ownership of the woods, land, and sky. The Jews in that ancient story are defiant of Nebuchadnezzar's rule, so in their own way threaten the *status quo*. In the O'Connor story, Mrs. Cope asserts her rule over the land much as Nebuchadnezzar does, insisting she owns it, but more than once, the boys voice their skepticism. Their defiance leaves her "shocked" and disoriented, "as if she had had a search light thrown on her."[5] The claim to rights, the claim to ownership, is not allowed to stand unquestioned. The children are prophets who unsettle the comfortable and presumptuous. One of the children notes, with reference to Mrs. Cope's farm, "It don't belong to nobody." And again, one insists she does not own the woods or the sky or this place because "'Gawd owns'" it all.[6] Similarly, stories often function prophetically, raising questions about our settled ways and self-assured ideas, challenging dubious assumptions, throwing a searchlight on us.

Prophets defy the establishment. They are iconoclasts. The woman's deepseated fear of fire—an echo of the Daniel story—suggests an awareness that her little farm could disappear in a moment, that her grip on the empire to which she lays claim is tenuous at best. Her young daughter, who threatens to beat up the boys, and the girl's eventual venture into the woods to "hunt" them with her toy guns suggest the impotence of the establishment as it tries

---

3 Flannery O'Connor, "A Circle in the Fire," in *The Complete Stories* (New York: Farrar, Straus and Giroux, 1971), 186. Full story, 175–193.
4 O'Connor, "A Circle in the Fire," 193.
5 O'Connor, "A Circle in the Fire," 186.
6 O'Connor, "A Circle in the Fire," 192, 186.

to maintain order by force and by doing so resist the disrupting activities of the "prophets." As if to emphasize this weakness, O'Connor's boy-prophets happily light the blaze themselves, sparing the Nebuchadnezzar-like Mrs. Cope the trouble. Mrs. Pritchard, who works on the farm, says more than once there is nothing Mrs. Cope can do about the boys' presence except, as her name suggests, cope with it.

In this short story, Black workers on the farm do not respond to Mrs. Cope's orders as she would like, nor do the children leave when she arranges for a milk truck to take them or when she threatens to call the sheriff. The children, Cope's employees, and the Jews in Daniel all ignore an overreaching monarch. A few times in O'Connor's "A Circle in the Fire," there is mention of Jews in Europe carted off in boxcars, alluding to the Shoah, or Holocaust. Though not a storyline developed in any detail, it does involve a loose parallel with Daniel in which an attack on representatives of the Jews, namely, Shadrach, Meshach, and Abednego, fails to destroy the chosen people. The word *holocaust* means destruction by fire. The woman fears fire, something mentioned repeatedly in the story, but the children are safe within the midst of it (last sentence), and O'Connor refers to the Daniel text to express this. The kids' wild, high shrieks of joy and fiery dance signal their rejection of this minor despot. They answer to "Gawd" alone. The three Jews "walked around in the midst of the flames, singing hymns to God and blessing the Lord" (3:24, NRSV, Catholic Edition), and "the three with one voice praised and glorified and blessed God in the furnace" (3:51).[7]

---

7 Greek versions of Daniel include additions, which appear in some canonical traditions. The Roman Catholic O'Connor uses this longer deuterocanonical text, which includes 3:24–45 (inserted between 3:23 and 3:24 of other editions), given the heading "The Prayer of Azariah" in the New Revised Standard Version Catholic Edition, and 3:46–90, titled "The Song of the Three Jews." These additions are important passages for O'Connor, who closes her story by picturing the ecstatic child-prophets dancing joyfully in the flames. Shorter editions of Daniel say nothing about the three Jews' worship of God while in the furnace. Their conflict with Nebuchadnezzar begins when the king orders all to worship a golden statue he sets up (Dan 3:1–7), but the three Jews, Daniel's friends Shadrach, Meshach, and Abednego, refuse to do so (3:8–12), and the celebratory nature of that defiance, elaborated in the Daniel additions, informs O'Connor's conclusion. For helpful backgrounds on these additions to Daniel, see, e.g., David A. deSilva, *Introducing the Apocrypha: Message, Context, and Significance* (Grand Rapids, MI: Baker Academic, 2002), 222–243; and Daniel J. Harrington, *Invitation to the Apocrypha* (Grand Rapids, MI: Eerdmans, 1999), 109–121.

O'Connor the artist creates these three child-prophets. She invents this story of a confrontation between Cope's dominion and God's dominion. In doing so, she suggests art is a form of resistance. Literature, like these boys, is potentially prophetic. One of its functions is to unsettle the comfortable, to challenge assumptions and reveal prejudices. The book we turn to next is unsettling in just this way. It, too, introduces an unlikely prophet and raises questions about what dominion over the earth means.

DOMINION OR DESPOTISM?

*The LORD God took the man, and put him into
the garden of Eden to dress it and to keep it.*
—Genesis 2:15, AV

Rabbits have prophets among them too. That "the man" in this section's epigraph caring for the garden of Eden is called Adam is a happy coincidence as we turn to the English writer Richard Adams (1920–2016). His novel *Watership Down* (1972) is perhaps my favorite book, or at least high on the list, usually contesting with Kenneth Grahame's *Wind in the Willows* (1908) for top honors. It's a bit odd I have such an affection for this story, about a courageous band of rabbits setting out from their warren in Sandleford (southcentral England) in search of a new home, because it makes me anxious. There are reminders of their fragility on each page as they encounter one obstacle after another and one enemy after another, who threatens their very existence. Like Adams's *The Plague Dogs* (1977), another favorite, it is a story of those who are dispossessed and vulnerable and whose survival owes much to the kindnesses of unlikely friends encountered during their journeys. I find both very challenging but equally rewarding. They are, to draw on Harold Bloom's terms, hard-earned pleasures: "Opening yourself to a direct confrontation with Shakespeare at his strongest, as in *King Lear*, is never an easy pleasure, whether in youth or in age, and yet not to read *King Lear* fully (which means without ideological expectations) is to be cognitively as well as aesthetically defrauded."[8] *Watership Down* is difficult, yes, but within the canon of animal literature, there are few better and more deserving to be read "fully."[9]

---

8 Harold Bloom, *How to Read and Why* (New York: Simon & Schuster, 2000), 22–23.
9 For analysis of *The Plague Dogs*, see Gilmour, *Creative Compassion*, 56–72, 118–120. On Adams's memoir *The Day Gone By: An Autobiography* (1990), mentioned below, see 176–182.

But what does a rabbit story have to do with the Bible and faith-motivated service? We are considering ways creative writers call attention to moral blind spots and instances of an empathetic gap. There are many examples in the history of the church of abuses, exclusions, and failures to care—anti-Semitism and racism, misogyny, intolerance of religious others, slavery, abuses toward formerly colonized Indigenous peoples, attempts to stifle and demonize members of the 2SLGBTQI+ community, and much more besides. Among the pressing dilemmas of the times is our collective treatment of the earth. There is no doubt the climate crisis is awakening many in the church to ethical questions about the care of God's good world, and many are developing theological bases for incorporating creation care into religious praxis.[10] Also emerging is an approach to animal ethics rooted in biblical and theological argument. The notion of Christian concern for nature generally and animals specifically has deep roots in the Christian tradition with exemplary figures like St. Francis of Assisi modeling compassion and a positive view of the material world, and yet despite that, the church has been slow to develop its thinking in these areas.[11]

Richard Adams was clear he never meant *Watership Down* "to be some sort of allegory or parable,"[12] though I suspect many readers experience it this way, as a fantastic tale that reveals as much about people as it does its nonhuman characters. I try to keep Adams's remark in view in the following pages, as well as Bloom's caution against reading with "ideological expectations," though I likely overreach on both counts. The results are my impressions on rereading the novel within the parameters of analysis described in the introduction of this book. What, if anything, does this story contribute to *my* understanding of Christian discipleship and biblical ethics?

---

10 For theological perspectives on creation care grounded in biblical exegesis, see, e.g., Richard Bauckham's *The Bible and Ecology: Rediscovering the Community of Creation* (Waco, TX: Baylor University Press, 2010); and *Living with Other Creatures: Green Exegesis and Theology* (Waco, TX: Baylor University Press, 2011).

11 Though a very selective list, among recent work on these topics providing broad orientation to issues involved are Andrew Linzey's *Animal Gospel* (Louisville, KY: Westminster John Knox, 2000); David L. Clough, *On Animals*, vol. 1, *Systematic Theology*; and *On Animals*, vol. 2, *Theological Ethics* (London: T & T Clark, 2012 and 2017). For studies of key thinkers representing a range of religious perspectives, see Andrew Linzey and Clair Linzey, eds., *Animal Theologians* (Oxford: Oxford University Press, 2023).

12 Richard Adams, introduction to the 2005 edition of *Watership Down* (1972; New York: Scribner, 2005), xvi.

Recognizing Bloom's concern about forcing books into predetermined categories and Adams's insistence there is no underlying parallel meaning (parable), I acknowledge my commentary is idiosyncratic, but I trust in keeping with the spirit of the novelist's tale. Adams celebrated nature and wrote movingly of the wonders of plants, insects, birds, and animals. He bemoaned the devastations resulting from human incursions into pristine lands, and this one-time president of the Royal Society for the Prevention of Cruelty to Animals deplored violence against helpless creatures. He traces this interest in advocacy to his childhood reading, with Hugh Lofting's Doctor Dolittle providing him with a role model. He found in those stories "warmth and humor," noting their author "obviously felt real compassion for animals. If I am up to the neck in the animal rights movement today, Dr. Dolittle must answer for it," and again, "there is nothing amiss with the Doctor's passionate concern about the abuse of animals. He turned me against circuses, fur coats and other such evil things—for life."[13]

Nor does reading *Watership Down* through a theological lens seem farfetched.[14] Those familiar with it, and with *The Plague Dogs*, are aware that the species on which these stories focus—rabbits, and dogs and a fox, respectively—have their own mythologies that sometimes parallel the biblical creation narratives. Taking these stories seriously, to read them "fully," as Bloom suggests, encourages reassessment of our own origin myths, which in turn urge respect for nature.

A LEPORINE PROPHET

In his 2005 introduction to *Watership Down*, Adams explains the inspiration for one of the story's heroes, Fiver, comes from the Trojan prophetess Cassandra, who was cursed by Apollo "always to tell the truth and never

---

13 Richard Adams, *The Day Gone By: An Autobiography* (1990; London: Penguin, 1991), 22, 106. For further remarks on Lofting and the Dolittle tales, see the introduction.

14 For a theologian's analysis of the novel, see the opening chapter of Stanley Hauerwas's *A Community of Character: Toward a Constructive Christian Social Ethic* (Notre Dame, IN: University of Notre Dame, 1981), titled "A Story-Formed Community: Reflections on *Watership Down*." The very structure of the novel, he argues, "provides an account of the narrative nature of social ethics that is seldom noticed or accounted for by most political and social theory" (12).

to be believed."¹⁵ The epigraph he uses for the opening chapter reports one occasion this happened:

Chorus: Why do you cry out thus, unless at some vision of horror?
Cassandra: The house reeks of death and dripping blood.
Chorus: How so? 'Tis but the odor of the altar sacrifice.
Cassandra: The stench is like a breath from the tomb.

—Aeschylus, *Agamemnon*¹⁶

Early in the story, Fiver is frantic, certain, though he knows not why, that the warren is doomed, and he pleads with his brother Hazel to do something. Hazel is reluctant but trusts his brother. He agrees to sound the alarm, and they eventually flee the Sandleford warren with any who wish to follow. As is the case with O'Connor's Daniel-inspired children, the eruption of a prophetic voice in an otherwise peaceful place is shocking and unsettling. Life in the warren is orderly, and most of its residents are contented. But the stakes of ignoring the prophet are high. Like Cassandra's disturbing vision, Fiver intuits something undefined but deadly: "'The field! It's covered with blood!' . . . 'It'll come . . . don't think it won't! I tell you, the field's full of blood.'"¹⁷

The curse of Cassandra echoes throughout the story, with Fiver on various occasions forewarning disaster. Most ridicule his second sight, but he is infallible, and those ignoring him do so to their peril. Others survive by heeding the call. So persistent is this Cassandra motif that it not only defines Fiver's relationship with the other rabbits and gives impetus to the unfolding plot, but it defines the reader's relationship to the book. The opening chapter's title—"The Notice Board"—invites them to *notice* warnings contained in the story. Consider the opening sentence of the novel: "The primroses were over." And then consider its closing sentence: "He reached the top of the bank in a single, powerful leap. Hazel followed; and together they slipped away, running easily down through the wood, where the first primroses were beginning to bloom."¹⁸ There is a death-to-life narrative trajectory to the story signaled by the seasonal cycle of these flowers, but only those attending to the notice

---

15 Adams, *Watership Down*, xii.
16 Adams, *Watership Down*, 3.
17 Adams, *Watership Down*, 7.
18 Adams, *Watership Down*, 3, 474.

board escape destruction and reach their promised land. The Cassandra-like Fiver is bound to tell the truth, and those with ears to hear survive, living to see the flowers blossoming in spring. But as a story that touches on humanity's often destructive treatment of nature, there are timely warnings for people as well, prompting consideration of our response to the environmental crisis. Our survival is in question too.

It is strange to insist there are lessons for us in *Watership Down* given there are relatively few mentions of humans in it. They are usually "off stage," their presence implied by things seen or smelled or experienced by the rabbits but not often met directly. Tellingly, there is only one positive interaction with a human character, which I discuss below. The rest are unmistakably negative.

As the story opens, Fiver senses something he describes as oppressive immediately after he and Hazel come upon the notice board. They see heavy posts, reeking of creosote and paint, and other signs of human presence: a hammer with a few nails left behind by workers, a cigarette butt.[19] The description of the sign includes suggestively violent terms. It has "hard straight letters that cut straight as black knives across its white surface," and later, someone compares its markings with thorns.[20] This foreshadows the violence experienced by the rabbits who choose to ignore Fiver's warning and remain in the Sandleford warren after Hazel, his brother, and their followers leave. The rabbits cannot read it, of course, but the sign announces a building project, and the first stage of that work is the gassing of the warren and the slaughter of the rabbits living there.

One survivor of that hellish destruction of the burrows describes the terrifying ordeal of workers stopping up the holes and pumping poisonous gas into the ground. Captain Holly's account is chilling: "'I saw Scabious—you remember Scabious? He came out of a hole along the hedge—one they hadn't noticed.... The men didn't see him for a few moments and then one of them stuck out his arm to show where he was and the boy shot him. He didn't kill him—Scabious began to scream—and one of the men went over and picked him up and hit him.... I wish I hadn't seen it.'"[21] Readers might wish the same, that they hadn't "seen" the episode on the page. But this is one of the ways Adams's books are so effective in awakening concern for animals—and affective. By allowing those entering the story to experience such brutalities

---

19 Adams, *Watership Down*, 6, 7.
20 Adams, *Watership Down*, 8, 44.
21 Adams, *Watership Down*, 154.

from the victims' point of view, he shifts perspective and so disorients readers. We don't just see homebuilders leveling the land and clearing out pests ahead of a construction project; we see named rabbits with personalities, we see other-than-human animals who experience fear and pain. Adams here and elsewhere invites an empathetic connection with nature.

READING RABBITS: AWAKENING RESPECT FOR THE NATURAL WORLD

What literature can do, argues theologian Andrew Linzey, even more than other fields of academic inquiry, "is to reconnect us with the world of animals": "No matter how much we may learn about animals from disciplines such as psychology and biology (for they have much to teach us), that knowledge cannot replace the insights that can come from the disciplined exercise of our imagination."[22]

That the editors of the anthology from which this citation comes are specialists in academic fields other than English literature—Linzey is a theologian, Tom Regan a philosopher—and yet turn to fiction to explore our moral relationships with other animals highlights the unique capacity of storytelling to awaken compassion for other species. Though not anthologized in this collection, Richard Adams's writings are certainly among the best that accomplish that reconnection Linzey describes. But how does he do it, and what, if any, relevance does his story have for a specifically *religious* ethic?

In *Watership Down*, the rabbits are metonymic, representing the whole of nature, and to the extent we see humans in the story, they are almost always viewed as a threat. They are enemies to rabbits just as much as weasels and foxes.[23] We see events through their eyes, a literary device that is usefully disruptive as it exposes attitudes and assumptions that warrant assessment and raises questions not often asked. As suggested, O'Connor's "A Circle of Fire" is a parable of fiction's capacity to unsettle norms, to interrupt habits of thought, to question entrenched beliefs, which is what we find in the Adams's tale. The construction of new homes that the notice board announces is, from

---

22 Andrew Linzey, "Preface," in *Other Nations: Animals in Modern Literature*, ed. Tom Regan and Andrew Linzey (Waco, TX: Baylor University Press, 2010), xviii.

23 The term *enemies* applies to humans a few times. See, e.g., Adams, *Watership Down*, 25.

Fiver's point of view, "oppressive," leading to his vision of a field of blood. Since most readers' sympathies naturally align with the rabbits, it is disorienting to read of people being the "oppressor." Even ordinary activities like building homes are potentially cruel and damaging and quite at odds with the images of Adam in the garden of Eden, tilling the soil and in communion with the animals who approach him (Gen 2:15, 19–20). To engage the novel on its own terms, by which I mean accepting the values it espouses, is humbling. Adams decenters humanity. We discover humanity's story is not the only story. When the rabbits pick up the scent of nearby people, or see their homes or cars, or hear their guns, we fear them, too, because we want these characters to succeed. And if there is a decentering of people, there is a simultaneous centering of other species. For a brief time—the time it takes to read the story—we suspend our fear of / disdain for / indifference toward other creatures and allow them to be the focus of our attention. When good storytellers achieve this, such moments potentially heighten a sense of moral obligation to our nonhuman neighbors. Though sadly neglected in Christian teaching, this shift of our attention seems appropriate. After all, the God of the Bible sends rain to places where no human beings live (see Job 38:27), suggesting a concern for creation independent of the image-bearers. This same God also expresses concern for animals as well as people (see, e.g., Jonah 4:11).

Watership Down does not include many direct references to the Bible, and yet the Bible is everywhere. Sometimes it is subtle, as in the fragment of a psalm that is part of a story one rabbit tells his friends. In it, the beloved hero of rabbit lore, El-ahrairah, begins to quote Psalm 146:3 ("Do not put your trust in princes").[24] Perhaps one reason this psalm is meaningful to El-ahrairah is its inclusivity: "Happy are those whose . . . hope is in the LORD their God, who made heaven and earth, the sea, and *all* that is in them" (146:5–6; italics added). Throughout the novel, we learn about the mythologies that shape the rabbits' worldview, and often they resemble the Genesis creation narratives and include echoes of other biblical texts. El-ahrairah is the most celebrated

---

24 Adams, *Watership Down*, 169. Hauerwas finds the rabbits' habit of telling stories, especially those about El-ahrairah, warrants attention: "We, no less than rabbits, depend on narratives to guide us . . . .. And this is particularly important to Christians, because they also claim that their lives are formed by the story of a prince. Like El-ahrairah, our prince was defenseless against those who would rule the world with violence. He had a power, however, which the world knew not. For he insisted that we could form our lives together by trusting in truth and love to banish the fears that create enmity and discord" (*A Community of Character*, 34–35).

figure in rabbit legends. The Lapine (rabbit language) glossary Adams provides explains he is a "rabbit folk hero" whose name means Prince with a Thousand Enemies, a term appearing in the Psalm fragment he cites.[25] The name first appears in the form of a compliment as Dandelion credits Hazel with being a leader like him. The narrator then explains El-ahrairah is to rabbits what Robin Hood is to the English or John Henry to American slaves and suggests his legendary trickery was possibly known to Odysseus and Brer Rabbit.[26] The stories about El-ahrairah often employ theological language, so the rabbits' practice of relating tales about his adventures amounts to a kind of religious ritual, and the allusions to and quotations of biblical passages ensure readers do not lose sight of this. For instance, in one of those stories, we read repeatedly of El-ahrairah's willingness to give his life for his people. He suffers for them, losing his whiskers, tail, ears, and even tries to take on himself all the diseases rabbits most fear.[27] John 15:13 seems to echo in the background: "No one has greater love than this, to lay down one's life for one's friends."

The epigraph for chapter 41, which includes a rabbit storytelling performance, invites us to consider Bluebell's tale an instance of this kind of religious ritual. The epigraph appears as follows in the novel:

> *Be not merciful unto them that offend of malicious wickedness. They grin like a dog and run about through the city. But thou, O Lord, shalt have them in derision. Thou shalt laugh all the heathen to scorn.*
>
> Psalm 59[28]

This is Psalm 59:5–8 as it appears in the Anglican *Book of Common Prayer*, with slightly adjusted punctuation and elisions. The full passage Adams cites as it appears in the *Book of Common Prayer* is as follows, with the lines he omits underlined: "<u>Stand up, O LORD God of hosts, thou God of Israel, to visit all the heathen, and</u> be not merciful unto them that offend of malicious wickedness. <u>They go to and fro in the evening,</u> they grin like a dog, and run about through the city. <u>Behold, they speak with their mouth, and swords are in their lips; for who doth hear?</u> But thou, O LORD, shalt have them in derision<u>, and</u> thou shalt laugh all the heathen to scorn."

---

25 Adams, *Watership Down*, 475.
26 Adams, *Watership Down*, 24.
27 Adams, *Watership Down*, 271–279.
28 Adams, *Watership Down*, 394. The layout is Adams's.

Adams's edits make sense in context. The phrase *God of Israel* is too narrow for a rabbit myth because it is *their* story told in this chapter, not Israel's. Furthermore, the distinction of those believing in Israel's God as opposed to other spiritualities (heathen) does not appear relevant as there are no rival worldviews depicted, which may account for the downplaying of that idea (i.e., by omission of the first mention of "the heathen"). The reference to enemies moving to and fro in the evening is perhaps not pertinent because those they consider enemies do not threaten only at certain times of the day. The enemies' words ("they speak") are of no concern to rabbits; it's their teeth and claws and guns that really matter. That the psalm equates Israel's enemies with dogs two times, at 59:6 in the epigraph and also at 59:14, is fitting because the story told about El-ahrairah in this chapter concerns a canine enemy. What is a simile in the psalm, with human enemies grinning like dogs, is literalized by the rabbits in their version of the story about "the most objectionable, malicious, disgusting [canine] brute," named Rowsby Woof.[29] Rabbits worry about actual dogs. This process of editing a psalm in this context creates a same-yet-different effect. Of course, rabbits are not people. They are not like the ancient Israelites who produced the psalm in the first place. But they are created beings who worship their creator in their own way, and so it is the language and imagery associated with worship reflects their form of being.

On the Creation of Rabbits

Though not part of the explanation provided in the novel's glossary, the opening El of the name El-ahrairah is suggestive, recalling a Hebrew term meaning "god" or "gods" (pl. Elohim). This loosely connects the rabbits' tales about their hero to those of the God of the Bible, and indeed, in accounts of El-ahrairah's exploits, this connection is obvious. Hazel asks Dandelion to tell the frightened group of rabbits who recently left their home warren a story to inspire them and give them courage.[30] The one he chooses begins with the declaration that Frith made the world. *Frith* means "sun," and is personified as a god by the rabbits, according to the glossary Adams provides. As in Genesis 1, this creator made the stars and the animals and the birds and also controls the waters. Like Isaiah 11:6–8, where we read of wolf and lamb, leopard and goat, calf and lion, cow and bear, and human infant and

---

29 Adams, *Watership Down*, 396.
30 Adams, *Watership Down*, 25–29.

snake cohabitating peacefully, and like Genesis 1:30, which says the creator provided green plants for all creatures to eat, so, too, in Frith's new world there is peace between those who later became enemies. All eat the abundant vegetation: "The sparrow and the kestrel were friends and they both ate seeds and flies. And the fox and the rabbit were friends and they both ate grass."[31] This scene is reminiscent of No Man's Land in *Doctor Dolittle's Post Office*, described by the piffilosaurus (see the introduction). There are other echoes of the biblical prehistory. El-ahrairah is guilty of a Babel-like hubris, "boasting" of his power and defying Frith (cf. Gen 11:1–9), which amounts to a fall. The result is banishment from a peaceful garden (cf. Gen 3:1–24). Frith looks for the hiding El-ahrairah just as God looks for the hiding Adam and Eve (Gen 3:8–9), and Dandelion's story tells of the rabbits "multiplying" and "wandering everywhere" (cf. Gen 1:22, 28; 8:17; 9:1, 7). He describes the creator Frith resting (cf. Gen 2:2–3), declaring, "'Be it so!'" (cf. "And it was so," Gen 1:7, 9, 11, 15, 24, 30), and promising never again to destroy all (cf. Gen 9:11, 15). Elsewhere, a story about El-ahrairah relates his interactions with Prince Rainbow, who "had the power of the sky and the power of the hills." As in Genesis, where we read of God setting the rainbow in the sky for a specific purpose (9:9–17), so here, Dandelion explains, the creator Frith appointed Prince Rainbow "to order the world as he thought best."[32] There is another, more direct allusion to the Noah story as well. One tale has the creator Frith going away on a journey, leaving the whole world to be covered with rain: "But a man built a great floating hutch that held all the animals and birds until Frith returned and let them out."[33]

A foundational belief of biblical religion is the origin of people in the creative acts of God, who "created humankind in his image, in the image of God he created them; male and female he created them" (Gen 1:27). It is a wonder God is mindful of human beings, writes the psalmist: "Yet you have made them a little lower than God, and crowned them with glory and honour" (Ps 8:4–5). But Adams's inclusion of an alternative origin story with its echoes of what some readers consider sacred texts disrupts the idea that humans *alone* matter. Through this device, he creates an imaginative space in which rabbits view themselves as the theological poets just cited view people.

---

31 Adams, *Watership Down*, 26.
32 Adams, *Watership Down*, 93, cf. 167.
33 Adams, *Watership Down*, 208.

Here and throughout, I argue fiction nurtures attitudes and values consistent with biblical ethics, and in this case, the story challenges the view that animals are meaningless, mere pests to be tolerated or exterminated, as though dominion over the earth were synonymous with despotism. In this literary world, rabbits are meaning-full, to the point they see themselves as an integral part of the creator's work, and to be sure, this is in keeping with the biblical story: "God saw *everything* that he had made, and indeed, it was very good" (Gen 1:31, italics added); "He [Christ] is the image of the invisible God, the firstborn of *all* creation; for in him *all* things in heaven and on earth were created . . . *all* things have been created through him and for him" (Col 1:15–16, italics added).

St. Paul and the Acts of the Animals

One of the direct references to the Bible in *Watership Down* achieves a similar effect to the creation myth told by Dandelion.[34] Chapter 8 is titled "The Crossing," and it relates the story of the band of rabbits escaping disaster as they realize a roaming dog is nearby. They are between it and the bank of a small river. Some of them can swim but not all. The smaller rabbits Fiver and Pipkin, the latter injured, are too weak to cross. While precariously caught between the dog and the flowing water, Blackberry sees a piece of wood floating and recognizes it is a possible means of escape: "'It must have drifted down the river. So it floats. We could put Fiver and Pipkin on it and make it float again. It might cross the river.'"[35] The situation is desperate, but they get Fiver and Pipkin on the makeshift raft, and some of the others push it to safety on the other side.

For an epigraph to this chapter, Adams cites Acts 27:43–44 in the Authorized Version: "The centurion . . . commanded that they which could swim should cast themselves first into the sea, and get to land. And the rest, some on boards and some on broken pieces of the ship. And so it came to pass, that they escaped all safe to land." The story related in chapter 8 follows that pattern, with those able to swim going ahead while those who cannot floating

---

34 There is also indirect theological content concerning animals. One of the epigraphs for chap. 21 is an excerpt from Dostoevsky's *The Brothers Karamazov* (1880): "Love the animals. God has given them the rudiments of thought and joy untroubled. Don't trouble it, don't harass them, don't deprive them of their happiness, don't work against God's intent" (Adams, *Watership Down*, 150).

35 Adams, *Watership Down*, 37.

to safety on that piece of wood. What interests me here is the effect on readers who know the story Luke relates in Acts 27. This chapter tells of the apostle Paul's harrowing journey to Rome after he appeals to the emperor (see Acts 25:11–12; 26:31–32). It was not an easy voyage: "The winds were against us" (27:4); "We sailed slowly for a number of days . . . as the wind was against us" (27:7); "Sailing past [Crete] with difficulty" (27:8); "Much time had been lost and sailing was now dangerous" (27:9); "'Sirs, I [Paul] can see that the voyage will be with danger and much heavy loss'" (27:10). This series of setbacks culminates in a terrible storm that runs the ship against a reef, after which the waves break up what remains of it (27:13–44). But all is not lost.

The first-person narrator, traditionally St. Luke, relates the moment of deepest despair: "When neither sun nor stars appeared for many days, and no small tempest raged, all hope of our being saved was at last abandoned" (27:20). It is at this point a miracle occurs. Paul speaks to the crew and his fellow prisoners, announcing that an angel of God stood by him and, furthermore, that God has granted safety to all those who sail with him (27:23–24). As the storm continues to rage, he reminds them many days later, "'None of you will lose a hair from your heads'" (27:34). Sure enough, the episode concludes with the narrator affirming, "And so it was that all were brought safely to land" (27:44).

God rescues the renowned apostle Paul and all those traveling with him. Adams's explicit alignment of the apostle's sea voyage with the rabbits' river crossing subtly dignifies his furry heroes, suggesting they, too, have worth, and they, too, are worthy of an unlikely, even miraculous, deliverance. Like the narrator of Acts, Adams's rabbits similarly feared they were doomed: "Hazel felt at a loss. . . . Then he looked at Pipkin, huddled into a fold of sand, more panic-stricken and helpless than any rabbit he had ever seen."[36] But the story does not end there, of course. Adams does not need to say it directly, but the unexpected appearance of that "piece of flat wood" floating down the river, that equivalent of the "pieces of the ship" the prisoners in Acts use to get safely out of the sea, is God-sent. God chooses to rescue the mighty apostle Paul through a hunk of wood and chooses to rescue two fragile rabbits the same way.[37]

---

36 Adams, *Watership Down*, 36.
37 Another example of apparent supernatural intervention, from the rabbits' point of view, occurs in a daring escape from the despotic General Woundwort. Bigwig warns the General that Frith sees his evil actions and in the same moment interprets the storm that rages as a form of divine aid (Adams, *Watership Down*, 359).

Just like the rabbits' creation story, the river crossing borrows a theological vocabulary to assert the animals' worth. God makes them and saves them. As we read, as we suspend disbelief for a short while, we enter an imaginative space that encourages us to consider animals differently than we might otherwise. Here, *they* are the heroes of the story, and *they* are the ones favored by God and afforded the dignity God's favor implies. This kind of reading experience potentially—maybe, just maybe—encourages us to pause before deliberately harming a rabbit. They matter too.

The Mortality and Afterlife of Rabbits

"Come away, come away death," sings the clown Feste in Shakespeare's *Twelfth Night*, "and in sad cypress let me be laid. / Fie away, fie away breath, / I am slain by a fair cruel maid. / My shroud of white, stuck all with yew, O prepare it" (2.4.50–55). The sad cypress coffin, like the sprigs from the yew tree on the shroud, is emblematic of death and mourning.[38] In *Watership Down*, the yew tree features prominently in chapters 14–17, which document a terrifying sequence of events conspicuously associated with human activity.

"Few trees," writes Thomas W. Laquer, "were so rooted in the deep time of the dead."[39] Laquer refers to "the long-lived European yew tree—*Taxus baccata*, the tree of the dead, the tree of poisonous seeds—that bears witness to the antiquity of the churchyard. . . . The yew of legend is old and lays claim to immemorial presence."[40] The yew tree took root in the mythologies of classical Greece and Rome and even in the lore of earliest Christianity, associated as it is with the passion of Christ, Ash Wednesday, and Palm Sunday.[41] Thomas Gray's 1751 poem about a church cemetery offers a further example of the trees' connection to Christian death rituals and reflection of them in the arts: "Beneath those rugged elms, / that yew tree's shade, / Where heaves the turf

---

38 See, e.g., the editorial notes in *Twelfth Night, The Arden Shakespeare*, ed. J. M. Lothian and T. W. Craik (1975; London: Thomson, 2006), 58n. 52; and *The Norton Shakespeare*, 2nd ed., ed. Stephen Greenblatt et al. (New York: Norton, 2008), 1812n. 5.

39 Thomas W. Laquer, *The Work of the Dead: A Cultural History of Mortal Remains* (Princeton, NJ: Princeton University Press, 2015), 135.

40 Laquer, *Work of the Dead*, 133.

41 Laquer, *Work of the Dead*, 135.

in many a moldering heap, / Each in his narrow cell forever laid, / The rude forefathers of the hamlet sleep."[42]

Assuming references to the yew tree in *Watership Down* carry the association of death and mourning just described, the imagery seems out of place at this point in the story because the rabbits just arrived at a peaceful warren and one that is a possible new home for them. In these chapters, Hazel, Fiver, and Bigwig meet a rabbit named Cowslip, who invites the travelers to join their warren. Fiver, however, is suspicious from the outset, recommending they have nothing to do with the strangers, and once inside, he sits alone, away from them.[43] This warren is large and dry but also strange. Its most conspicuous feature is a burrow larger than any they've seen before, "with several tree roots running across the roof and it was these that supported the unusual span [of the hall]."[44]

Fiver alone is wary of Cowslip and the others living there. As noted, he is a Cassandra-like prophet whose messages go unheeded. He refuses to stay in the warren overnight, and when Hazel later finds him, Fiver "was sitting half concealed under the low spread of a yew tree."[45] He later recalls his dark visions while "under the yew tree."[46] Fiver knows there is "something unnatural and evil twisted all round this place" and that "the man," the nearby farmer who leaves food out for the rabbits, has something to do with the doom he senses. His use of the word "twisted" and mention of "*wire* netting" in remarks about "the man" clearly foreshadow the snaring of Bigwig a few pages later.[47] Fiver also explains why the great open hall in the warren frightens him: "'I tell you [Hazel] I'll have nothing to do with the place. . . . The roof of that hall is made of bones.'"[48] Hazel insists they're not bones but roots, but he fails to understand the prophet's message. Yew trees are a commonplace in European graveyards, so the mingling of their roots with the bones of the dead makes this an appropriate descriptor for Fiver's vague fears of certain death. When Fiver explains he'd rather be outside this terrifying burrow, sitting where he is—"'A yew

---

42 Thomas Gray, "Elegy Written in a Country Churchyard," in *The Norton Anthology of English Literature*, 10th ed., vol. C, *The Restoration and the Eighteenth Century* (New York: Norton, 2018), 998. Full poem, 998–1001.
43 Adams, *Watership Down*, 68, 75.
44 Adams, *Watership Down*, 73.
45 Adams, *Watership Down*, 87.
46 Adams, *Watership Down*, 151.
47 Adams, *Watership Down*, 88. Italics added.
48 Adams, *Watership Down*, 89.

tree gives good shelter, you know'"⁴⁹—instead of going below ground, he is, in effect, the visitor to a cemetery contented to be above ground, mourning the dead who are below, among the bones and roots, which is to say the residents of this warren. The connection between the bones and the roots continues. Hazel later dreams of "the roof made of bones," and when Fiver gives a great speech warning against taking over the warren for themselves, he insists it would mean taking "'a roof of bones, hung with shining wires!'"⁵⁰ One such shining wire almost kills Bigwig, and the description of the near-fatal injuries he sustains recalls the prophet's chosen tree: "The projecting point of one strand of [the snare wire] had lacerated his neck and drops of blood, dark and red as *yew* berries, welled one by one down his shoulder."⁵¹

By weaving yew tree symbolism into a rabbit story, symbolism so widely associated with rituals of mourning, Adams seems to invite readers to treat the death of all creatures with appropriate gravitas. But he doesn't stop there. A further way Adams uses a theological vocabulary to lend his rabbits dignity is by the inclusion of a form of afterlife. It is understated but elegant. *Watership Down* closes with the sad but sweet account of Hazel's death. While he dozes and dreams, a buck enters his burrow and asks Hazel if he recognizes him: "'Yes, my lord,' he said. 'Yes, I know you.'" The stranger knows Hazel has been "'feeling tired,'" and says he can help, and invites the hero to join his Owsla, the ruling circle: "'We shall be glad to have you and you'll enjoy it. If you're ready, we might go along now.'"⁵² Though not named, we recognize the stranger to be El-ahrairah, the rabbit folk hero featured in the species' mythology as a favorite of Frith, the sun god. As they leave the burrow together, Hazel realizes "he would not be needing his body any more, so he left it lying on the edge of the ditch." He watches his friends on Watership Down as they pass, and the stranger tells him, "'You needn't worry about them. . . . They'll be all right—and thousands like them. If you come along, I'll show you what I mean.'"⁵³ Together they slip away, running easily through the woods and primroses. Adams thus challenges the view that rabbits are expendable. Their lives have meaning, too, from their origin in the creative acts of a god through to fullness of purpose ("'join my Owsla'") and peace

---

49 Adams, *Watership Down*, 89.
50 Adams, *Watership Down*, 106, 117.
51 Adams, *Watership Down*, 110. Italics added.
52 Adams, *Watership Down*, 474.
53 Adams, *Watership Down*, 474.

("'you'll enjoy it'") in the afterlife. The fantasy invites a shift in perspective. To accept the narrative logic of the story is to see beauty and value in burrows and primroses. Perhaps it even encourages a fresh look at Genesis 1:24, challenging us to take the words more seriously than is often our habit: "And God said, 'Let the earth bring forth living creatures of every kind: cattle and creeping things and wild animals of the earth of every kind.' And it was so. God made the wild animals of the earth of every kind, and the cattle of every kind, and everything that creeps upon the ground of every kind. And God saw that it was good."

Empathizing with Rabbits

If Adams is successful in convincing readers to pause and consider the plight of rabbits and other species, if only for the moments we hold the book in our hands, it is also possible his depictions of some human activities present themselves to us as morally suspect. In addition to the environmental degradation and cruelty to rabbits evident in the clearing of the Sandleford warren, there are scenes involving the hunting of rabbits that are difficult to read owing to their graphic nature and Adams's effective use of a more-or-less unfamiliar point of view. We experience the hunts, so to speak, along with the rabbits. We see it through their eyes, not those of the hunters. The ones doing the snaring and shooting are not the focus. As characters in a story, they are flat compared with the rabbits and decentered as the focus of our attention.

Adams generates empathy for the anthropomorphized animals by depicting their physical and emotional distresses, friendships, sense of community, and longing for peace and flourishing in forms readers recognize. We see something of ourselves in them. We saw already that even their sense of cohesion as a species, even among rabbits from different warrens, is the result of a shared story, a grand narrative that encompasses them all, a myth of origin that provides a sense of purpose and a way of making sense of their surroundings. This recognition of a shared creaturely experience—we, too, hunger and thirst, love and hate, and grow old and die—is one way Adams urges compassion for other species. Another is by showing ways we harm them. We are among the *elil*, or enemies, to use their language, one of *u harair*, or the thousand, a collective term for all who harm rabbits.[54] They

---

54 Adams, *Watership Down*, 4n.

face enemies within the natural world, of course, like the crow and fox. There are several examples of encounters with predators.[55] Humans, however, are the most dangerous of the *elil*, and Adams seems to stress the horrors they inflict. One emotively charged instance of this is an episode involving a trap specifically designed to catch rabbits.

> Bigwig was lying on his side, his back legs kicking and struggling. A length of twisted copper [snare] wire, gleaming dully in the first sunlight, was looped round his neck and ran taut across one forepaw to the head of a stout peg driven into the ground. The running knot had pulled tight and was buried in the fur behind his ear. The projecting point of one strand had lacerated his neck and drops of blood, dark and red as yew berries, welled one by one down his shoulder. For a few moments he lay panting, his side heaving in exhaustion. Then again began the struggling and fighting, backward and forward, jerking and falling, until he choked and lay quiet.[56]

Adams lingers over the rabbit's injuries in this episode, which is nine pages long, and then reminds readers of it later in the story. Bigwig survives, but owing to his past injuries, he is more vulnerable to predators: "The snare had left him weak and overwrought"; "They were all on edge. . . . Bigwig and Buckthorn smelled of blood."[57] The same is true of Hazel, who recovers after a farmer shoots him. He carries the consequences of his wounds for the rest of his life: "'Yes, he *has* got something the matter with that leg, you see,' said Doctor Adams. 'But he could perfectly well live for years, as far as that goes.'"[58] We wince at moments in the story when animals bleed because we bleed, too, and empathize with their pains. But Adams does not let us forget those wounds are human-caused.

His descriptions of Bigwig's injuries and distress in the chapter titled "The Shining Wire" are graphic (struggling, lacerated, panting, choked, etc.) and emotionally charged in the account of his friends' frantic, panicked efforts to help. Also emphasized is the power difference between the human hunter (a gun, a metal wire) and the fragile rabbits' bodies. The hunter even resorts to trickery. He manipulates the wild rabbits in the nearby warren by feeding them to keep them close by. He also shoots animal predators to lull rabbits

---

55 See, e.g., Adams, *Watership Down*, 41–43, which tells of a crow attacking Fiver and Pipkin.
56 Adams, *Watership Down*, 110.
57 Adams, *Watership Down*, 123, 125.
58 Adams, *Watership Down*, 459.

into a false sense of security. It is ultimately a trap because he sets snares in the area to ensure a regular supply of meat and fur. As noted, before they reach the area with the snare, Fiver is wary. He anticipates "mysterious trouble" that involves "being deceived."[59] Before we learn any of the hunter's strategy, Hazel and the others observe a strangeness about their hosts in this warren. The first one they encounter, Cowslip, baffles them as they observe his "unnatural gentleness" and "unusual smell." Furthermore, his demeanor "had a kind of melancholy which was perplexing," and a manner that was "strange, clouded."[60] This stress on their unusual behavior recurs throughout this episode: "Hazel felt oddly perplexed"; "'There *is* something strange about these rabbits.'"[61] Adams makes clear the actions of this hunter-farmer, and by extension all instances of human interference with nature, are destructive and cruel.[62]

As we read about the damage caused to the snared Bigwig, we come to dread the appearance of that human hunter. There is stress on the "humanness" of this elaborate trapping scheme: a snare wire fastened to a "man-smelling peg"; "the man would come soon. Perhaps he was already coming, with his gun, to take poor Bigwig away." As Fiver put it, that whole man-manipulated warren is a "'death hole,'" snares everywhere, every day.[63] Reading about broken animal bodies is a reminder we, too, are creatures of flesh and blood, and in that moment of recognition, there is the possibility of ethical reflection. Adams's disdain for humanity's indifference and cruelty toward animals is unmistakable. The rabbit Captain Holly seems to reflect the author's views when he says, "'All other elil do what they have to do, and Frith moves them as he moves us. They live on the earth and they need food. Men will never rest till they've spoiled the earth and destroyed the animals.'"[64] At the same time, Adams acknowledges people's capacity to protect and show compassion to other species, and the one beautiful example of this in the novel deserves notice.

---

59 Adams, *Watership Down*, 53.

60 Adams, *Watership Down*, 63, 66. There are repeated examples of ways this manipulated group of rabbits differs in terms of their behavior and worldview compared with Hazel and his followers (see 62–118).

61 Adams, *Watership Down*, 76. 81. Italics original. On another occasion, Hazel and his friends meet rabbits kept in cages on a farm, and they, too, act in ways strange to those born in the wild. See, e.g., Adams, *Watership Down*, 216, 217.

62 Cf. the account of a farmer shooting Hazel and the lingering injuries resulting from it (*Watership Down*, 222, 243–247, etc.).

63 Adams, *Watership Down*, 112, 113, 115.

64 Adams, *Watership Down*, 115.

A Model of Human Kindness to Other Species

The title of chapter 48 is "*Dea ex Machina*," the feminine form of the more familiar term *deus ex machina*, a god from a machine. The term refers to the ancient Greek theater when some dramatists arranged for a god to be lowered onto the stage by a mechanical apparatus. The god resolves whatever dilemmas characters in the play face. By extension, a *deus ex machina* now refers to an author's unlikely solution to plot difficulties. Adams uses the feminine form as his title because "the god" introduced is a farm girl named Lucy Cane, who rescues Hazel from a cat and then, with the family doctor's help, takes him back home to Watership Down.[65] That this literary device refers to an *unlikely, improbable* resolution (as the term *deus ex machina* usually indicates) is telling. By this point, late in the novel, readers do not expect an act of kindness from a human. Lucy is the first to show concern toward any of the rabbits in Hazel's band.[66] The significance of the moment is highlighted further by the presence of the family's physician, Dr. Adams, who visits the girl's home. This is certainly the author's playful way of writing himself into the story. He does the same thing in *The Plague Dogs*.[67] Dr. Adams encourages the child's natural inclination to be kind to animals, just as Richard Adams the author encourages readers to do through his fiction.

---

65 Adams, *Watership Down*, 456, 459.

66 The only exception is a passing remark about someone caring for the orphaned General Woundwort when he was a youngster (Adams, *Watership Down*, 304). Regarding Lucy's role in the story, Lisa Sainsbury observes, "In a book which on the whole renders humanity an acquisitive and brutal enemy of the land it seems significant, considering that editions continue to be published for children, that hope is carried by a human child" (*Ethics in British Children's Literature: Unexamined Life*, Perspectives on Children's Literature [London: Bloomsbury, 2013], 121). For Sainsbury's analysis of the novel, see 111–122, 127–131.

67 In *The Plague Dogs*, Adams is playfully self-effacing as one character chides the author's rabbit book: "'Well-intentioned amateurs like that chap Richard Adams—fond of the country—reasonably good observer—knows next to nothing about rabbits—hopelessly sentimental—everyone starts thinking rabbits are marvellous when what they really need is keeping down if they're not to become an absolute pest to the farmer'" (*The Plague Dogs* [1977; Toronto: Vintage, 2016], 485–486). The charge does not go unchallenged. Another character comes to the defense of such sentimentality. For more on this scene from *The Plague Dogs*, see the discussion in Gilmour, *Creative Compassion*, 56–72. Part of the joke in the excerpt just cited is that the speaker is Ronald Lockley, a real-life ornithologist and naturalist whose research on rabbits is one of Adams's sources for *Watership Down*, as he explains in his acknowledgments (unnumbered page, front matter). He cites or summarizes Lockley's research at four points in the novel itself.

THE MEEK SHALL INHERIT THE EARTH

By means of this self-reference, Adams the author signals the values he holds with respect to human-animal relations and those he urges on those immersed in *Watership Down*. When Lucy first rescues Hazel, she holds the injured rabbit and explains to her father that she wants to show him to Dr. Adams: "She knew that Doctor thought of her as a proper farm girl—a country girl. When she showed him things she had found—a goldfinch's egg, a Painted Lady fluttering in a jam jar or a fungus that looked exactly like orange peel— he took her seriously and talked to her as he would to a grown-up person. To ask his advice about a damaged rabbit and discuss it with him would be very grown-up."[68] Her father is reluctant but allows the girl to keep the rabbit until the doctor comes. Dr. Adams, as mentioned, takes the girl to Watership Down, where they release Hazel, not realizing, of course, it is the rabbit's home.[69] Hazel's account of the events leading to his safe return seems improbable to the others; they have a hard time believing it because the very idea of people being kind to rabbits is too fantastic.[70] The scene affirms an inclination to be compassionate toward animals and to support wildlife whenever possible.

There are occasional moments when Adams comments directly on harms to nature resulting from human actions. In one such aside, he mentions the increasing noise in our world, which is "too high" for some species to tolerate. In the last half century, he continues, "the silence of much of the country has been destroyed."[71] This kind of direct address is rare. Far more effective is the atmosphere Adams creates in which the wonders and fragility of the animals and grasses and flowers and trees and insects speak for themselves. Our admiration for them swells, and awareness of our callousness and indifference, even cruelty, increases at the same time. Perhaps, I imagine Adams hoping, readers allowing themselves to visit Watership Down in imagination will choose to tread more lightly in the places where they live.

A PARABLE

As mentioned, Richard Adams insisted he never meant *Watership Down* to be allegorical or parabolic. It's just a story. However, as I draw these few notes

---

68 Adams, *Watership Down*, 456–457.
69 Adams, *Watership Down*, 459.
70 Adams, *Watership Down*, 463–464. For Bigwig, the idea of Hazel riding in a "hrududu," a motor vehicle, is the most difficult part of the story to believe.
71 Adams, *Watership Down*, 130.

on the book to a close, I stray into a deliberate misreading of this rabbits' tale, much as I did with Flannery O'Connor's "A Circle in the Fire." Parables are, to use one standard textbook definition, short fictional stories, or vignettes, "illustrating a moral or spiritual lesson."[72] Most associate the term with the New Testament Gospels because it was Jesus's preferred way of communicating with followers, which is why I turn to a biblical studies textbook for a definition. As another puts it, "Jesus' teaching about the kingdom frequently took the form of punchy and pointed stories, which (following the gospel-writers themselves) we call 'parables'. Nor were they simply childish illustrations, earthly stories with heavenly meanings. . . . They were explanations for actions, invitations to new perspectives, and even weapons of political discourse designed to shock as much as to inform. The parables were centred on God, God's people, and God's word."[73] Even definitions in reference works outside biblical studies recognize the connection to the Gospels: "A parable is a very short narrative about human beings presented so as to stress the tacit analogy, or parallel, with a general thesis or lesson that the narrator is trying to bring home to his audience. The parable was one of Jesus' favorite devices as a teacher; examples are his parables of the good Samaritan and of the prodigal son."[74]

I realize the risk of reading far too much into Adams's choice of terms in his introduction to the 2005 edition of *Watership Down*, but it's one I take just the same. The phrase in question goes as follows: "I want to emphasize that *Watership Down* was never intended to be some sort of allegory or parable. It is simply the story about rabbits made up and told in the car [to my young daughters]."[75] What interests me is the redundancy of this sentence with his inclusion of both "allegory" and "parable." Abrams and Harpham, writing for students of literature and literary criticism, define *allegory* as a narrative in which "the agents and actions, and sometimes the setting as well, are contrived by the author to make coherent sense on the 'literal,' or primary, level of signification, and at the same time to communicate a second, correlated order of signification." A parable, they go on to explain, like a fable, an

---

72 Mark L. Strauss, *Four Portraits, One Jesus: A Survey of Jesus and the Gospels*, 2nd ed. (Grand Rapids, MI: Zondervan, 2020), 642.
73 N. T. Wright and Michael F. Bird, *The New Testament in Its World: An Introduction to the History, Literature, and Theology of the First Christians* (Grand Rapids, MI: Zondervan, 2019), 204.
74 Abrams and Harpham, *A Glossary of Literary Terms*, 11.
75 Adams, *Watership Down*, xvi.

exemplum, or some proverbs, is a "species of allegory" but distinctive in its length.[76] They illustrate the broader umbrella term *allegory* with reference to longer works such as John Dryden's *Absalom and Achitophel* (1681), John Bunyan's *The Pilgrim's Progress* (1678), and the third book of Jonathan Swift's *Gulliver's Travels* (1726), about the voyage to Laputa and Lagado. When they illustrate parable within the same entry, they emphasize it is "a very short narrative" and use Jesus's "terse" parable of the fig tree (Luke 13:6–9) as their illustration.[77]

Strauss also distinguishes allegory and parable. At times, he explains, assuming the terms are one and the same has resulted in overly elaborate readings of Jesus's parables, noting Augustine's colorful interpretation of the story of the good Samaritan as an example. "While most parables are not allegories," he concludes, "many parables have allegorical elements, especially those parables related to Jesus' preaching about the kingdom of God."[78] Many prefer to think of parables as similitudes or extended similes, some with and some without allegorical meanings. Furthermore, as Wright and Bird's definition makes clear, Jesus's parables addressed weighty subject matter, not "simply childish illustrations."

Adams refuses the term *parable*, but it wouldn't have suited anyway, even if he meant the story to be read as one. *Watership Down* is not "a very short narrative" (Abrams and Harpham), but is instead a very long novel, well over 450 pages in the 2005 Scribner edition. So why did he introduce the word? The point he makes in that introduction is clear. Don't overthink it. It's just a story. An elaborate allegorizing interpretation strategy is not necessary. But the word *allegory* in that note to the reader would have been sufficient to make that point. So why add the other term? I suspect Adams adds the word *parable* in that note because of its association with the teachings of Jesus and especially because so many of the Gospel teachings grouped under the heading *parables* capture quintessential values embedded in the novel. Parables illustrate "a moral or spiritual lesson," as Strauss puts it, and by introducing

---

76 Abrams and Harpham, *A Glossary of Literary Terms*, 8, 10. Cf., e.g., the entry on parable in X. J. Kennedy, Dana Gioia, and Mark Bauerlein, *The Longman Dictionary of Literary Terms: Vocabulary for the Informed Reader* (New York: Pearson Longman, 2006): "A brief narrative that teaches a moral. The parables found in Christian literature, such as 'The Prodigal Son' (Luke 15:11–32), are classic examples of the form" (110).

77 Abrams and Harpham, *A Glossary of Literary Terms*, 9–11.

78 Strauss, *Four Portraits*, 540. On Augustine, see 539.

the term in his introduction, even though formally it does not apply, Adams invites reading *Watership Down* through an ethical lens.

The rabbits who journey from the warren in Sandleford to Watership Down are fragile with few defenses against human incursions and predatory animals, which makes one of the episodes in the novel noteworthy in the present context as we consider Christian ethics and the mandate to love and serve our neighbors as ourselves. The scene in question concerns a mouse. Soon after Hazel and Fiver's bedraggled crew arrive at Watership Down, one of them sounds a warning after sighting a kestrel above. The rabbits take cover in the burrows to escape the dangerous bird, but while they look through the opening, knowing the hunting raptor is overhead, they see another creature in danger: "'See the mouse?' said Silver suddenly. 'There, look. Poor little beast.' They could all see the field mouse, which was exposed in a patch of smooth grass. It had evidently strayed too far from its hole and now could not tell what to do. The kestrel's shadow had not passed over it, but the rabbits' sudden disappearance had made it uneasy and it was pressed to the ground, looking uncertainly this way and that. The kestrel had not yet seen it, but could hardly fail to do so as soon as it moved. 'Any moment now,' said Bigwig callously."[79]

The incident follows a long series of hardships endured by the rabbits. Serious physical injuries and the constant dread of threats real and imagined left them exhausted by this point in the story. And so it is that after Adams builds the tension so effectively with respect to this latest threat that what follows is completely unexpected: "On an impulse, Hazel hopped down the bank and went a little way into the open grass. Mice do not speak Lapine [rabbit language], but there is a very simple, limited *lingua franca* of the hedgerow and woodland. Hazel used it now. 'Run,' he said. Here; quick.'"[80] This was no small gesture. At the very moment the mouse scurries into the burrow opening, running between Hazel's legs to get there, and before Hazel could spring back from the opening of the hole, "the kestrel, all beak and talons, hit the loose earth immediately outside like a missile thrown from the tree above. It scuffled savagely and for an instant the three rabbits saw its round, dark eyes looking straight down the run."[81] This is not the end of the story about the mouse's relationship with Hazel and the other rabbits. With the

---

79 Adams, *Watership Down*, 144–145.
80 Adams, *Watership Down*, 145.
81 Adams, *Watership Down*, 145.

danger passed, the mouse expresses his gratitude to Hazel and offers to help the rabbits in any way he can.[82]

The episode intrigues me because it shows the rabbits in a middle position; they are weaker than the predatory bird but strong enough to give the mouse what he most needs. Hazel's act of hospitality and kindness is costly. He and the others share what little they have, namely, their burrow. This spirit of generosity to a vulnerable fellow creature is consistent with the ethical ideals found in the Gospels, most familiarly in parables. Just mentioning the term *parable* with reference to the novel, even though in the negative, is suggestive. Adams subtly plants an ethical seed. When we read *parable*, we think of Jesus's teachings that urge a liberality of temperament, a generosity toward those most vulnerable as in, for instance, the parable of the good Samaritan. And then we see Hazel and the others enacting that very altruism.

When Hazel risks his life to rescue the field mouse, one of his companions asks the obvious question: "'I know you're not stupid, but what did we get out of that? Are you going in for protecting every mole and shrew that can't get underground?'"[83] Eventually the new friendship with the mouse proves useful to Hazel's community, but that is not what motivated the chief rabbit to risk all by encountering the hunting raptor: "'Well, I'll admit I hadn't any particular idea when I went out to help it.'"[84] There was no expectation of reward, no demand on the mouse to reciprocate, and Bigwig's baffled query—*what did we get out of that?*—implies awareness that mice have nothing to offer anyway. Here again, fiction captures something of the atmosphere of the gospel ethic. Love, do good, lend, "expecting nothing in return" (Luke 6:35). The motivation to help those who are helpless, to reach out to the margins and offer what we can from our own middle positions, needs to come from elsewhere.

---

82 Adams, *Watership Down*, 149. There is a similar story involving the rabbits' efforts to save a distressed seagull (see 163, 164, etc.). This bird, named Kehaar, plays an important role in saving the warren later in the story.
83 Adams, *Watership Down*, 145.
84 Adams, *Watership Down*, 146.

CHAPTER EIGHT

The Gospel of the Imagination, or the Imaginary Gospel

So where is God?
Well, while I hope God is with those of us who live such comfortable lives, I know God is with the poorest and most vulnerable. In the slums and cardboard boxes where the poor have to play house. In the doorways as we step over the divine on our way to work. In the silence of a mother who has unknowingly infected her child with a virus that will end both their lives. God is in the cries heard under the rubble of war, in the bare hands digging for air. God is with the terrorized. At sea with the desperate, clinging onto drowning dreams. God is with the refugee. I hear his only son was one. God is with the poor and the vulnerable, and God is with us if we are with them.

—Bono[1]

Creative writers integrate biblical content to works of fiction for all kinds of reasons, and it is not necessarily religious or ethical in intent. Stephen King includes a booklist in the peek-behind-the-artistic-curtain that is *On Writing: A Memoir of the Craft*. Questions about the kinds of books he reads often come up, he explains, and in place of the simplest response ("Everything I can get my hands on"), he offers here a more specific answer he describes as "the

---

1 Bono, *Surrender: 40 Songs, One Story* (Toronto: Penguin Random House Canada, 2022), 531. Italics original.

best books I've read over the last three or four years."[2] He added to that list for subsequent editions of *On Writing*, and in the latest, sandwiched between "Tolstoy, Leo: *War and Peace*" and "Wallace, David Foster: *Infinite Jest*," he has "Various Hands: *King James Bible*."[3] No surprise there. The Bible often appears in his novels. The prominence of the Lazarus story from John's Gospel, used as section epigraphs in *Pet Sematary* (1983), comes to mind, as does discussion about the seven seals of the book of Revelation at a key moment in *Under the Dome* (2009). Not all books engaging biblical texts gesture toward Mystery, to return to Middleton's term noted in the introduction, in the kinds of ways explored in the previous chapters. At the same time, as I hope to have shown, not all gestures toward Mystery look particularly religious.

Consider again two authors encountered earlier. Good writers know good writing. Salman Rushdie—as likely as any to win the Nobel Prize in Literature himself one day—is a self-described "enthusiastic [Bob] Dylan worshipper."[4] Following the announcement, he lauded the Swedish Academy's decision to honor the songwriter with the Nobel Prize in Literature. "From Orpheus to [Faiz Ahmad] Faiz, song and poetry have been closely linked," he tweeted on October 13, 2016, after the announcement. "Dylan is the brilliant inheritor of the bardic tradition. Great choice." Rushdie's novels reflect this admiration, too, with a mix of obvious and not-so-obvious references to the singer and his lyrics to be found. For instance, a character in *The Golden House* recites "the whole of 'Sad-Eyed Lady of the Lowlands,' as reverently as if it were a companion piece to [John Keats's] 'La Belle Dame sans Merci.'" The narrator tells us he's a latter-day A. J. Weberman, investigating secrets with the same obsessive determination as that famed "garbologer" rummaging through Dylan's trash for clues about song meanings.[5] But read carefully when playing spot-the-Dylanism in Rushdie's writing: "Over ice cream, Uncle Ray spoke up. Judy hadn't been the only woman to visit him up in the woods. 'There's been somebody else,' he said, with difficulty. 'Woman name of Hatty, Carole

---

2 Stephen King, *On Writing: A Memoir of the Craft* (2000; New York: Scribner, 2020), 285.

3 King, *On Writing*, 295.

4 Salman Rushdie, *Joseph Anton: A Memoir* (New York: Random House, 2012), 30.

5 Salman Rushdie, *The Golden House* (Toronto: Alfred A. Knopf, 2017), 48–49, 36. Bob Dylan's song "Sad-Eyed Lady of the Lowlands" appeared on the album *Blonde on Blonde* (1966). See *Lyrics*, 211–212. For a brief introduction to A. J. Weberman, see the entry about him in Michael Gray, *The Bob Dylan Encyclopedia* (New York: Continuum, 2006), 693.

Hatty, knows there's a few of us scattered about them woods.'"⁶ Elsewhere in this novel there is a character named Sara, which is the same spelling as Dylan's first wife. She is described as "beautiful but sly. Sly-eyed lady of the Fenlands."⁷ Whoever has ears to hear, let them hear.

Rushdie's most intriguing reflections on Bob Dylan—and here I admit taking liberties, squeezing commentary out of fiction—appear in his 1999 novel *The Ground beneath Her Feet*. There is something of Dylan (and Jim Morrison and Freddie Mercury) in the novel's rock god Ormus Cama, "the youthful proselytizer of the here and now . . . the poet of the actual [who] saw visions of the otherworld and was transformed into an oracle."⁸ If pressed to encapsulate Dylan's career in a sentence, one could do worse.

For those who approach Dylan with an interest in religious studies and theology, that remark touches on a valued quality of the Nobel laureate's writing, illustrated by an excerpt from his memoir: "New York City was cold, muffled and mysterious, the capital of the world. On 7th Avenue I passed the building where Walt Whitman had lived and worked. I paused momentarily imagining him printing away and singing the true song of his soul. I had stood outside of Poe's house on 3rd Street, too, and had done the same thing, staring mournfully up at the windows. The city was like some uncarved block without any name or shape and it showed no favouritism. Everything was always new, always changing. It was never the same old crowd upon the streets."⁹

Bob Dylan succeeds where most others fail. We also walk familiar city streets but rarely see and feel so much. Michelangelo imagined magnificent sculptures locked in stone, and similarly Dylan suspects hidden mysteries, "like some uncarved block," in the banalities of that urban landscape. We meet two very different kinds of people in this scene. There are those swept up in the ever-shifting sidewalk mobs. If it's never the same old crowd, they're clearly on the move, stopping for nothing. They contrast with the poets Walt Whitman and Edgar Allan Poe sitting at their writing desks and with the author, who "paused momentarily" on 7th Street and "stood outside" 3rd to

---

6 Salman Rushdie, *Fury* (Toronto: Vintage, 2001), 121. He alludes to Dylan's "The Lonesome Death of Hattie Carroll," on *The Times They Are a-Changin'* (1964). See *Lyrics*, 95–96.

7 Rushdie, *Fury*, 31.

8 Salman Rushdie, *The Ground beneath Her Feet* (Toronto: Vintage, 1999), 418.

9 Dylan, *Chronicles*, 103. For more of Dylan's pursuit of the true music of the soul, captured in his sometimes mysterious prose, see *The Philosophy of Modern Song* (New York: Simon & Schuster, 2022).

listen for those great American poets, singing their songs of the soul. That's what poets do. That's what novelists, like those considered in the earlier chapters of this book, do. They stop, look, and wonder, whereas the rest of us hurry along, unaware of nearby treasures encased in rock.

Dylan knows of others who pause and look. In the near context, he mentions Woody Guthrie (cf. chap. 1), Kris Kristofferson, Graham Nash, Joni Mitchell, and Johnny Cash, among others. They also sing true songs of the soul while busy pedestrians pass beauty by, hearing little else than traffic noise and the hubbub of the city. Maybe it's why we value artists in the first place. Maybe it's why we ragged clowns follow behind. It's a shadow *you're* seeing (we say to Whitman or Poe or Cash or Mitchell or Dylan) that *we're* chasing.[10]

What has any of this to do with the theological imagination and gestures toward Mystery in literature? Dylan, after all, is a song and dance man, not a religious thinker, and famously uneasy with exaggerated assessments of his art. It ain't me, babe: "I know I ain't no prophet / An' I ain't no prophet's son."[11] That's all true, but I still associate Dylan's art with religious contemplation. But what I find in his music is not theological *content* so much as a *posture* vis-à-vis the mundane. The worlds described in Dylan songs are somehow thicker than my own. There's something substantial beneath the veneer. His is a world of ghosts: "On the same block was the Bull's Head, a cellar tavern where John Wilkes Booth, the American Brutus, used to drink. I'd been in there once and saw his ghost in the mirror—an ill spirit."[12] Poe and Whitman are among the ghosts, sitting at their desks, pens in hand. Treasures everywhere, just waiting for the artist to carve them out of stone.

To listen to Dylan's *Highway 61 Revisited* (1965) or *Blood on the Tracks* (1975) or *Rough and Rowdy Ways* (2020) is to step out of the passing crowd for the five or ten minutes of a song's duration. It is to stand beside him as he looks up at the apartment windows wondering what's behind. On my own, I don't see Whitman or Poe or anything half so "mysterious" as what he describes. That's why spending time with such artists matters. We need them to look through the surface of things, to peer behind the curtain. And so it is we occasionally hear a *something* in the arts we scarcely have words to describe. I want to say "Visions of Johanna" or "Key West (Philosopher

---

10 Cf. Dylan's "Mr. Tambourine Man," *Bringing It All Back Home* (1965). See *Lyrics*, 152–153.
11 Dylan, *Lyrics*, 29. Cf. Amos 7:14.
12 Dylan, *Chronicles*, 25.

Pirate)" and a hundred other Dylan songs are prophetic, but I don't know why. It's not about entertainment or not just about entertainment. Instead, it's about an awakened imagination. It's a whiff of enchantment in an otherwise unenchanted world. It's a looking at but also a looking through.

Dylan and other writers considered in this book are among the most important theologians in my life not because they teach me doctrine but because they tune the radio. Static gives way to a clearer signal. They create spaces for mysteries, give permission to look past the obvious. An awakened imagination makes contemplation of spiritual realities possible. Art, for me at least, is a necessary first step. For me, there is no openness to religious mysteries without "Where Are You Tonight? (Journey through Dark Heat)," discussed in chapter 5, or "Red River Shore" or "Series of Dreams." Everyone's playlist is a bit different, of course. Each one in the crowd at Pentecost heard the apostles speaking their own language.

LITERARY PRECEPTORS

We looked to Lewis and Lofting in the introduction for preliminary insights on literature's capacity to enrich our lives. These artistic preceptors illustrated, among other things, ways creative writings mingle with our own experiences in meaningful ways and help us envision a kinder, gentler world. We also considered throughout selections by other writers helping to close empathetic gaps and navigate the demands of Christian discipleship. Stories help us connect with the "least of these."

"I believe that deep and close reading of literature," writes Robert P. Waxler, "can help us to understand ourselves and the world around us, that we need fiction to give our so-called real life meaning, and that reading narrative fiction remains crucial to the making of a humane and democratic society."[13] This is no less true for religious readers of fiction. We return in this concluding chapter to the main idea put forward in the introduction, namely, that attention to artistic "commentaries" on the Bible is important for an inclusive,

---

13 Robert P. Waxler, *The Risk of Reading: How Literature Helps Us to Understand Ourselves and the World* (New York: Bloomsbury, 2014), 13. Waxler discusses these issues with reference to a diverse series of nineteenth- and twentieth-century works, among them Mary Shelley's *Frankenstein* (1818), Lewis Carroll's *Alice in Wonderland* (1865), Ernest Hemingway's *Old Man and the Sea* (1952), and Chuck Palahniuk's *Fight Club* (1996).

Other-oriented, and compassionate Christianity. Stories disrupt habitual patterns of thought. They embody the injustices and kindnesses Scripture describes. They reveal blind spots in our ethical outlook and bring to the surface otherwise hidden failures to care. Stories help concretize abstract values, recommend models of behavior to emulate, and awaken emotion and sympathies motivating right action. They urge us to go beyond sympathy and toward empathetic connection. Such conditioning to care potentially translates into right action once we put the books back on the shelf. For this reason, the notion of reading fiction as a spiritual discipline, as suggested in the introduction, does not seem overly hyperbolic. There is much to gain by exercising our imaginative faculties, engaging the arts, and seeking there whatever is true, honorable, just, pure, pleasing, commendable, excellent, and worthy of praise (Phil 4:8).

In his 1867 essay "The Imagination: Its Functions and Its Culture," George MacDonald, with a nod to Joel 2:28 and Acts 2:17, reminds us of the importance for the religious life of a mind nourished with creativity and invention.

> Cultivate the mere intellect as you may, it will never reduce the passions: the imagination, seeking the ideal in everything, will elevate them to their true and noble service. Seek not that your sons and your daughters should not see visions, should not dream dreams; seek that they should see true visions, that they should dream noble dreams. Such out-going of the imagination is one with aspiration, and will do more to elevate above what is low and vile than all possible inculcations of morality. Nor can religion herself ever rise up into her own calm home, her crystal shrine, when one of her wings, one of the twain with which she flies, is thus broken or paralyzed.[14]

The imagination is no mere add-on to the religious life but rather part of it ("one of her wings"). Reason alone, the intellect alone, is insufficient. "I believe," says the desperate father to Jesus, with reference to an ailing child, "help my unbelief!" (Mark 9:24)—this in response to Jesus's claim that all things are possible for the person of faith. The cognitive dissonance here is

---

14 George MacDonald, "The Imagination: Its Functions and Its Culture," first published in *British Quarterly Review* 46, no. 91 (July 1867): 45–70. Editors Shelley King and John B. Pierce include the essay in *The Princess and the Goblin and Other Fairy Tales* (Peterborough, ON: Broadview, 2014), 327–355. The excerpt cited is from p. 347. MacDonald is rarely read today. For an introduction to his work, see, e.g., Daniel Gabelman, *George MacDonald: Divine Carelessness and Fairytale Levity* (Waco, TX: Baylor University Press, 2013); and Timothy Larsen, *George MacDonald in the Age of Miracles: Incarnation, Doubt, and Reenchantment* (Downers Grove, IL: IVP Academic, 2018).

palpable. Desperation faces an assertion about God's interest in human affairs and God's willingness to intervene. The father's struggle is all too familiar. Unbelief intrudes on belief, doubt on trust, fear on hope. Mystery has more to do with spirituality than reason and logic. There are limits to the apologist's arguments. They do not bring solace in moments of extreme crisis, and *Help my unbelief!* is often the best prayer, often the only prayer we have.

The utterance of such a prayer is an exercise of the imagination. I plant a flag on ground I do not see and claim it as my own. As Puddleglum says to the witch, "'I'm on Aslan's side even if there isn't any Aslan to lead it. I'm going to live as like a Narnian as I can even if there isn't any Narnia.'"[15] Faith is the conviction of things not seen, as the author of Hebrews puts it (11:1). This is a surety in something beyond sight, and without any kind of empirical assurance, it involves an engagement of the imagination. If a religious worldview begins in sensory and measurable experience, it certainly does not end there. As MacDonald notes in the same essay, "To inquire into what God has made is the main function of the imagination. It is aroused by facts, is nourished by facts, seeks for higher and yet higher laws in those facts; but refuses to regard science as the sole interpreter of nature, or the laws of science as the only region of discovery."[16] It ought to come as no surprise this theologian and one-time clergyman is best remembered for his fairy tales and children's fiction.

CALEB PLUMMER'S CRICKET: SOME CHIRPINGS ABOUT DICKENS AND THE IMAGINATION

"'What's the use of stories that aren't even true?'"[17] So asks a villain in a Salman Rushdie novel, a sinister figure determined to silence the spinners of yarns. Rushdie writes of what he knows. Real-world villains put that question to him all the time, and unfortunately, as the brutal attack on Rushdie in the summer of 2022 reminds us, some remain unmoved by his attempts to explain why works of the imagination matter and why censorship is dangerous.

Calls to silence Rushdie through assassination originated in other-than-Christian religious extremism, but Christianity is not immune to a similar

---

15 C. S. Lewis, *The Silver Chair* (1953; New York: HarperCollins, 1994), 182.
16 MacDonald, "The Imagination," 327.
17 Rushdie, *Haroun and the Sea of Stories*, 155. Cf. 20, 22.

devaluing of the arts. From England's Puritan-dominated seventeenth-century parliament closing theaters through to conservatives in our own day banning books and movies deemed offensive, suspicion about such creativity runs deep in Christian circles. "What's the use of stories that aren't even true?" is a question often asked.

Rushdie is hardly alone among writers celebrating and defending their craft, and I invite you to consider the case of Caleb Plummer. He is a minor character, part of a minor storyline, in a minor work in the Charles Dickens catalog. As though reinforcing this sense of the inconsequential, his home is small, his resources few, his hair thinning. He is even diminutive in appearance, with the adjectives "little" and "meagre" attached to him on his first appearance in the story.[18] And in the world of Dickens's fiction, a world of large books with sprawling, elaborate plots populated with exaggerated, bigger-than-life saints and sinners, Caleb Plummer seems to shrink further yet. If many can rattle off a dozen or so Dickens characters without much effort, I suspect fewer recognize the name Caleb Plummer or the 1845 novella in which he appears, *The Cricket on the Hearth: A Fairy Tale of Home*. Even the title stresses the small and insignificant. A cricket. A mere insect. How important can that be?

But let's not look away too soon. Crickets, after all, are associated with luck in a number of cultures,[19] and according to Dickens, they "are potent Spirits, even though the people who hold converse with them do not know it . . . and there are not, in the unseen world, voices more gentle and more true, that may be so implicitly relied on, or that are so certain to give none but tenderest counsel, as the Voices in which the Spirits of the Fireside and the Hearth address themselves to human kind."[20] Throughout this story, a cricket's chirruping is the sound of "welcome" and domestic contentment. For one married couple, its song is the assurance of a spouse's love and affection.[21] A cricket silenced, however, is a terrible thing. We see this when that same happy couple entertains a visitor to their home, the vile Mr. Tackleton. He is

---

18 Charles Dickens, *The Cricket on the Hearth* (1845), in *A Christmas Carol and Other Stories*, ed. Robert Douglas-Fairhurst (Oxford: Oxford University Press, 2006), 177.

19 Traditionally, notes Douglas-Fairhurst, "crickets have even been kept in small cages to prevent luck from escaping the house" (in Dickens, *Cricket on the Hearth*, 431n. 172).

20 Dickens, *Cricket on the Hearth*, 189.

21 Dickens, *Cricket on the Hearth*, 173.

cynical about love and marriage, and the moment he arrives, the cricket goes silent. This man even kills crickets when he finds them on his own hearth.[22]

There's a cricket in Caleb Plummer's home, too, and it is his story that interests me here. Dickens's *Cricket on the Hearth* is in part a story about storytelling, one contemplating the capacity of the imagination to ameliorate bad situations and bring out the good in people. Fictions enchant an otherwise dark world, something fittingly illustrated through the work of Caleb and his daughter, Bertha. They are toy makers. Toys are fictions that awaken joy in children and create worlds of pure fantasy.[23] But Caleb Plummer's artistry involves far more than dolls and children's entertainments. He is desperately poor, his wife is dead, he lives with Bertha in absolute squalor, and their employer (Tackleton) is a tyrant. Adding to his sorrows, his beloved daughter is blind. What is a loving father to do? Caleb's course of action is extreme. He shelters her from the truth about their harsh circumstances by creating an elaborate alternate reality.[24]

Caleb, much like Dickens himself, holds spellbound those who encounter his stories. "I have said that Caleb and his poor Blind Daughter lived," says the narrator, in a small, shabby, rotting dwelling, but "I should have said that Caleb lived here, and his poor Blind Daughter somewhere else—in an enchanted home of Caleb's furnishing, where scarcity and shabbiness were not, and trouble never entered."[25] Caleb, we're told, "was no sorcerer, but in the only magic art that still remains to us, the magic of devoted, deathless love, Nature had been the mistress of his study; and from her teaching, all the wonder came."[26] And so it is the girl knows nothing of the discolored

---

22 Dickens, *Cricket on the Hearth*, 175, 182.

23 In their doll-making skills and desire to make children happy, Caleb and his daughter contrast sharply with their employer, Mr. Tackleton, who owns the toy shop where they work. In him we have a kind of fictionalizing devoid of love and indeed one that is cruel. His favorite toys are those that frighten children. He cares nothing for kids, and his only interest is making money.

24 Dickens's depiction of the blind Bertha is complicated and even vexing in many respects. As Elisabeth G. Gitter observes, through her humiliating passion for Tackleton, her vulnerability to deception, and punishing exclusion from the fairy-tale ending because conventionally ineligible for marriage owing to her blindness, Dickens "make[s] light of darkness" ("The Blind Daughter in Charles Dickens's 'The Cricket on the Hearth,'" *Studies in English Literature, 1500–1900* 39, no. 4 [1999]: 686). On Bertha's ineligibility for marriage, see, too, 675, 680.

25 Dickens, *Cricket on the Hearth*, 188.

26 Dickens, *Cricket on the Hearth*, 188.

walls and ceilings, or the moldering beams of their home; knows nothing of Caleb's quickly graying hair, and the evidence of hard work, worry, and age on his stooped body. So complete is the ruse, she believes the rags he wears to be the finery of a nobleman and their miserly, brutal employer to be the family's benefactor and guardian angel. Caleb's storytelling keeps her safe from the harsh, precarious realities of their dire situation.

Did Caleb do the right thing? We're made to wonder. The time comes when the whole house of cards crashes down on father and daughter. When Bertha discovers the truth, she is initially heartbroken: "'Oh why,' cried the Blind Girl, tortured, as it seemed, almost beyond endurance, 'why did you ever do this! Why did you ever fill my heart so full, and then come in like Death, and tear away the objects of my love! Oh Heaven, how blind I am! How helpless and alone!' Her afflicted father hung his head, and offered no reply but in his penitence and sorrow."[27] Like Rushdie, Dickens has us asking, *What's the use of stories that aren't even true?*, and we might conclude there's no use at all were it not for the reentrance at this moment of the central character: "She had not been but a short time in this passion of regret, when the Cricket on the Hearth, unheard by all but her, began to chirp."[28] A trusted friend is by her side at that moment, explaining all. Tell me what my home is, Bertha asks her. It is a poor place, very poor and bare indeed. The house will scarcely keep out the wind and rain another winter. Tell me what my father is like, Bertha asks. He is an old man, worn with care and work, spare, dejected, thoughtful, gray-haired. I see him now, despondent and bowed down.[29] Detail by detail, slowly but surely, the fiction evaporates.

But then an unexpected reaction from the girl who knows for the first time the real facts about their precarious existence. With the cricket chirruping quietly, with her friend laying bare the painful details behind the heartwarming fiction, an epiphany. She goes to her dejected father and cries, "'It is my sight restored. It is my sight! . . . I have been blind, and now my eyes are open. I never knew him! To think I might have died, and never truly seen the father who has been so loving to me!'"[30] She is still physically blind. The sight she refers to is of a different and far more important kind.

---

27 Dickens, *Cricket on the Hearth*, 228.
28 Dickens, *Cricket on the Hearth*, 228.
29 Dickens, *Cricket on the Hearth*, 229.
30 Dickens, *Cricket on the Hearth*, 229–230.

Dickens, it seems to me, sets a trap for readers. We're ready to think Caleb cruel for perpetuating a lie, and even he second-guesses himself before all comes to light. He fears he will be the cause of the girl's broken heart because after leading her to think their nasty employer is generous and kind, the girl fell in love with the man.[31] But Dickens comes to the defense of creativity, the arts, and storytellers. Caleb, we discover, is not solely responsible for the dream he weaves. The unobtrusive presence of the titular orthoptera singer is the magical heart of this fairy tale: "All [this fiction, the narrator tells us,] was Caleb's doing. . . . But he too had a Cricket on his Hearth; and listening sadly to its music when the motherless Blind Child was very young, that Spirit had inspired him with the thought that even her great deprivations might be almost changed into a blessing, and the girl made happy by these little means."[32] Again, as Dickens explains, in the unseen world there are no voices gentler and truer, more reliable, or more certain to give nothing but the tenderest counsel than crickets.

The proof is the illumination Bertha experiences. Though initially horrified at discovering that much of what she thought to be true was a lie, she gains far more. The story ends with the girl still physically blind but having "seen" her father anew, understanding now the depths of his love and self-sacrifice. Now she truly sees: "'I am NOT blind, father, any longer!'"[33]

A story points beyond itself to a higher truth, much like the parabolic fictions Jesus tells throughout the Synoptic Gospels. Caleb and Bertha Plummer's relationship, held together as it is by a story, is an analogy of the relationship between author and audience.[34] On one level, it is a celebration of the capacity of art to help us imagine a better world and to transform the world in which we live, and Dickens's praise for works of imagination is explicit and attached to these two characters in particular: "Caleb Plummer and his Blind Daughter," he writes, "lived all alone by themselves, as the Story-books say—and my blessing, with yours to back it I hope, on the Story-books, for saying anything in this workaday world!"[35] In this instance, the workaday world understands true love better thanks to Caleb's cricket-inspired artistry.

---

31 Dickens, *Cricket on the Hearth*, 208, 210 cf. 228.
32 Dickens, *Cricket on the Hearth*, 189.
33 Dickens, *Cricket on the Hearth*, 230.
34 See, e.g., Scott Moncrieff, "*The Cricket* in the Study," *Dickens Studies Annual* 22 (1993): 150.
35 Dickens, *Cricket on the Hearth*, 188.

Like Dickens's better-known seasonal tale *A Christmas Carol*, there is a conversion story in *The Cricket on the Hearth*. As mentioned, Caleb's employer is an awful man. Tackleton is cynical and miserly, indifferent to the needs of others, cruel to children, and even willing to crush crickets underfoot, and yet he goes through a Scrooge-like transformation. His very body marks both his problem and his potential for reform. We're told he always has one eye wide open and one eye nearly shut.[36] He simultaneously sees and does not see, which is surely an important descriptor given the presence of Caleb's daughter. She is fully blind, literally blind, and yet sees all that really matters by the end of the story. Tackleton is both sighted and benighted, one eye open, one eye shut. Do we recognize anything of ourselves in this half-sighted character, seeing some things but shutting out others? We see such play on sight and blindness elsewhere. Scrooge's conversion after the ghostly visits caused some people to laugh at him, but he didn't mind: "Knowing that such as these would be blind anyway, he thought it quite as well that they should wrinkle up their eyes in grins, as have the malady in less attractive forms."[37] Of course, there are Gospel roots to this imagery. How did Tiny Tim behave?, asks Mrs. Cratchit: "'As good as gold,' said Bob, 'and better. Somehow he gets thoughtful, sitting by himself so much, and thinks the strangest things you ever heard. He told me, coming home, that he hoped the people saw him in the church, because he was a cripple, and it might be pleasant to them to remember upon Christmas Day, who made lame beggars walk and blind men see.'"[38] In their very different ways, these two Dickens Christmas stories invite us to contemplate our own blindness and turn our thoughts to the one who gives sight.

The Cricket on the Hearth is not universally beloved by the critics. Aside from "a few glowing passages of domestic description," observes Edgar Johnson, it "is a weak book." Furthermore, with reference to the storyline just considered, he finds "Caleb Plummer's loving deception in describing their bleak hovel to his blind daughter as a cheerful cottage, and portraying the snarling Tackleton as a benevolent eccentric, overflows with an excess of

---

36 Dickens, *Cricket on the Hearth*, 181.
37 Dickens, *Cricket on the Hearth*, 83.
38 Charles Dickens, *A Christmas Carol, in Prose: Being a Ghost Story of Christmas*, ed. Richard Kelly (1843; Peterborough, ON: Broadview, 2003), 87. Cf. e.g., Mark 8:22–26; John 5:1–10.

sentimental pathos."³⁹ That may be. But the story still points beyond itself. Caleb's kind fiction deepens the love between father and daughter and by that metric serves a higher and an even spiritual good: "A new commandment I give unto you, That ye love one another; as I have loved you, that ye also love one another" (John 13:34, AV). And perhaps—and here is a thought for those advocating censorship and those reluctant to approach the arts as a potential resource for spiritual enrichment—perhaps we do well to listen, if ever so lucky as to hear a cricket chirping on our own hearth. *What's the use of stories that aren't even true?* It's a question worth pondering and one leading us to add our blessing on the storybooks for having something to say in this workaday world.

---

39 Edgar Johnson, *Charles Dickens: His Tragedy and Triumph* (New York: Simon & Schuster, 1952), 1.579–580. See, too, Peter Ackroyd, *Dickens: A Memoir of Middle Age* (London: Vintage, 2012): "those who were seeking to find evidence of Dickens's fading powers pounced upon it as an example of what one critic called 'sentimental twaddle'" (266; full discussion, 263–266). I disagree.

Afterword
Censorship and The Far Side *of Religion*

This was a psalter in whose margins was delineated a world reversed with respect to the one to which our senses have accustomed us. As if at the border of a discourse that is by definition the discourse of truth, there proceeded, closely linked to it . . . a topsy-turvy universe, in which dogs flee before the hare, and deer hunt the lion.

—Umberto Eco, *The Name of the Rose*[1]

What's the use of stories that aren't even true? For those concluding there's none, there's sometimes the concomitant assumption danger lurks within them. If there's no wisdom beyond the stained-glass windows, there's no point looking beyond the church walls. Whatever's out there must be folly and so best avoided. Censorship is the logical next step for some. In this afterword, I argue we lose too much by turning away from works of the imagination, by picking and choosing what to read or watch based on arbitrary criteria. My choice of illustration is a bit silly, but I hope it underscores that some moral outrages distract us from issues that really matter, like those Jesus refers to in Matthew 25:10–36.

"NATURALLY, A MANUSCRIPT"[2]

The speaker in this chapter's epigraph is a Benedictine novice named Adso of Melk, narrator of Umberto Eco's 1980 novel *The Name of the Rose*, who, in

---

1 Umberto Eco, *The Name of the Rose*, trans. William Weaver (Italian original, 1980; San Diego, CA: Harcourt, 1984), 76.

2 These all-cap words appear on an unnumbered page in the front matter to Umberto Eco's *Name of the Rose*. Fitting words to begin a detective story set in an abbey with a scriptorium and library. An earlier version of this argument appeared as "The Far Side of Religion: Notes on the Prophet Gary Larson," *Direction* 39, no. 2 (2010): 220–233. I adapt and expand on it here with the editor's kind permission.

1327, accompanied the Sherlock Holmes-like monk William of Baskerville to a wealthy Italian abbey. They are in the scriptorium, visiting the workstation of the recently deceased illuminator Adelmo of Otranto, and Adso describes the strange drawings Adelmo placed alongside the biblical Psalms. He reports a long list of bizarre images: bird-feet heads; animals with human hands on their back; zebra-striped dragons; quadrupeds with serpentine necks; monkeys with stags' horns; armless men with other human bodies emerging from their backs like humps; humans with horses' heads and horses with human legs; fish with birds' wings and birds with fishtails; monsters with single bodies and double heads or single heads and double bodies; cows with cocks' tails and butterfly wings; women with heads scaly as a fish's back; centaurs; elephants; manticores; "sequences of anthropomorphic animals and zoomorphic dwarfs joined, sometimes on the same page, with scenes of rustic life in which you saw, depicted with such impressive vivacity that the figures seemed alive, all the life of the fields"; a towered city defended by monkeys; and on and on it goes.[3]

What is startling about the scene Adso describes, especially in the context of a fourteenth-century monastery, is the location of these pictures, appearing as they do *alongside* the sacred Scriptures. This inverted world "where houses stand on the tip of a steeple and the earth is above the sky" intrigues Adso, who finds himself "torn between silent admiration and laughter, because the illustrations naturally inspired merriment, though they were commenting on holy pages."[4] Some are not so impressed, particularly Jorge of Burgos, who finds such indulgences in the fantastic an evil, one even justifying murder. Jesus, he argues, "did not have to employ such foolish things to point out the strait and narrow path," and further, "Nothing in his parables arouses laughter." Humor and laughter, in Jorge's view, "is weakness, corruption, the foolishness of our flesh." William of Baskerville, on the other hand, is far less severe, suggesting, "Marginal images often provoke smiles, but to edifying ends." As in sermons, William continues, "to touch the imagination of devout throngs it is necessary to

---

3 Eco, *Name of the Rose*, 76–77. For a marvelous tale involving several such phantasmagorical creatures, see Eco's *Baudolino*, trans. William Weaver (Italian original, 2000; Toronto: Harcourt, 2002).

4 Eco, *Name of the Rose*, 78.

introduce exempla, not infrequently jocular." Similarly, "the discourse of images must indulge in these trivia."⁵

Allow me to be the first—I think this safe to say—to describe the great cartoonist Gary Larson as an illuminator not unlike Adelmo of Otranto who could take "known things" and from them "compose unknown and surprising things, as one might join a human body to an equine neck." Like this medieval illuminator, who "worked only on marginalia,"⁶ Gary Larson also writes *alongside* other texts, including the sacred Scriptures. He does not do so literally, doodling in the margins of actual Bibles (as far as I know) but rather figuratively, taking familiar ideas, characters, and stories, biblical in origin, and repeating, retelling, redrawing those scenes to "provoke smiles." The extent of this biblical and religious-themed content in Larson's work might surprise casual readers of the cartoon, and as a widely disseminated pop-culture art form, engagement with sacred subject matter warrants consideration. As a starting point, the observations of academics in another field suggest a way forward.

The American biologist and naturalist Edward O. Wilson describes Larson as "the madcap sage of the biological sciences" and credits the cartoonist with an important insight: "Nature is part of us and we are part of Nature."⁷ Primatologist Jane Goodall agrees, suggesting, "Gary's cartoons help us to see things with a new perspective, above all to realize that we humans, after all, are just one species among many, just one small part of the wondrous animal kingdom."⁸ Here we have a constructive way to think about the theological content of these cartoons. Just as Larson bridges the gap and blurs the boundaries between the biological species, so, too, he allows the distance between the spiritual and the mundane to melt away. There is an odd proximity between the everyday and commonplace on the one hand, the mysterious and extraordinary on the other. God and gods, Satan and devils, angels and biblical characters mingle with regular flesh-and-blood folk in this topsy-turvy cartoon universe, along with aliens, zombies, and talking gorillas.

---

5 Eco, *Name of the Rose*, 81, 474, 79. See, too, the long exchange between Jorge and William on this subject on pp. 473–479.

6 Eco, *Name of the Rose*, 76.

7 Edward O. Wilson, "Foreword," in Gary Larson, *There's a Hair in My Dirt! A Worm's Story* (New York: Harper, 1998), n.p.

8 Jane Goodall, "Foreword," in Gary Larson, *The Far Side Gallery 5* (Kansas City, MO: Andrews and McMeel, 1995), n.p.

AFTERWORD

A WORLD REVERSED TO OUR SENSES: GARY LARSON'S TOPSY-TURVY UNIVERSE

Ask anyone who read newspapers during the 1980s and '90s, and they can recall at least one *Far Side* cartoon, or, to use a neologism for the sake of convenience, Lartoon. The series remains a fixture in popular culture long after Larson's retirement. By his count, there are 4,337 *Far Side* cartoons, the first published on December 31, 1979, the last on January 1, 1995.[9] What is surprising is the extent of religious material found in these pages. How does his engagement with rather sobering subject matter function on a comedic level? For humor to be effective, cartoonists, like other comedians, must deal with cultural commonplaces. Jokes only work to the extent that audiences recognize a twist on what is otherwise normal. Everyone knows "nervous little dogs" do not make espresso to prepare for their day, which is what makes this Lartoon funny (2.341). Such departures from normalcy permit a momentary escape from realism and grant permission to indulge in the absurd. Because most readers bring basic knowledge of the "religion script" to their reading of *The Far Side*—angels are good, devils are bad, God is all-powerful, hell involves suffering and heaven bliss, and so on—the unanticipated visual gags and turns of phrase shifting away from the usual rhythms of religious narrative surprise and entertain.

And so it is we find the caption "Acts of God" beneath a picture of God juggling (2.367), a flying saucer with a fish symbol on the back bumper (2.570), and caterpillars offering a beautiful butterfly to an entomologist with a net (2.510). In each instance, the cartoonist takes something broadly familiar to a mass audience and swerves from the accustomed sense. Of course, the expression "acts of god" usually indicates something other than a divine song and dance man in everyday speech. Similarly, though there are no words accompanying the picture of extraterrestrials flying through space, the joke still works because most North American drivers know a fish bumper sticker is a religious symbol representing Christianity; the image is an *ichthus*, a fish.

---

9 Gary Larson, *The Complete Far Side*, vol 1: 1980–1986, vol. 2: 1987–1994 (Kansas City, MO: Andrews McMeel Publishing, 2003), 1.xvi. All subsequent references to this collection appear in text. Complementing this delightful body of work, Larson's post-*Far Side* book, *There's a Hair in My Dirt! A Worm's Story*, is a must-read for fans. For examples of Larson's work, including some post-retirement drawings, see the official website, www.thefarside.com.

AFTERWORD

Apparently, aliens identify their religious beliefs in the same way, though their *ichthus* has four eyes! The image of pagans presenting a sacrificial human to some god or monster, like Fay Wray to King Kong, comes to mind as we look at caterpillars summoning Professor Crutchfeld with a gong. We see him approaching the terrified, tied-up butterfly, and the caption reads, "The little caterpillars had done well this time in their offering." All such scenes are part of our collective cultural capital. We recognize the norms behind the cartoons and enjoy the deviations from them. Larson's genius lies in his ability to manipulate our expectations.

I think we can say more about the religious content in Lartoons, however. Trying to explain the attractions of the natural world, indeed the allure known to biologists, zoologists, entomologists, and everyone else looking under rocks, up trees, down holes, and under water to find some specimen to observe, Larson offers this explanation: "Very simply, it's the obsession to capture and to hold, if only for a few moments, some living, natural wonder, to observe it, examine it, have it touch your skin, feel its heartbeat against your hand—to 'drink it in' before it once again slips back over *that invisible wall that separates Us from Them*" (1.181; italics added). By *the natural world*, Larson has in mind insects, birds, and animals, and in fact, he makes this comment after an account of chasing a three-foot-long lizard while in Indonesia, which, incidentally, got away from him. This remark offers an insight to Gary Larson's comical world that extends well beyond human curiosity about nonhuman species. So often in these cartoons, we find ourselves looking at and reading about—and then despite ourselves, imagining—things that are either unreal or impossible or inaccessible to us in some sense. We are privy to the private thoughts of plants and animals, the emotional states of inanimate objects, or conversations between extraterrestrials and vampires. Fictitious literary characters and long-dead historical figures also come to life; they speak and act and so are accessible to *Far Side* readers, if only for a moment before slipping back over that *invisible dividing wall*.

Also hidden away from everyday experience are the decidedly private, psychological dimensions of existence, human or otherwise. Larson cartoons reveal the deepest fears, longings, and beliefs of a world of characters. Usually, we bury our emotional lives behind a veneer of respectability; we are socialized to keep certain matters hidden away from onlookers. Not here. Personal failings and social ineptitude, our pathetic romantic insecurities or overbearing self-confidence, every manner of embarrassment and shameful cowardice, pure folly and stupidity, not to mention that nagging but rarely indulged desire we have to place "a single drop of hydrochloric acid on the back of a [colleague's] neck" (2.356) or scare and humiliate peers in some other way (for suggestions, see 1.303; 1.306)—all this and much more parades through Larson's panels. They reveal much about human existence that is less than cool and far from noble—behaviors, beliefs, attitudes, desires, and fears usually secreted away behind *that invisible wall*.

My concern here is the religious content of Gary Larson's *The Far Side*. Spiritual beings, those experiencing the afterlife for better or worse, and biblical characters are all beyond the reach of our senses. They, too, are over that invisible wall, as it were, as unfamiliar to our everyday lives as vampires, cave dwellers, and the private thoughts of Leonardo da Vinci's dog ("So where's my dinner? . . . One of the Great Masters indeed" [2.263]). Here, too, we also deal with something analogous to Larson's longing to take hold of that three-foot lizard. Religions attempt to bring near a "wonder" that is otherwise beyond our grasp, to bridge the mundane and the supernatural. The New Testament refers to belief in "things not seen" (Heb 11:1). Larson's dialogues with religion also explore "things not seen," though he chooses to remove that *invisible wall*, giving devils and angels faces.

BRINGING RELIGION WITHIN REACH

The terms *anthropomorphism*, thinking of animals as we would people, and *zoomorphism*, thinking of people as we would animals, involve, among other things, uses of language that attempt to remove the gap between species. Anthropomorphism and zoomorphism are commonplace in these comic panels, with animals acting and speaking like humans and humans behaving like animals. As Jane Goodall puts it, "Larson blithely reverses the roles of human and nonhuman so that, as you browse through a collection you find on one page a Gary Larson human carelessly squishing a foolish dog (yapping when the man of the house is trying to watch the World Cup), and on another, a Gary Larson elephant carelessly squishing a foolish human."[10] These role reversals provide much of the humor, of course, as species do the most unexpected things. In this world, spiders die by suicide (1.159), snakes

---

10 Goodall, "Foreword," n.p.

attend movies (1.138), elephants sit around campfires (1.567), and worms attend parties and flirt with other guests (1.438). At the same time, humans are bestial/insectival/birdlike in all kinds of ways. A similar pattern emerges in *The Far Side*'s religious content with the humanizing of otherwise out-of-reach spiritual beings and phenomena, thus casting them in recognizable forms. A few examples of this humanizing and familiarizing pattern in Lartoons illustrate the point.

Death, Heaven, and Hell

Life after death is a recurring subject in *The Far Side* universe, and three general patterns deserve notice. First, Larson's cartoons often literalize popular religious ideas and metaphors. Here we find actual wolves wearing sheep's clothing/costumes to aid the hunt (1.312; 1.461; cf. Matt 7:15). Such concretizing of metaphor is widespread, particularly in depictions of postmortem experience, which capitalize on popular, fanciful notions about the nature of heaven and hell—clouds, wings, haloes, harps, and white robes on the one side; fire, horned red devils with tails, heat, and grief on the other.

Second, death generally involves continuity, as one's habits, behaviors, and interests in life follow one to a particularly well-suited heaven or hell, as the case may be. If a hippie goes to heaven, it only makes sense that he sits on a cloud with long hair, sunglasses, and sandals, with his harp plugged into an enormous amp (1.22), whereas for flies, now buzzing around with haloes, heaven is a big bowl of potato salad (1.416). A bowler in hell must naturally face a wider-than-usual lane with only two pins standing on the opposite corners, while the devil says mockingly, "Whoa! Another split? . . . What a bummer!" (2.249). Jazz great Charlie Parker must endure New Age music in his private torment (2.276), whereas those sent to "scientist hell" face a room marked "Psychics, Astrologists & Mediums Eternal Discussion Group" (2.600). Before learning his postmortem fate, Colonel Sanders approaches the pearly gates only to find statues of chickens gracing the entranceway: "Uh-oh" (2.379). These highly individualized afterworlds include some surprises. Not only is there a customized room for homicidal maniacs and terrorists but also one for "people who drove too slow in the fast lane" (2.166). Of course, the coffee in hell is cold, something only a coffee drinker would appreciate: "Oh, man! . . . They thought of *everything!*" (2.511; italics original).

Third, Larson's presentations of postmortem existence dull the terrors of hell and make dull the pleasures of heaven. A man in glory with halo and wings sits by himself on a cloud wishing he brought a magazine (1.451). The fate of the damned involves little more than petty nuisances (cold coffee), monotony (blowing bubbles for all eternity [2.567]), irritation (a maestro in a room full of banjo players [1.190]), rich irony (dogs carrying mailbags and picking up after themselves [1.582]), and of course heat ("Hot enough for ya?," says one of the damned to another, with the caption "Nerds in hell" [2.91]). It's not all fun and games for Satan either, forced as he is to put up with the invasive interviewing techniques of Mike Wallace (2.381), an incompetent painter ("999"; 2.454), residents playing with the thermostat (2.381) and ordering pizza (2.177), and various graffiti insults: "Satan is a warm and tender guy," "Hey, you call this hot?" and so on (2.543).

Anthropomorphizing God

The Far Side God is rather human—an old man, to be precise—in most Lartoons. He has a body (e.g., 1.418; 1.529); plays game shows (and well, needless to say; 1.418); uses a phone (2.454: "And for the rest of his life, Ernie told his friends that he had talked with God"); and operates a computer, complete with a "smite" button (2.347), presumably when sitting in his den (1.554). Since the divine creator of the universe is spirit, remote, unimaginable, and beyond day-to-day experience, Larson washes away that invisible line and represents the deity in terms all recognize, which is to say anthropomorphic. His God is powerful yet limited in these cartoons, creating a world that is half-baked (1.529) and losing his keys (1.207) and a contact lens (1.479). After dropping a jar marked "humans" into the newly created world, a voice from the clouds mutters "uh-oh" as people run merrily away (1.243). God has a sense of humor, too, sprinkling in some "jerks" to the new creation, "just to make it interesting" (2.562).

The origin of the universe is a recurring theme in *The Far Side*, especially if we include both religious-themed Lartoons referring to creation and various scenes inspired by evolution and related matters like dinosaurs, cave dwellers, continental drift / plate tectonics, and Darwin. Larson's version of divine creation expands on the rather succinct, unembellished accounts found in Genesis, suggesting more of a process. God practices his creative techniques as a child, even causing a minor explosion when trying to make a chicken on one occasion, leaving feathers scattered all over his bedroom (1.616; making snakes, by comparison, is "a cinch" [2.302]). He thinks on his feet when creating animals, pausing to consider, for instance, whether to put "a 'happy face' on the uvula" of the great white shark (2.389). After making pairs of zebras, giraffes, pigs, rabbits, and other nonpredatory species, he looks at his handiwork and muses, "Hmmmmm . . . not bad, not bad at all . . . Well, now I guess I'd better make some things to eat you guys" (2.237).

Specific and Generic Religious References

Literary and historical figures appear regularly in *The Far Side*. Among fictional characters, we find some from *The Wizard of Oz*, Herman Melville's *Moby-Dick*, Mary Shelley's *Frankenstein*, Virgil's *Aeneid* (the Trojan horse), *Humpty Dumpty*, *King Kong*, Oscar Wilde's *The Picture of Dorian Gray*, Victor Hugo's *The Hunchback of Notre-Dame*, and Edgar Rice Burroughs's Tarzan stories, to name but a few. Historical figures include Genghis Khan, Albert Einstein, and Lewis and Clark. Characters from biblical stories also appear. God is in many, as noted, but he is not alone. Noah is the most frequently represented biblical character, featuring in at least nine panels by my count (1.8; 1.29; 1.53; 1.177; 2.24; 2.40; 2.116; 2.206; 2.594). Others include the serpent and/or Adam and/or Eve in the garden of Eden (1.104; 1.549; 2.126; 2.387); Jonah (1.65); Jesus (2.547); Moses (2.158; 2.456); Samson (2.383); the three wise men (1.486; maybe also 1.503); and if we take the pyramid/Egypt/slave panels as a reflection of biblical stories, the Israelites (1.39; 1.151; 1.502; 2.585).

Other panels provide glimpses into religious life bearing little or no resemblance to the major religious traditions. These include, to name but a few, "chicken cults," with robed birds gathered around a freshly roasted bird, their sacrificial victim (1.614); astral-traveling water buffaloes (2.6); Cowintology ("just take one of our brochures" [2.7]); witch doctors (2.9); rain dancing (2.17); reincarnation, with reference to Shirley MacLaine (2.19); and appliance healers ("I command the foul demons that have clogged this vacuum cleaner to come out!" [1.597; underlining original]).

RESPONDING TO THE FAR SIDE OF RELIGION

So how should we react to all this, as readers who take religion seriously, as academics in religious studies, or as practitioners of specific faith traditions?

AFTERWORD

Allow me to address this in the negative, with a suggestion of how *not* to respond. I mentioned earlier that evolution is a recurring subject for Larson, appearing alongside various other indicators of the earth's age. My favorite has the caption "Continental drift whiplash" (1.297), and the picture shows two continents colliding, catching people standing on either side unawares, causing them to stumble. There are many others (e.g., 1.77; 1.198; 1.236; 1.255; 1.287). Larson's frequent references to biological evolution provide a hilarious backdrop for one letter of complaint included in *The Complete Far Side*. The writer, representing the "Center for the Study of Secular Humanism," complains that Larson combines a brachiosaurus and *homo habilus*[11] in the same drawing—sort of, since it represents the dinosaur's footprint with the flattened, club-holding hunter at its base (1.296). The writer criticizes the drawing, calling it ludicrous "since Brachiosaurus existed 60,000,000 years before Homo Habilus or any form even remotely resembling the human form came on the scene." This disgruntled reader then adds, "This is exactly what the 'Creationist' would like us to believe; that evolution was a one-shot deal instead of a process that took place over billions of years." I suspect most evolutionary scientists and creationists reading this would find the complaint absurd and marvel that the letter lacks even a hint of irony in its concern for "truth and historical accuracy" and the dissemination of "specific information to the public at large."[12] What does this scientist expect from a cartoonist who blames cigarette smoking for the extinction of the dinosaurs (1.264)?

There is clear genre confusion at play in such a response. *The Far Side* is not a doctoral dissertation or university textbook, and so it does not matter that a brachiosaurus stepped on a *homo habilis* any more than it matters that cows fly in these pages. This angry letter is not an isolated case. Larson's cartoons generated numerous negative reactions over the years, with readers critical of certain drawings and recurring themes for all kinds of reasons. This includes concerns about the religious content, even leading some to threaten boycotts of newspapers carrying the panels (see e.g., 1.471). To react to these cartoons this way misses the point, which is, in my view, that there is no point. To take offense is to commit Jorge of Burgos's error of equating humor with

---

11 In the cartoon, the spelling is *habilis*. *Homo habilis* appears again in a cartoon depicting an anthropologist's dream: "a beautiful woman in one hand, the fossilized skull of *Homo habilis* in the other" (1.428).

12 The letter appears alongside the cartoon, at 1.296. The writer even carbon copies the letter to Carl Sagan!

ridicule of the "target," levity with sacrilege. For instance, I think it's safe to say Gary Larson wouldn't condone torture in real life, so a cartoon referring to this subject is not an obvious window into the man's views on the subject. Similarly, religious-themed cartoons are playful, not theological statements with any agenda attached.

Then again, maybe I'm wrong. Perhaps we should take the religious content in these cartoons more seriously. Maybe the comedian, actor, and musician Steve Martin is on to something in remarks about the theological significance of *The Far Side*:

> Many Larson scholars like to cite panel 108, caption 16, as proof of the existence of a deity. However, the exact nature of the deity is contradicted by several other panels. Scholars working at the Institute of Talking Dogs offer panel 247, with its image of two men standing on white clouds of heaven talking out of earshot of the deity, as proof of Larson's *theory of semi-omniscience*. In another panel depicting heaven, the newly deceased are issued harps, indicating a *benevolent un-musical mover*. However, the two men in the previous panel do not have harps, they have a gun. So how does a supreme being regarded as a *benevolent un-musical mover* fit into the *theory of semi-omniscience*, especially when the devil, who is handing out accordions, is revealed to be a blithe humorist (panel 42, caption 16)?[13]

Clearly, we need more theological analysis of *The Far Side*. Or is that less? To return to Eco's novel *The Name of the Rose* as I close this section, I take note again of William of Baskerville's views on humor and religion. Defending the margin illustrations of the biblical illuminator Adelmo, he reminds the humorless Jorges of Burgos that some ancient Christian authorities prized laughter and absurdity for what it might reveal. "God can be named only through the most distorted things," some argue, and "the more the simile becomes dissimilar, the more the truth is revealed to us under the guise of horrible and indecorous figures, the less the imagination is sated in carnal enjoyment, and is thus obliged to perceive the mysteries hidden under the turpitude of the images."[14] This does not impress Jorges, who continues his murderous efforts to rid the monastery of laughter, nor will it resolve all the theological conundrums we grapple with, as Steve Martin makes clear, but it might just be enough to conclude that laughter is good and edifying, even when the subject matter is sacred.

---

13 Steve Martin, "Foreword," in *The Complete Far Side*, 1.vii.
14 Eco, *Name of the Rose*, 80.

AFTERWORD

Though some might still find *The Far Side* offensive, it deserves notice, to state the obvious, that the universe found in these comics is theistic and broadly biblical, which is more than one can say about most others. It is irreverent, perhaps, but with no real agenda that I can see beyond humor. Like Umberto Eco's narrator Adso, who finds himself "torn between silent admiration and laughter, because [Adelmo's] illustrations naturally inspired merriment, though they were commenting on holy pages,"[15] we recognize the sacred in the playful Larson panels and occasionally do not know how to react. Lartoons bring religion and its characters close, making them like us. These marginal images provoke smiles, potentially to edifying ends. This is not sacrilege but rather an attempt to look behind the invisible wall that separates *us and them*.

ARE POPULAR CULTURE AND THE ARTS REALLY SO DANGEROUS?

There is a fine line between playfulness and insensitivity in the depiction of religious content. Art easily offends and leaves us with difficult questions. With reference to Lartoons, for instance, can we laugh at God and still revere him? Can we laugh at other people's notions of God and still love those people? Gary Larson knows firsthand that some Christian readers find his work offensive. At one point, he mentions Christians among a long list of groups troubled by his work (2.452). Though fortunately not as violent, Larson's experiences parallel those of Danish artist Kurt Westergaard, whose cartoon featuring Mohammed in the *Jyllands-Posten* in a September 2005 issue outraged many Muslims. Religionists are not alone, however, in finding the mix of comedy and serious subject matter troubling. Larson "incurred the wrath" of many others: the Inuit, or Eskimos, as he calls them ("I'm still not exactly sure why"); cat lovers ("I know why"); mental health organizations ("Shouldn't they have been reaching out to me?"); and Amnesty International among them.

My attempt to argue that *The Far Side* is just innocent fun—and not theologically dangerous or significant—will not convince all. For some, censorship, not laughter, is the best course. Either ignore *The Far Side* altogether, or read it selectively. While this might not seem consequential because most do not run

---

15 Eco, *Name of the Rose*, 78.

across *The Far Side* on a regular basis, consistency requires a similar response to all art forms, and this is consequential. The challenge here is the endless list of potentially offensive paintings and drawings, sculptures and dances, literature, films, television shows, plays, and music. Should Christians ignore popular culture and the arts outright? Is censorship the best way forward? Personally, I do not believe it is because of the tendency to throw out too much.

The austere Malvolio in William Shakespeare's delightful comedy *Twelfth Night, or What You Will* is a classic wet blanket, an insufferable moralist quick to find fault in others and voice disapproval when they have too much fun. The mischievous and fun-loving Maria calls him "a kind of puritan" (2.3.125). Few take him seriously. Sir Toby, for one, dismisses Malvolio's self-righteousness out of hand: "Dost thou think because thou art virtuous there shall be no more cakes and ale?" (2.3.103–104).

The Puritans, and those like Malvolio who resembled their strict demeanor, were easy targets for theatrical comedy in the late sixteenth and early seventeenth centuries, but this religious sect proved to be more than a mere irritant in the following decades. In 1642, just twenty-six years after William Shakespeare's death, the Puritan-influenced English Parliament closed all public theaters in the country. They found much to complain about in these places, with sexuality of particular concern. The Puritan preacher John Northbrooke published an attack on the theater that is representative of their sentiments: "Satan hath not a more speedie way and fitter schoole to work and teach his desire, to bring men and women into his snare of concupiscence [sexual desire] and filthie lastes [lusts] of wicked whoredome."[16] The theaters finally reopened in 1660, and though the Puritans' political influence diminished by this time, this pattern of suspicion about the popular arts persisted.

Jump ahead a few centuries to 1807 and 1818 and the publication of *The Family Shakespeare* by Henrietta Maria Bowdler and her brother Thomas Bowdler, who explain their reasons for editing Shakespeare the way they do: "It must . . .be acknowledged, by his warmest admirers, that some defects are to be found in the writings of our immortal bard. . . . Many words and expressions occur which are of so indecent a nature as to render it highly desirable that they should be erased." Said differently, the Bowdlers took out the naughty bits. Swearing, flippant treatment of religious subjects, bodily

---

16 Taken from Jack Lynch, *Becoming Shakespeare: How a Dead Poet Became the World's Foremost Literary Genius* (London: Constable, 2008), 15. The citation below from *The Family Shakespeare* appears on p. 178.

functions, and of course, sex—the Bowdlers excised or changed anything they deemed indecent and improper for respectable families. Somehow, Lady Macbeth's cry of "Out, crimson spot!" in *The Family Shakespeare* does not pack the same rhetorical punch as the original.

Here we have two extreme reactions before us—avoid Shakespeare altogether or bowdlerize his work beyond recognition. It is hard to imagine a world without Shakespeare's jolly Falstaff, neurotic Hamlet, or the deluded Lear, not to mention Larson's cows, but many insist the Puritans and the Bowdlers got it right; the world is better off without these characters and stories as Shakespeare constructed them, and the same goes for other artists and entertainers with questionable content. What we really need is a world without cakes and ale!

Such religious and social conservatives, past and present, insulate themselves against coarse language and sexual innuendo but in the process sacrifice far more. Shakespeare's villains, tragic heroes, and comic figures embody quintessential qualities of the human condition. We recognize ourselves in his depictions of friendship and rivalry, self-sacrificing love, and self-serving ambition. Shakespeare captures such things as the joys of romantic love, religious hypocrisy, existential despair, and fear of the grave. He teaches us what it means to be human, with all its private/internal/psychological and public/external/social complexities. Is this really such a bad thing?

My concern is not really the prudishness of seventeenth- and nineteenth-century English readers but more generally Christian responses to works of the imagination. As said, many in our day fear film, television, literature, comics—all the so-called "secular" arts—just as much as the pious of earlier generations, equally convinced that in these media "Satan hath not a more speedie way and fitter schoole to work and teach his desire." Without denying that Christians need to be thoughtful consumers of literature and the arts, something mentioned more than once already, I disagree with proponents of censorship and book bans and those urging retreat into religious subcultures. The reason is that inclusion of sex, swearing, drug use, violence, irreverent religious references, and the like does not necessarily make movies, television, literature, or comics bad, any more than the absence of such things makes them good. Furthermore, films and literature without such content might be immoral on other, less obvious grounds. Interestingly, concern over the anti-Semitic overtones of Shakespeare's *Merchant of Venice* (Shylock) did not bother Puritan or Victorian readers.

I find this issue far more troubling than the Bard's occasional bawdy jokes. Moral censure tends to be selective.

A better way forward, in my view, is thoughtful engagement that focuses on the quality of art, not the presence or absence of particular subject matter. Thinking about what is honorable, just, pure, pleasing, commendable, excellent, and worthy of praise (Phil 4:8) involves more than averting one's eyes or plugging one's ears at opportune moments. If someone's top criteria for measuring artistic merit is the absence of sexual references and swearing, for instance, they might conclude *The Passion of the Christ* is a good film (it isn't) and *Jesus of Montreal* a bad one (it isn't). If someone else prizes explicit Christian content over all else, they might replace Jane Austen on their shelves with the Left Behind series. Shudder.

We also do well to change our expectations and seek out meaning and truth in literature and film, as argued throughout this book. We might just find the "secular" arts turning our thoughts to what is honorable, just, pure, pleasing, commendable, excellent, and worthy of praise. I learn far more about the evils of systemic injustice and the ameliorating potential of simple acts of compassion from Charles Dickens than sermons. This is not a criticism of the preachers in my life but rather a comment about the power of the novel and this specific storyteller. Christians should celebrate good art rather than simply tolerate "safe" art. Larson is good art. Shakespeare or Larson censored and bowdlerized in any fashion is not Shakespeare or Larson at all. Yes, Christians must be discerning and critical consumers of literature, but censorship is too clumsy a tool for this task.

Works Cited

Abrams, M. H., and Geoffrey Galt Harpham. *A Glossary of Literary Terms* 11th ed. Stamford, CT: Cengage, 2015.
Ackroyd, Peter. *Dickens: A Memoir of Middle Age*. London: Vintage, 2012.
Adams, Richard. *The Day Gone By: An Autobiography*. 1990. London: Penguin, 1991.
———. *The Plague Dogs*. 1977. Toronto: Vintage, 2016.
———. *Watership Down*. 1972. New York: Scribner, 2005.
Alter, Robert. *Canon and Creativity: Modern Writing and the Authority of Scripture*. New Haven, CT: Yale University Press, 2000.
Ashworth, Andrea. "Afterword." In Jean Rhys, *Wide Sargasso Sea*, 149–160. London: Penguin, 2019.
Bailey, Kenneth E. *Jacob and the Prodigal: How Jesus Retold Israel's Story*. Downers Grove, IL: InterVarsity, 2003.
Bauckham, Richard. *The Bible and Ecology: Rediscovering the Community of Creation*. Waco, TX: Baylor University Press, 2010.
———. *Living with Other Creatures: Green Exegesis and Theology*. Waco, TX: Baylor University Press, 2011.
Belletto, Steven. "The Beats." In *The World of Bob Dylan*, edited by Sean Latham, 169–180. Cambridge, UK: Cambridge University Press, 2021.
Bhabha, Homi. *The Location of Culture*. London: Routledge, 1994.
Blomberg, Craig L. *Interpreting the Parables*. 2nd ed. Downers Grove, IL: IVP Academic, 2012.
Bloom, Harold. *How to Read and Why*. New York: Simon & Schuster, 2000.
Bono. *Surrender: 40 Songs, One Story*. Toronto: Penguin Random House Canada, 2022.
Booth, Wayne C. *The Company We Keep: An Ethics of Fiction*. Berkeley: University of California Press, 1988.
Brontë, Anne. *Agnes Grey*. 1847. Edited by Robin L. Inboden. Peterborough, ON: Broadview, 2020.
———. *The Tenant of Wildfell Hall*. 1848. Edited by Lee A. Talley. Peterborough, ON: Broadview, 2009.
Brontë, Charlotte. *Jane Eyre*. 1847. Edited by Richard Nemesvari. 2nd ed. Peterborough, ON: Broadview, 2021.
Buechner, Frederick. *Speak What We Feel (Not What We Ought to Say): Reflections on Literature and Faith*. New York: HarperSanFrancisco, 2001.
Bunyan, John. *The Pilgrim's Progress*. 1678, 1684. Oxford World's Classics. Edited by W. R. Owens. Oxford: Oxford University Press, 2003.

WORKS CITED

Caron, Timothy P. "'The Bottom Rail Is on the Top': Race and 'Theological Whiteness' in Flannery O'Connor's Short Fiction." In *Inside the Church of Flannery O'Connor: Sacrament, Sacramental, and the Sacred in Her Fiction*, edited by Joanne Halleran McMullen and Jon Parrish Peele, 138–164. Macon, GA: Mercer University Press, 2007.

Cavanaugh, Christine. "Auguries of Power: Prophecy and Violence in *The Satanic Verses*." *Studies in the Novel* 36 (2004): 393–404.

Cavill, Paul, and Heather Ward, with Matthew Baynham, Andrew Swinford, John Flood, and Roger Pooley. *Christian Tradition in English Literature: Poetry, Plays, and Shorter Prose*. Grand Rapids, MI: Zondervan, 2007.

Chitham, Edward. *A Life of Anne Brontë*. Oxford: Blackwell, 1991.

Clark, Roger Y. *Stranger Gods: Salman Rushdie's Other Worlds*. Montreal: McGill-Queens University Press, 2001.

Clough, David L. *On Animals*. Vol. 1. *Systematic Theology*. London: T & T Clark, 2012.

———. *On Animals*. Vol. 2. *Theological Ethics*. London: T & T Clark, 2017.

Colledge, Gary L. *God and Charles Dickens: Recovering the Christian Voice of a Classic Author*. Grand Rapids, MI: Brazos, 2012.

Collmer, Robert G. "John Bunyan." In *The Oxford Handbook of English Literature and Theology*, edited by Andrew W. Haas, David Jasper, and Elisabeth Jay, 575–589. Oxford: Oxford University Press, 2007.

Cott, Jonathan, ed. *Bob Dylan: The Essential Interviews*. New York: Wenner, 2006.

Defoe, Daniel. *Robinson Crusoe*. 1719. Edited by Evan R. Davis. Peterborough, ON: Broadview, 2010.

deSilva, David A. *Introducing the Apocrypha: Message, Context, and Significance*. Grand Rapids, MI: Baker Academic, 2002.

Detweiler, Robert, and David Jasper, eds., with S. Brent Plate and Heidi L. Nordberg. *Religion and Literature: A Reader*. Louisville, KY: Westminster John Knox, 2000.

Dickens, Charles. *A Christmas Carol, in Prose: Being a Ghost Story of Christmas*. 1843. In *A Christmas Carol*, edited by Richard Kelly. Peterborough, ON: Broadview, 2003.

———. *The Cricket on the Hearth: A Fairy Tale of Home*. 1845. In *A Christmas Carol and Other Stories*, edited by Robert Douglas-Fairhurst, 163–242. Oxford: Oxford University Press, 2006.

———. *The Old Curiosity Shop*. 1841. London: Arcturus, 2011.

———. *Oliver Twist, or, The Parish Boy's Progress*. 1838. London: Penguin, 2002.

Dore, Florence. "American Literature." In *The World of Bob Dylan*, edited by Sean Latham, 147–157. Cambridge, UK: Cambridge University Press, 2021.

Dylan, Bob. *Chronicles: Volume One*. New York: Simon & Schuster, 2004.

———. *The Lyrics 1961-2012*. New York: Simon & Schuster, 2016.

———. *The Nobel Lecture*. New York: Simon & Schuster, 2017.

———. *The Philosophy of Modern Song*. New York: Simon & Schuster, 2022.

Eagleton, Terry. *Literary Theory: An Introduction*. Anniversary edition. Minneapolis: University of Minnesota Press, 2008.

Eco, Umberto. *Baudolino*. 2000. Translated by William Weaver. Toronto: Harcourt, 2002.

———. *The Name of the Rose*. 1984. Translated by William Weaver. San Diego, CA: Harcourt, 1980.

Evans, Craig A. *Jesus and the Ossuaries: What Jewish Burial Practices Reveal about the Beginning of Christianity*. Waco, TX: Baylor University Press, 2003.

Exum, J. Cheryl. *Plotted, Shot, and Painted: Cultural Representations of Biblical Women.* 2nd rev. ed. 1996. Sheffield, UK: Sheffield Phoenix, 2012.

Ferguson, Everett. *Backgrounds of Early Christianity.* 3rd ed. Grand Rapids, MI: Eerdmans, 2003.

Findley, Timothy. *Not Wanted on the Voyage.* 1984. Toronto: Penguin, 1996.

Frye, Northrop. *The Great Code: The Bible and Literature.* 1981. San Diego, CA: Harvest, 2002.

———. "The Search for Acceptable Words." In *Spiritus Mundi: Essays on Literature, Myth, and Society*, 3–26. Bloomington: Indiana University Press, 1976.

Gabelman, Daniel. *George MacDonald: Divine Carelessness and Fairytale Levity.* Waco, TX: Baylor University Press, 2013.

Gaskell, Elizabeth. *The Life of Charlotte Brontë.* Oxford World's Classics. Edited by Angus Easson. Oxford: Oxford University Press, 1996.

Gilmour, Michael J. "Animal Imagery in Charles Dickens's *Dombey and Son*." *Bhatter College Journal of Multidisciplinary Studies* 3 (2013): 55–61.

———. "The Bible and Popular Music." In *The Bloomsbury Handbook of Religion and Popular Music*, 2nd ed, edited by Christopher Partridge and Marcus Moberg, 67–76. London: Bloomsbury, 2023.

———. "Bob Dylan's Bible." In *The Oxford Handbook of Reception History of the Bible*, edited by Michael Lieb, Emma Mason, Christopher Rowland, and Jonathan Roberts, 355–368. Oxford University Press, 2010.

———. *Creative Compassion, Literature and Animal Welfare.* Basingstoke, UK: Palgrave Macmillan, 2020.

———. "The Far Side of Religion: Notes on the Prophet Gary Larson." *Direction* 39, no. 2 (2010): 220–233.

———. "Raging against the Machine: Tom Morello's Nightwatchman Persona and the Sound of Apocalypse-Inspired *Schadenfreude*." In *Anthems of Apocalypse: Popular Music and Apocalyptic Thought*, edited by Christopher Partridge. 43–54. Sheffield, UK: Sheffield Phoenix Press, 2012.

———. "Some Novel Remarks about Popular Culture and Religion: Salman Rushdie and the Adaptation of Sacred Texts." In *The Bible in/and Popular Culture: A Creative Encounter.* Semeia Studies, edited by Philip Culbertson and Elaine Wainwright, 13–25. Atlanta: SBL, 2010.

Gitter, Elisabeth G. "The Blind Daughter in Charles Dickens's 'The Cricket on the Hearth.'" *Studies in English Literature, 1500-1900* 39, no. 4 (1999): 675–689.

Goodall, Jane. "Foreword." In Gary Larson, *The Far Side Gallery 5.* Kansas City, MO: Andrews and McMeel, 1995.

Gray, Michael. *The Bob Dylan Encyclopedia.* New York: Continuum, 2006.

Green, Mitchell S. "Learning to Be Good (or Bad) in (or through) Literature." In *Fictional Characters, Real Problems: The Search for Ethical Content*, edited by Garry L. Hagberg, 282–301. Oxford: Oxford University Press, 2016.

Greenblatt, Stephen, Walter Cohen, Jean E. Howard, and Katherine Eisaman Maus, eds. *The Norton Shakespeare.* 2nd ed. New York: Norton, 2008.

Greenblatt, Stephen, Katharine Eisaman Maus, and George Logan, eds. *The Norton Anthology of English Literature.* Vol. B. 10th ed. New York: Norton, 2018.

Greenblatt, Stephen, and James Noggle, eds. *The Norton Anthology of English Literature.* Vol. C. 10th ed. New York: Norton, 2018.

Gribble, Jennifer. *Dickens and the Bible: "What Providence Meant."* New York: Routledge, 2021.

Guthrie, Woody. *Bound for Glory*. 1943. New York: Penguin, 1983.

Hagner, Donald A. *Matthew 14-28*. WBC 33B. Dallas: Word, 1995.

Hammond, Gerald, and Austin Busch, eds. *The English Bible: King James Version*. Vol. 2. *The New Testament and the Apocrypha*. Norton Critical edition. New York: Norton, 2012.

Hanger, Nancy C. "The Excellent Absurdity: Substitution and Co-Inherence in C. S. Lewis and Charles Williams." *Mythlore* 34 (1983): 14-18.

Harrington, Daniel J. *Invitation to the Apocrypha*. Grand Rapids, MI: Eerdmans, 1999.

Hass, Andrew W., David Jasper, and Elisabeth Jay, eds. *The Oxford Handbook of English Literature and Theology*. Oxford: Oxford University Press, 2007.

Hauerwas, Stanley. *A Community of Character: Toward a Constructive Christian Social Ethic*. Notre Dame, IN: University of Notre Dame, 1981.

Hauerwas, Stanley, and Ralph C. Wood. "How the Church Became Invisible: A Christian Reading of American Literary Tradition." In *Invisible Conversations: Religion in the Literature of America*, edited by Roger Lundin, 159-186. Waco, TX: Baylor University Press, 2009.

Heylin, Clinton. "Saved! Bob Dylan's Conversion to Christianity." In *Wanted Man: In Search of Bob Dylan*, edited by John Bauldie, 128-134. New York: Citadel, 1991.

———. *Trouble in Mind: Bob Dylan's Gospel Years, What Really Happened*. New York: Lesser Gods, 2017.

Hosseini, Khaled. *And the Mountains Echoed*. Toronto: Viking, 2013.

Hutcheon, Linda. *A Theory of Adaptation*. New York: Routledge, 2006.

Jeffrey, David Lyle. *Houses of the Interpreter: Reading Scripture, Reading Culture*. Waco, TX: Baylor University Press, 2003.

———, ed., *A Dictionary of Biblical Tradition in English Literature*. Grand Rapids, MI: Eerdmans, 1992.

Johnson, Edgar. *Charles Dickens: His Tragedy and Triumph*. 2 vols. New York: Simon & Schuster, 1952.

Johnson, Luke Timothy. *Hebrews: A Commentary*. NTL. Louisville, KY: Westminster John Knox, 2006.

Kaplan, Fred. *Dickens: A Biography*. Baltimore, MD: The Johns Hopkins University Press, 1998.

Kennedy, X. J., Dana Gioia, and Mark Bauerlein. *The Longman Dictionary of Literary Terms: Vocabulary for the Informed Reader*. New York: Pearson Longman, 2006.

King, Stephen. *On Writing: A Memoir of the Craft*. 2000. New York: Scribner, 2020.

Knight, James. "'I Ain't Got No Home in This World Anymore': Protest and Promise in Woody Guthrie and the Jesus Tradition." In *Call Me the Seeker: Listening to Religion in Popular Music*, edited by Michael J. Gilmour, 17-33. New York: Continuum, 2005.

Kogawa, Joy. *Obasan*. 1981. Toronto: Penguin, 2003.

Kutzer, M. Daphne. *Empire's Children: Empire and Imperialism in Classic British Children's Books*. New York: Garland, 2000.

Lane, Richard J. *The Postcolonial Novel*. Themes in 20th Century Literature and Culture. Cambridge, UK: Polity, 2006.

Laquer, Thomas W. *The Work of the Dead: A Cultural History of Mortal Remains*. Princeton, NJ: Princeton University Press, 2015.

Larsen, Timothy. *George MacDonald in the Age of Miracles: Incarnation, Doubt, and Reenchantment.* Downers Grove, IL: IVP Academic, 2018.

Larson, Gary. *The Complete Far Side.* Vol. 1: 1980–1986 and Vol. 2: 1987–1994. Kansas City, MO: Andrews McMeel Publishing, 2003.

———. *There's a Hair in My Dirt! A Worm's Story.* New York: Harper, 1998.

Lemon, Rebecca, Emma Mason, Jonathan Roberts, and Christopher Rowland, eds. *The Blackwell Companion to the Bible in English Literature.* Chichester, UK: Wiley-Blackwell, 2012.

Lewis, C. S. *All My Road before Me: The Diary of C. S. Lewis 1922–1927.* Edited by Walter Hooper. San Diego, CA: Harvest, 1991.

———. *The Collected Letters of C. S. Lewis.* Vol. 1. *Family Letters, 1905–1931.* Edited by Walter Hooper. New York: HarperCollins, 2000.

———. *The Collected Letters of C. S. Lewis.* Vol. 2. *Books, Broadcasts, and the War, 1931–1949.* Edited by Walter Hooper. New York: HarperCollins, 2004.

———. *The Collected Letters of C. S. Lewis.* Vol. 3. *Narnia, Cambridge, and Joy 1950–1963.* Edited by Walter Hooper. New York: HarperCollins, 2007

———. *The Lion, the Witch and the Wardrobe.* 1950. New York: HarperCollins, 1994.

———. "The Novels of Charles Williams." 1949. In *On Stories: And Other Essays on Literature*, edited by Walter Hooper, 21–28. New York: Harcourt, 1982.

———. *Perelandra.* 1943. London: HarperCollins, 2005.

———. *Poems.* 1964. New York: HarperOne, 2017.

———. *Prince Caspian: The Return to Narnia.* 1951. New York: HarperCollins, 1994.

———. *The Silver Chair.* 1953. New York: HarperCollins, 1994.

———. *Surprised by Joy: The Shape of My Early Life.* 1955. Boston: Houghton Mifflin Harcourt, 2012.

———. *That Hideous Strength: A Modern Fairy-Tale for Grown-Ups.* 1945. London: HarperCollins, 2005.

Lindop, Grevel. *Charles Williams: The Third Inkling.* Oxford: Oxford University Press, 2015.

Linzey, Andrew. *Animal Gospel.* Louisville, KY: Westminster John Knox, 2000.

———. "Preface." In *Other Nations: Animals in Modern Literature*, edited by Tom Regan and Andrew Linzey, ix–xx. Waco, TX: Baylor University Press, 2010.

Linzey, Andrew, and Clair Linzey, eds. *Animal Theologians.* Oxford: Oxford University Press, 2023.

Lofting, Hugh. *Doctor Dolittle's Post Office.* 1923. In *Doctor Dolittle: The Complete Collection.* Vol. 1: 427–709. New York: Aladdin, 2019.

———. *Victory for the Slain.* 1942. Sandness, UK: Walmer, 2020.

———. *The Voyages of Doctor Dolittle.* 1922. In *Doctor Dolittle: The Complete Collection.* Vol. 1: 1–314. New York: Aladdin, 2019.

Lothian, J. M., and T. W. Craik, eds. *Twelfth Night.* The Arden Shakespeare. 1975. London: Thomson, 2006.

Lynch, Jack. *Becoming Shakespeare: How a Dead Poet Became the World's Foremost Literary Genius.* London: Constable, 2008.

MacDonald, George. "The Imagination: Its Functions and Its Culture." In *The Princess and the Goblin and Other Fairy Tales*, edited by Shelley King and John B. Pierce, 327–355. Peterborough, ON: Broadview, 2014.

Mai, Anne-Marie. "World Literature." In *The World of Bob Dylan*, edited by Sean Latham, 158–168. Cambridge, UK: Cambridge University Press, 2021.

Manguel, Alberto, and Gianni Guadalupi. *The Dictionary of Imaginary Places*. Toronto: Vintage, 2001.
Marciniak, Katarzyna. *Alienhood: Citizenship, Exile, and the Logic of Difference*. Minneapolis: University of Minnesota Press, 2006.
Martin, Steve. "Foreword." In Gary Larson, *The Complete Far Side*. Vol. 1: 1980–1986 and Vol. 2: 1987–1994. Kansas City, MO: Andrews McMeel Publishing, 2003.
Marx, John. "Postcolonial Literature and the Western Literary Canon." In *The Cambridge Companion to Postcolonial Literary Studies*, edited by Neil Lazarus, 83–96. Cambridge, UK: Cambridge University Press, 2004.
Maynard, John. "The Brontës and Religion." In *The Cambridge Companion to the Brontës*, edited by Heather Glen, 192–213. Cambridge, UK: Cambridge University Press, 2002.
McCarron, Andrew. *Light Come Shining: The Transformation of Bob Dylan*. New York: Oxford University Press, 2017.
McGrath, Alister. *C. S. Lewis—A Life: Eccentric Genius, Reluctant Prophet*. Carol Stream, IL: Tyndale House, 2013.
Middleton, Darren J. N. *Theology after Reading: Christian Imagination and the Power of Fiction*. Waco, TX: Baylor University Press, 2008.
Moncrieff, Scott. "*The Cricket* in the Study." *Dickens Studies Annual* 22 (1993): 137–153.
Newman, Barbara. "Charles Williams and the Companions of the Co-inherence." *Spiritus: A Journal of Christian Spirituality* 9, no. 1 (2009): 1–26.
O'Connor, Flannery. "A Circle of Fire." In *The Complete Stories*, 175–193. New York: Farrar, Straus and Giroux, 1971.
Porter, Stanley E. "Sheep and the goats, Parable of the." In *Dictionary of the Bible and Western Culture*, edited by Mary Ann Beavis and Michael J. Gilmour, 485–486. Sheffield, UK: Sheffield Phoenix Press, 2012.
Prior, Karen Swallow. *On Reading Well: Finding the Good Life through Great Books*. Grand Rapids, MI: Brazos, 2018.
Resseguie, James L. *Spiritual Landscape: Images of the Spiritual Life in the Gospel of Luke*. Peabody, MA: Hendrickson, 2004.
Rhys, Jean. *Wide Sargasso Sea*. 1966. Norton Critical edition. Edited by Judith L. Raiskin. New York: Norton, 1999.
Rogovoy, Seth. *Bob Dylan: Prophet, Mystic, Poet*. New York: Scribner, 2009.
Rushdie, Salman. *Fury*. Toronto: Vintage, 2001.
———. *The Golden House*. Toronto: Alfred A. Knopf, 2017.
———. *The Ground Beneath Her Feet*. Toronto: Vintage, 1999.
———. *Haroun and the Sea of Stories*. London: Granta, 1990.
———. *Joseph Anton: A Memoir*. New York: Random House, 2012.
———. *The Moor's Last Sigh*. Toronto: Vintage, 1996.
———. *The Satanic Verses*. New York: Picador, 1988.
———. *Step across This Line: Collected Nonfiction, 1992–2002*. Toronto: Knopf, 2002.
Sainsbury, Lisa. *Ethics in British Children's Literature: Unexamined Life*. Perspectives on Children's Literature. London: Bloomsbury, 2013.
Sakamoto, Kerri. "Introduction." In Joy Kogawa, *Obasan*, vii–ix. Toronto: Penguin, 2003.
Schmidt, Gary D. *Hugh Lofting*. Twayne's English Authors Series 496. New York: Twayne, 1992.

Sharma, Shailja. "Salman Rushdie: The Ambivalence of Migrancy." *Twentieth Century Literature* 47 (2001): 596–618.
Shelton, Robert. *No Direction Home: The Life and Music of Bob Dylan*. London: Penguin, 1987.
Snodgrass, Klyne R. *Stories with Intent: A Comprehensive Guide to the Parables of Jesus*. 2nd ed. Grand Rapids, MI: Eerdmans, 2018.
Sounes, Howard. *Down the Highway: The Life of Bob Dylan*. Updated edition. New York: Grove, 2021.
Spargo, R. Clifton, and Anne K. Ream. "Bob Dylan and Religion." In *The Cambridge Companion to Bob Dylan*, edited by Kevin J. H. Dettmar, 87–99. Cambridge, UK: Cambridge University Press, 2009.
Spivak, Gayatri Chakravorty. "Three Women's Texts and a Critique of Imperialism." *Critical Inquiry* 12, no. 1 (1988): 243–261.
Stoneman, Patsy. "The Brontë Myth." In *The Cambridge Companion to the Brontës*, edited by Heather Glen, 214–241. Cambridge, UK: Cambridge University Press 2002.
Strauss, Mark L. *Four Portraits, One Jesus: A Survey of Jesus and the Gospels*. 2nd ed. Grand Rapids, MI: Zondervan, 2020.
Streete, Gail Corrington. *The Strange Woman: Power and Sex in the Bible*. Louisville, KY: Westminster John Knox, 1997.
Thomas, Richard F. *Why Bob Dylan Matters*. New York: Dey Street, 2017.
Tolkien, J. R. R. *Return of the King*. 1955. London: HarperCollins, 1999.
Warner, Marina. *Fantastic Metamorphoses, Other World: Ways of Telling the Self*. Oxford: Oxford University Press. 2002.
Waxler, Robert P. *The Risk of Reading: How Literature Helps Us to Understand Ourselves and the World*. New York: Bloomsbury, 2014.
Webb, Stephen H. *Dylan Redeemed: From* Highway 61 *to* Saved. New York: Continuum, 2006.
Williams, Charles. *Descent into Hell*. 1937. London: Charles Williams Society, 2018.
———. *The Greater Trumps*. 1932. London: Charles Williams Society, 2019.
Wilson, A. N. *The Mystery of Charles Dickens*. New York: HarperCollins, 2020.
Wilson, Edward O. "Foreword." In Gary Larson, *There's a Hair in My Dirt! A Worm's Story*. New York: Harper, 1998.
Wimsatt, William K., Jr., Jand Monroe C. Beardsley. "The Affective Fallacy." 1949. Reprinted in *The Norton Anthology of Theory and Criticism*, edited by Vincent B. Leitch, William E. Cain, Laurie A. Finke, Barbara E. Johnson, John McGowan, and Jeffrey J. Williams, 1387–1403. New York: Norton, 2001.
Wood, Ralph C. *Literature and Theology*. Nashville, TN: Abingdon, 2008.
Wright, N. T., and Michael F. Bird. *The New Testament in Its World: An Introduction to the History, Literature, and Theology of the First Christians*. Grand Rapids, MI: Zondervan, 2019.
Zaleski, Philip, and Carol Zaleski. *The Fellowship: The Literary Lives of the Inklings*. New York: Farrar, Straus and Giroux, 2015.

Index of Subjects

adaptation of texts, xxxvi, 54, 64–80
alcohol, alcoholism, xxi, 28 n. 16, 29, 32, 35, 39, 40 n. 57, 112, 123, 124 n. 65
angel, angels, xxvi, xi, 1, 4, 12, 67–74, 111, 121, 124–26, 128, 141, 171, 172, 174
animal cruelty, xxiv–xxv, 33, 49–50, 132, 134–35, 143–44, 146–47, 149

Beatitudes, the, frontmatter (Matt 5:3–14), 82. *See also* Sermon on the Mount, the
Beatles, the, 72 n. 38
blindness (literal), 163–66
blindness (metaphorical), xxxvii, xl, 26, 27, 42, 46, 48 n. 21, 127 n. 2, 131, 160

Cassandra, the prophetess, 132–34, 143
censorship, xlii, 161, 167, 169–83
children's literature, xxiv, xxvii, 4 n. 10, 61, 64, 84–103
church(es), xxviii–xxix, xxxiv–xxxv, xxxviii, xl, 8, 18–20, 26–27, 32, 38, 41, 60–62, 105–7, 117, 122, 123, 131, 142–43, 166, 169
colonialism, xxiv n. 25, 41–80

Daniel, the prophet, 128–30
devil, devils (Lucifer, Satan), 40 n. 57, 61, 67–79, 86, 92, 94, 95 n. 32, 105, 113, 118, 124, 171, 172, 175, 176, 179, 181, 182
disciple, discipleship, xv, xxxix–xliii, 63, 81, 104–8, 131, 159
Doctor Dolittle, xxiii–xxvii, 132, 139
domestic abuse, xl, xliii, 33–34, 111–12

dominion, 48–52, 111–12, 128, 130, 140
drunkenness. *See* alcohol

empathy, empathetic gap, xii, xxx–xxxvii, 29, 34, 109, 131, 135, 145–49, 159–60
environment, environmental degradation, xxvii, 130–53
ethical criticism, xli–xliii

Far Side, The. See Larson, Gary
Fatwa. See Rushdie, Salman

gamblers, gambling, 5, 6, 40 n. 57, 111, 115–19, 122–25
generosity, xxxix, 7–8, 20–21, 109, 122, 153
Genesis, book of, xxi, xxiii–xxvii, 48–51, 68 n. 20, 130, 136, 138–40, 145, 176
great depression, the, 8, 10, 14, 21
greed, 42, 48, 125

Hebrews, book of, xxxiii–xxxiv, 161
hospitality, 109, 111, 153
humor, 169–80
hypocrisy, 3, 18–20, 46, 104, 106, 123 n. 63, 182

imagination, xvi–xxx, xxxv, xxxviii, xli–xliii, 23–26, 110, 135, 139, 142, 155–67
inhospitality, 18–19, 26, 41, 42, 59–64

Japanese, abuse and internment of during World War II, 59–64

Lady Wisdom and Lady Folly (book of Proverbs), 31, 36–40

INDEX OF SUBJECTS

literary influence, 65–66, 86–87, 106–7, 114
literature as commentary on the Bible and theological topics, xvi, xxx–xli, 159–61
literature and processing life's challenges, 23–26
Lucifer. *See* devil, devils

margins (metaphoric), xliii–iv
mental illness, 15–17, 125, 180
Mercury, Freddie, 157
money. *See* wealth

Oxford University, x, xvii–xx

palimpsest, 87, 104, 106–7
parable(s), xxxvi, xxxvii n. 53, 2–4, 6–9, 19, 121–22, 127–30, 131–32, 135, 149–53, 170
poverty, 1–22, 109–26, 163–65
prayer, xiii, xxviii–xxix, xxxii, 44–45, 62–63, 86, 124–25, 161
pride, 19, 68 n. 20, 123, 13
prophets, 128–29

rabbits, 127–53
racism, 41–80, 127 n. 2, 131
reading as spiritual discipline, xxxii, 160
Rolling Stones, the, 71, 72 n. 38

Satan. *See* devil, devils
Sermon on the Mount, the, 9, 10, 41, 82, 83, 103. *See also* Beatitudes, the
sex, sexuality, sexual orientation, xxxvii n. 52, xl, xliii, 42, 68 n. 20, 131, 181–83
Scripture as script, scriptural patterns, 103–8
sheep and goats (Jesus's teaching about), frontmatter (Matt 25:31–46), xxxvii–xli, 2–3, 20, 22, 41, 56, 63, 82, 109
Skid Row, 10, 59
slavery, xxxiv, 11, 42–56
substitution. *See* Williams, Charles
sympathy, xii, xxxi, 160

temptation, tempter(s), 40 n. 57, 108, 109, 110, 115–17, 124

unemployment, 8, 13, 4–21

war, xvii–xxiv, xxvii–xxix, 9, 14, 59–64, 155
wealth, 1, 9, 12–13, 47–48, 111, 116 n. 23
worship, worshipping, xxxii, 61, 105, 108, 129 n. 7, 138

yew trees, 142–44, 146